BEFORE
THEY LEAVE THE STAGE

Interviews with eighteen men of God

KEITH BATSTONE AND ALUN EBENEZER

In memory of John Blanchard

© Day One Publications 2023

ISBN 978-1-84625-741-4

British Library Cataloguing in Publication Data available

Published by Day One Publications
Ryelands Road, Leominster, HR6 8NZ
Telephone 01568 613 740
North America Toll Free 888 329 6630
email—sales@dayone.co.uk
website—www.dayone.co.uk

The stage and lectern images on the cover are used under licence from Shutterstock.com

Cover design by smallprint

Printed by 4edge Limited

It is a joy for believers to share the stories of how God worked over the course of their lives and the lessons they have learned. But sadly, we often lose those stories when believers become elderly and then pass from this world. This little treasure of a book captures the stories of eighteen godly men—most of them faithful pastors whose godly friendship I treasure—so that we can trace the fingerprints of our faithful God and end in glorifying him while, by the Spirit's grace, becoming more sanctified ourselves, for the aim of this book is ultimately that we would grow in hating sin more, loving Christ more, and pursuing the King's highway of holiness more.

Dr Joel R. Beeke
President, Puritan Reformed Theological Seminary
and Pastor, Heritage Reformed Congregation
Grand Rapids, Michigan

If you are anything like me, you would love to spend an hour or two getting to know ministers whose lives and preaching you've long admired—from a distance. But you have always assumed that is impossible, since you will never actually meet them. If so, this is just the book for you! Here are eighteen grace-packed mini-biographies that are the next best thing to sitting at the feet of men who have served Christ faithfully for many decades. We get to overhear them talking about God's multi-coloured grace working in, around, and through their very varied lives and diverse personalities. *Before They Leave The Stage* is as instructive as it is encouraging, and challenging. A treat not to be missed!

Sinclair B. Ferguson

These men belong to a generation that had to fight for the gospel itself in their churches and ministries. They won the day for us and we stand on their shoulders. I am glad to own them as my models, teachers, mentors and friends. May God give us another generation like them.

Ian Parry
Pastor of Grangetown Baptist Church, Cardiff

Contents

The images at the beginnings of the chapters are from screenshots from the interviews

Introduction

What, Why, Who and When

What

Throughout the spring and into the summer of 2021 Christians from the UK and beyond were tuning in to a series of online interviews each Sunday evening called *Before They Leave The Stage*. The interviews featured retired pastors, and one evangelist, from England, Scotland and Wales, in their 70s, 80s and 90s. The interviews were transmitted through the YouTube Channel of the Heath Evangelical Church, Cardiff and would not have been possible without the technical skills of Tim Cross and Tom Davey, who gave up their Sunday evenings throughout the four months the series aired.

My father-in-law, Keith Batstone, and I conducted the interviews, and neither of us would claim to be Michael Parkinson or Jeremy Paxman! It was not very professional or slick. Just two interviewers and one interviewee, each Sunday evening in three different parts of the country, sat in our kitchens, studies and lounges. There were times when the internet lagged, cats miaowed, phones rang and screens froze. But it wasn't the style that was important, it was all about the substance.

This book is those interviews adapted in printed form, and we are very grateful to Rhonda Frost for transcribing them. Some of the men interviewed have provided additional information that we didn't have time to cover in the forty-five-minute interviews, which we have tried to include.

Each of the men interviewed has his own chapter, sandwiched between this Introduction and a final chapter by Keith Batstone setting out common themes and lessons that came from the series. The usual pattern on the night was for me to introduce the man, start and end the interview, while my father-in-law did most of the interviewing. My introduction to each man is at the beginning of their chapter.

Introduction

Why

Over the last few years many people I have known, loved, looked up to and who influenced me, have died and gone to glory. I am quite conscious there are others in that generation who over the next few months and years will be joining them. It is a generation that seems to know God in a way that I don't and have proved God in a way that I haven't. So we thought it would be really good to sit down with them and listen to what they have to say *'before they leave the stage'*.

Moreover, there can be a danger with my generation, and the ones following, that we think we know best and that two thousand years of church history has been waiting for our arrival on the scene. Lost among all our tweets, instagram posts and blogs are these older men who have faithfully stood and served for the last forty to fifty years. It would do us good to heed the advice given in Proverbs 13:1, *'A wise son hears his father's instruction, whereas a fool despises it.'*

However, the intention was not to be nostalgic about the 'good old days' or to give the younger generations a 'kick in'. With more distractions, worldliness and ungodliness, it is really hard to stand as a Christian today. We simply wanted younger generations to look at these men and see that there is much to know. In the words of the hymn writer Isaac Watts we do not have to live at *'this poor dying rate'*. By listening to these men on those Sunday evenings throughout the Spring of 2021, and by reading this book, I trust the aim has been that we will have a higher view of God, become more serious about Him, have a greater desire for Him and a resolve to really go after Him.

We took the title for the series from Shakespeare's play, *As You Like It*, where Jaques famously says,

All the world's a stage,
And all the men and women merely players;
They have their exits and their entrances ...

It is important to say, we were in no way likening these great preachers to 'players', actors or performers. The point was that they were nearing their exit from the stage, brought poignantly home when John Blanchard, whom we had interviewed on 21st March 2021, died less than two months later on 14th May. His interview with us was his last 'public' engagement and reinforced to us the importance of the series.

Besides, it was not only Shakespeare who likened this world to a stage. Calvin, in his commentary on the Psalms, said, *'The whole world is a theatre for the display of the divine goodness, wisdom, justice, and power …'*.

Who

We spoke to seventeen ministers and one full time evangelist in total, all with different personalities, temperaments and gifts. You will no doubt pick up as you read each chapter, that among other things, they have different views on eschatology, church government and baptism. But in all of them there was a 'sameness' of spirit, and every one of them mentioned Lloyd-Jones!

The list of men we interviewed is not exhaustive. We realise there are many more we could have included. The eighteen men were ones we knew best and had access to. Three others declined due to health reasons or did not feel able to participate, which goes some way towards explaining why there is not an Irishman present!

When

The interviews went out live on Sunday evenings between 8.15 pm and 9 pm. The first episode was on 28th February and the last one aired on 27th June. It made a difference that the interviews happened during COVID-19 lockdown restrictions, as even those who could go out to church for a distanced meeting were still unable to meet up with friends and have fellowship afterwards. Many people got in touch to say how lovely it was to go home after church and wait for quarter past eight. As lockdown lifted, some people chose to listen to the interviews later in the week, but there was something exciting about watching them live, with a cup of tea and a piece of toast, not knowing what was going to happen!

On average, nearly seven thousand people of all ages tuned in to each interview. The young people in my own church in London thoroughly enjoyed listening to these 'old men', many of whom became their new heroes.

We are convinced that God was in this series and desire that these testimonies be heard far and wide. We hope and pray this book will extend the reach of their stories for His glory.

Keith Batstone and Alun Ebenezer
November 2022

Chapter 1

Basil Howlett

Introduction

Basil Howlett kicked off the series, and it is hard to think of a better man to open the batting. I first came across Mr Howlett when I was a student at Aberystwyth University and he came to preach at the Christian Union. More recently, since I've been a member at Amyand Park Chapel in Twickenham, I have heard him preach many times at our church and he has become one of my heroes. He climbs the pulpit in his 80s, on a stick, full of arthritis, then tells the children stories about his recent missionary trips to Lokichogio and Myanmar! Whenever I hear him preach I am struck by how much this man loves the gospel and the mercy he has been shown by God. He has also written an excellent book called *1966 and all that*.

Background

He was born in 1940 in Norwich in the county of Norfolk. For many of his relatives, Norfolk was the centre of the universe, and they never left it all their lives. His earliest memories were of the Second World War. The Anderson shelter for the whole row of houses where he lived was in his garden, and as a young child he remembers being in that shelter night after night as bombs fell on the city. He recalls one particular night vividly when his mother could not get the family into the shelter in time. He shielded under the dining room table as first the front door was blown in, then the back door, followed by the windows all cracking and cups falling off the shelves. Norwich was decimated that night and a number of people in the area were killed. Just two hundred yards up the road a house was virtually destroyed and the mother and her young baby girl were rescued from that house by air raid wardens. Basil was very glad about that because the young lady who was rescued has been his wife for the last fifty-eight years!

Growing up at that time was tough and his parents were poor. The family home was a small terraced house with no bathroom and the toilet was some distance away from the house. Food was scarce and toys and sweets were almost non-existent. After the war, Basil's father lost his job for a while and when he managed to get work again it was 'piece work', which meant he only got paid for the work he did. So when his father took off the top of his thumb one day at work in an accident, he went to the hospital, had it bandaged up, and then went straight back to work again.

Basil passed the 11-plus exam and got a place at the City of Norwich Grammar School. The family was so poor that before he went to school in the morning he would do a newspaper round, then when he came home from school at night he would do another one. On Saturday mornings he would do a butcher's run delivering meat. He desperately wanted to go into the sixth form and then go to university, but his parents couldn't afford another school blazer and so he had to leave school and get a job in order to contribute to the family budget.

Basil was very envious of those young people who could stay on in the sixth form and were then able to go to university. He became bitter and fell in with a rough gang and got into terrible ways. He got a job in the sales office of a flour milling company and when he was about 18 one of the sales representatives had a very bad accident and they wanted someone to go out and meet the customers. Basil was the only person in the sales office who could drive, and so at the age of 18 he was given a company car and told, 'Get on with it, do what you can.' In those days a young fellow of 18 with a car was a rare thing, so it enabled him to sin more easily and it was a very bad time in his life.

At the same time, his parents were taking him to church three times a Sunday: morning service, afternoon Sunday school and Bible class, and then the evening service. But the gospel was never preached. Week after week he would sit there, never being convicted of sin because the gospel just wasn't preached. It had no influence on him at all. However, three things did shake him.

Conversion

Firstly, the gang that Basil was part of raced cars or motorbikes from Norwich to Newmarket and back to see who could do it in the fastest time. One night his friend turned his car over and was killed. It was the first funeral service Basil ever attended and as he saw the coffin he was struck by the thought that it could easily have been him in there.

The second thing that convicted him was that his parents, although very poor, were very hospitable. Every Sunday night after church they would invite people into the home and at the end of the evening they would sing. One night Basil heard them singing, '*Long my imprisoned spirit lay fast bound in sin and nature's night; Thine eye diffused a quickening ray, I woke, the dungeon filled with light; my chains fell off, my heart was free.*' He remembers thinking, 'I'd love to be free.' He was drinking too much, swearing, cursing and doing many other things he is now ashamed of, and the only help his minister gave him was to tell him to try harder. He clearly had no idea how deep the pit Basil was in or how helpless he was.

Thirdly, Margaret, the young lady who lived up the road who had been rescued from the bombed house, had been very ill with TB and recovered. After that she started attending the same church as Basil and all the fellows in the church were speaking about her. She was so beautiful and demure. Basil thought he'd 'chat her up' one night and see if he could get friendly with her, but she told him that he was living a mad life and there was no way that he could be her boyfriend. That shook him a bit.

Then one Sunday night a visiting speaker came to the church and he broke the rule: he preached the gospel, and that really did convict Basil of his sin. He really felt dreadful and was angry at first, but then the preacher told him the only way to be saved from his sin was through the Lord Jesus Christ, and that was how Basil was converted. The preacher never came again. He was never allowed to.

The Call and Training

Soon after Basil's conversion he was at a service one night. By this time the church had a new minister who was better than the previous one and had a warmth about his preaching. That night God clearly called Basil to give up his work and train to be a pastor. Basil was almost 20. He had never preached before in his life, but he knew that this gospel he had heard, which had saved him from a wretched life, he had to preach for the rest of his life.

Basil applied to a college to train for the ministry, but his minister insisted he went to the same college he had gone to, Manchester Baptist College. Unbeknown to Basil, it was the most liberal Baptist College in the whole country at that time, and for his first year he was just bowled over by the false teaching. He thought his lecturers were clever men, and as they had been appointed by the denomination they must be right. All the zeal that he had to preach the gospel evaporated for a while. When he went back for the second year there he hadn't prayed or read his Bible for months and was in a bad way. One of his fellow students, a man named Rex Cousins, said to him one night, 'Are you coming to hear Martyn Lloyd-Jones tonight at the Free Trade Hall in Manchester?' Such was Basil's ignorance, he said, 'Who's he?' But he was persuaded to go and hear this man Lloyd-Jones and has never forgotten that evening. In Basil's own words:

If it's possible theologically, which it is not, that was my second conversion that night. Lloyd-Jones preached on 1 Corinthians 2. There were maybe three thousand people there and he preached in an amazing way. I spent the sermon gripping my chair as he swept away all the delusions of modernism and then emphasised, '*I determined not to know anything among you except Jesus Christ and Him crucified.*' It was amazing. At the end of the message this congregation of three thousand was totally silent and nobody moved. We knew that God had met with us. After a while Mr Wise, a surgeon who led the meeting, came back onto the platform and said, 'Now friends, it's time for us to go home quietly and remember what we've learned.' I remember walking back with three other students to the college, about two or three miles, in total silence except for the occasional comment, 'Wasn't that amazing!' We knew that night that God had spoken to us and we'd never be the same again.

As a result of that night, a battle began at the college. The Principal was a man who had been brought up among the strict Baptists in Suffolk but had turned right against the faith and was now violently opposed to evangelicals. Alun McNabb (see Chapter 3) recommended that Basil bought *A Commentary on Romans* by Robert Haldane, his first book by the Banner of Truth. Alun was a student there at the college and another student, Peter Garner, kept Banner of Truth books in a case hidden under his bed because the Principal hated having reformed books on the premises.

Evangelical students had a particularly hard time in sermon classes. On one occasion when one of the evangelical students had finished preaching, the Principal slammed his books down on the table and stormed out of the room shouting, 'We've failed with you, we've failed,' only because the student preached the gospel. It really was a tough time for Basil and the others, but God brought them safely through.

Ministry

Cheltenham (July 1964 to August 1983)

His first church was in Cheltenham. He didn't go there alone because by then the young lady who had been rescued from the bombed house, and had previously told him to 'get lost', was his wife. Quite by accident he bumped into her in Cambridge when he was with a fellow student looking around. She was training there to be a radiographer. He thought he would start writing to her as in those days there were no mobile phones or emails. They got friendly and decided to marry. He was inducted into the church in Cheltenham on 11th July 1964, one day before his 24th birthday, and married Margaret on 18th July, the following Saturday. Quite a week!

The church in Cheltenham was a new church plant on a housing estate just a short distance away from GCHQ, the government spy centre. A number of people in the church spoke Russian. One of the young people in those days eventually married a man who was fluent in Russian and he turned out to be Geoffrey Prime who was imprisoned for thirty-eight years for spying for the Russians. There cannot be many ministers who have had to deal with a pastoral issue where a wife had just discovered her husband was a spy!

Chapter 1

The church was a real mixed bag. It was a church plant by a liberal church and an evangelical church working together, a kind of buffer between the two. In the congregation, alongside people who had never been converted were some fine evangelicals. Basil's first pastoral problem arose when the church secretary told him that during the interregnum the church had agreed to welcome a couple into membership and asked if Basil would receive them next Sunday at the communion service. Basil thought he had better go and see this couple beforehand and has never forgotten what happened when he did. The lady told him how she got messages in the graveyard from the dead and how she had been involved in 'astral travelling', which is another spiritualist term. Basil had no idea what he was up against and, totally bewildered as a young pastor, asked to pray with the couple before he left. As he prayed and mentioned the name of the Lord Jesus Christ, the wife went almost wild and he knew he had been in the presence of something very unclean. So much so, he felt he could not go straight home to his new wife and had to cycle around Cheltenham for a little while trying to get this out of his mind. His first pastoral problem of telling the church secretary he could not receive this couple into membership was followed hard by his second when the church secretary said, 'If you won't bring them into membership, I will!' Nowadays Basil would have stood up against him, but being only 24 at the time and new, he found it hard to do. Today he would advise the average 24-year-old to be an assistant pastor to begin with, but at the time few churches—only the very large ones—had assistants.

During his first few years in Cheltenham there were a number of moves to get him out. There was one woman who had a meeting in her house of all the disenchanted people in the church who wanted to get rid of him. She eventually gave up and phoned Basil to say she was leaving to go to another church, a rank and file liberal church, because there was a better class of people there!

Another man swore at him as he left the service on Basil's first Christmas Day there and shouted, 'If it's the last thing I do, I'll get you out of this church.' The same man turned up at Basil's house on Boxing Day and repeated the same threat.

On top of all this the Baptist Union, which the church was part of, was riddled with heresy at that time. Howard Williams, the president of the Union, had denied the resurrection, then later on Michael Taylor, who was then the principal of the college Basil had been to, actually denied the deity of Christ. The Baptist Union did nothing about it, and so the church resigned from the Baptist Union. Consequently, the church was evicted from the building and Basil, Margaret and their two young boys, were thrown out of the manse. Pastors in those days were very poorly paid and the church in Cheltenham had very little money. Basil remembers one day Margaret asking him to go through his pockets to see if he had any odd coins to buy a loaf of bread for the weekend. They didn't have a bank account and were down to the last one and sixpence (7½ pence today). Basil recalls, 'Those were tough days, really tough.'

Despite such a difficult start, Basil survived there for nineteen years and all of his four children were born while he was in Cheltenham. Eventually half of those opposed to him left and the other half were wonderfully converted. Great blessing came following an alarming incident. A man who had been a prisoner in Dartmoor knocked on the manse door one Saturday morning begging for money. When Basil offered him food and a tract instead of cash he screamed a torrent of abuse and hideous blasphemies at him and threatened to kill him. Following that, the man stood outside the manse in the centre of Cheltenham on many nights, shouting abuse, brandishing a knife and threatening to cut Basil's throat. He had a very close encounter with him one night when he was outside the house. It was a scary time, especially as Basil and Margaret by now had a young family. The church officers pledged themselves to meet every Saturday morning to pray for the family's protection and the conversion of this man.

They never saw this man converted, and in fact he did another stint in Dartmoor, but following that time of intense prayer they did see some amazing conversions: a retired professor of Aberdeen university, who had opposed Basil so much to start with, and on his first Sunday said, 'What can an old fellow like me learn from a young fellow like you?' wrote to Basil with the glorious news that he and his wife had been converted; there were students who went on to serve the Lord on the mission field; Mary, the wife of a brutal husband, who had spent most nights at the bingo hall, became eager to be with the Lord's people.

There was Keith, who was illiterate: he was drawn into the chapel as he passed by and heard hearty singing and his life was transformed. Soon after, he was witnessing to his mates and told them he would 'knock their ****** blocks off' if they did not come and hear the preacher! Basil praised him for his evangelistic zeal but gently told him, as a faithful saint had told him after he was converted, and as Paul told the Ephesians (4:29), that there are certain words we try not to use now that we are Christians.

Then there was Granny Smith who had been a motorcycle dispatch rider in the First World War. She smoked heavily, swore profusely and was very much involved in spiritism and the occult. Neither Basil nor her family will ever forget the night this wizened old lady of 84, with a severe curvature of the spine, almost ran to get baptised; or her tears of joy the following Christmas Day when she told them she was celebrating her first 'real' Christmas.

Vastly different, but equally wonderful, was Brother Benedict, a Roman Catholic monk who, when he was a patient in hospital, met two members from the church. When they heard that he had occasional compassionate leave from the monastery to visit his dying mother they invited him to come to church. One Sunday, to Basil's amazement, he saw him there in his monk's habit. On a subsequent Sunday Brother Benedict realised that even after twenty-five years in the monastery he was still unsaved and he cried to the Lord for mercy and was saved. He eventually left the monastery and was baptised. One of his duties was to look after the monastery library, so during the intervening time he regularly put gospel books Basil gave him from the church bookstall into the library, including the volume *Romans: Atonement and Justification* by D. M. Lloyd-Jones (much to the Doctor's delight!).

Every conversion is an amazing miracle, but probably the most amazing was Jane's. It certainly led to the most astounding prayer meeting Basil has ever known. She was the mistress of the high priest of a witches coven, involved in unspeakably vile conduct, but in the early hours of one

Sunday morning, driving home after another night of debauchery at a secret meeting in the forest, she happened to hear the name 'God' on the car radio and was shaken to the core as it dawned on her that one day she would have to face God and be judged. After a sleepless night she drove into Cheltenham looking for a church, but as she was about to enter the chapel her nerve failed her. After a restless Sunday afternoon she came back in the evening and heard the gospel and was gloriously saved. She ran down the aisle weeping to tell Basil that God had met with her and rescued her from a wretched life. Two weeks later she came to her first-ever prayer meeting and during the prayer time she sang a hymn which she had heard the previous Sunday, *'I need Thee every hour, most gracious Lord.'* She sang the whole hymn slowly with tears of sorrow for her past life and joy for her new life in Christ. At which point the prayer meeting 'took-off' as one after another person praised God for his mercy to Jane and pleaded with him to do a similar miracle in the lives of many others. According to Basil, 'We lost all sense of time, we were "in heaven" and knew that God was with us and no one wanted to go home.'

As for the church building, they had to change premises three times. In 1970 they had to leave Hester Way Baptist Church due to eviction by the Baptist Union and moved to Golden Valley Chapel, a disused Anglican church, which they were able to purchase with an anonymous gift. Basil still does not know who the donor was as he/she made the gift through a solicitor. Then in July 1976, due to growth, they had to find a larger premises and were able to lease, then purchase, North Place Chapel in the centre of Cheltenham. This was formerly a Countess of Huntingdon church which had become redundant. It was a 500-seater with a manse attached. Basil recalls, 'We had some amazing meetings there when the building was full. God was so good.'

Copse Road Chapel, Clevedon (September 1983 – August 1993)

After nineteen years, he moved to Clevedon in Somerset, which at the time was in Avon. He went there to preach for a holiday Sunday, and over lunch the secretary told him their pastor was retiring and asked if Basil would consider being their new pastor. The church had previously had trouble with the Charismatic Movement and in response to that they had drawn up a booklet which more or less excluded any experience of the Holy Spirit. Basil said he could not possibly sign the booklet, which, he added, neither could Spurgeon, George Whitefield, John Wesley, nor Martyn Lloyd-Jones. Despite Basil thinking that was that, a couple of weeks later the secretary wrote to him and said, 'Forget the booklet, will you still come to be the pastor?' So he moved to Clevedon and was there for ten years.

Despite seeing some blessing in Clevedon, that was the toughest period of his ministry. At the same time as being pastor of the church, he was president of the Fellowship of Independent Evangelical Churches (FIEC). Preaching three times a week, undertaking all the pastoral visitation and doing the work of the FIEC was hard enough, but on top of that the church had enormous problems, including having to deal with a man who attended the chapel who turned up at his house to confess he had been sexually abusing children who came to the church. The man's parents were members at the church and the father was one of the most reformed men mentally you could ever meet. But Basil had always had doubts about him and felt that something was not quite right. When they came to Basil's house one Sunday evening after their son had confessed to him about abusing children, the mother of course was distraught. But the father sat at the other end of the settee and did not even bother to put his arm around her to comfort her, which convinced Basil there was something seriously wrong. Not long afterwards, on a Sunday morning, the man had been taking part in the communion service. In the afternoon he left his wife and went to live permanently with a woman with whom he had been having an affair which had been going on for years under the guise of a reformed profession.

It was a really horrendous time and soon after that Basil's health finally broke down. He had been preaching in Portishead on a Tuesday night and had a violent nose bleed. He got himself home in the car but at midnight his nose was still bleeding. Margaret thought enough was enough and took him to the hospital where they told him plainly that he was a walking time bomb and insisted he went to see his GP. When the GP asked him what he was doing for the rest of the week, Basil said he was going away to the FIEC conference where he had to chair some meetings. The doctor told him that before he went anywhere she would need to do some more tests on him. When he asked if they could wait until he got back, she said, 'Yes by all means, *if* you get back!'

Borras Park Evangelical Church, Wrexham (September 1993 – September 2000)

After Clevedon, Basil moved to Borras Park in Wrexham. One morning he had a telephone call, out of the blue, from the man who was acting as moderator for Borras Park, saying, 'What would you say, Basil, if I told you that Borras Park Church Wrexham were thinking of you as their next pastor?' It was a total shock. He had never been to Wrexham in his life and all he knew about Borras Park was that Hywel Rees Jones had been pastor there.

He was in Wrexham for seven years. It was really beautiful and they were very happy there. The singing was magnificent and the elders were supportive and prayed regularly with him. He and Margaret thought they would be there until they retired, when they would then maybe move a little bit away from Wrexham to give the new man space, but stay on in North Wales. After all, only a madman would leave North Wales to go somewhere like Reading!

Carey Baptist Church, Reading and the World!

Basil had no intention of going to Reading. He had just been in Thailand and was shocked how missionaries generally in Thailand had little pastoral care. He saw in a missionary magazine that the director of the mission was advertising for someone to assist him with the pastoral care of missionaries. Basil said to his wife that he thought of applying for that job, to which she replied that he was too old and too deaf! In a conference in London shortly afterwards he relayed the story to Jonathan Stephen, commenting how honest and helpful wives could be! He assumed from that remark that Basil was thinking of applying for a job because he was keen to move from Wrexham—which was not the case at all.

Nevertheless, Basil was invited to Carey to be the associate pastor. Carey was a big church and were looking for someone to help pastor the church. At first Basil totally dismissed the idea, but the more he and Margaret prayed about it, the more convinced they became that this was God's will. So in October 2000 they went to Reading.

For the first time in thirty-six years he was not preaching at least three times a week most weeks and had a church office and administrator to deal with administrative matters. This gave him time to teach at London Seminary and to take Pastors' Conferences, Bible Conventions and college lectures in other parts of the world.

He and Margaret had begun going to India in 1992 and went most years until 2001 when they were evicted from the country and banned for fifteen years. That was heart-breaking for both of them. The authorities had picked up that Basil had been regularly preaching there. Through this experience Basil discovered the quickest way to get through disorderly crowds waiting to board planes at airport gates in India, who know nothing about polite British queues, was to be 'marched' through by armed guards! They were allowed back into India in 2016 and 2018.

Despite being devastated at being expelled from India, in God's amazing providence opportunities arose to minister in many other countries. Probably the most remote place they went to was Lokichogio on the border of north-west Kenya and South Sudan where the Middle East Reformed Fellowship (MERF) have a training centre for pastors. The flight from Nairobi to Lokichogio was on a small Mission Aviation Fellowship (MAF) plane. Basil and Margaret went there several times and thank God for the privilege, but they also were greatly moved and challenged by spending time with the Lord's people in Myanmar and Cambodia. The Christians were so courageous and joyful in the face of suffering.

In 2009 Basil retired from being a pastor at Carey Baptist Church but continues itinerant ministry in the UK and, until lockdown, in other countries. His last foreign visit was to the Cambodian jungle for the opening of a Christian Centre started by his friend Chhinho whose family suffered so much during the Pol Pot genocide.

Advice

After such a remarkable ministry, Basil's advice to young men going into the ministry today is invaluable. His greatest advice is for young ministers to value the helpfulness of really godly members. It was the support of these people who kept him going. He remembers one particular couple from his time in Clevedon. The man was the director of a building merchants and they had a beautiful house just outside Bristol. He and Margaret would just go there for an evening for supper and confide in them, share their burdens and pray with them. To Basil, the support of people like that was wonderful and he would encourage young ministers to prize highly such members and value their council.

Encouragements

Basil believes there are definitely reasons to feel encouraged by the state of the church in the UK today. He feels there are a number of very promising young men going into the ministry, for which we should praise God. There are also more churches now with a plurality of elders and there is more help these days for pastors' wives. Margaret was thrown in at the deep end, whereas now there are more opportunities for ministers' wives to meet up together, and he is thankful that the FIEC has appointed a ladies' worker. Back in their day there was no meeting held specifically for pastors' wives to encourage them.

The Westminster Fellowship

By contrast, Basil had the Westminster Fellowship which took place on the first Monday of every month except for the summer months. He found these a great blessing and he and Margaret had an agreement that she would never be sick, never give birth and never die on the first Monday of the month! They were not to be missed, even though it meant driving all the way from Cheltenham to London, and later from Clevedon to London. Maybe two hundred ministers would go. Lloyd-Jones would ask someone to lead in prayer and then would leave the meeting open. They had just one general rule: theological questions in the morning and pastoral questions in the afternoon. They were special sessions and dealt with an amazing number of subjects. It was very moving and one saw Lloyd-Jones at his best there. The man had a great sense of humour and an incredible knowledge of the Bible. All the years Basil went to the Westminster Fellowship he never once saw Lloyd-Jones open the Bible, but in discussion, if someone said that in Deuteronomy 26 it says so-and-so, he would say, 'Oh yes, but what about verse 19?' Phenomenal! And if ever the discussion lacked power during the day, then to be there for the summing up and the final prayer was moving beyond measure. Lloyd-Jones knew what many of the young men were going through, battling against liberalism in their churches, and the care he showed them was quite wonderful.

Legacy

As far as Basil is concerned, his legacy is his passion to preach the gospel of the Lord Jesus Christ. He has never forgotten the sheer wonder of the fact that the Lord Jesus Christ saved him. He loves the children's hymn, *'It is a thing most wonderful, almost too wonderful to be, that God's own Son should come from heaven, and die to save a child like me,'* and substitutes the word 'child' in the last line with 'wretch'. Wherever he goes to preach, he preaches this gospel as though people have never heard it before. He maintains that in one of the services each Sunday, the gospel should be preached very plainly and clearly to people.

The Need of the Hour

As for the need of the hour, Basil is convinced it is for people to be on their knees pleading with God to intervene and pour out His Spirit. People should be crying out for God to revive us. It alarms him that there are many professing Christians who never ever go to a prayer meeting.

It also troubles him that there are some people who give their testimonies without ever mentioning sin. He wants to say to these people, 'But what has He saved you from? You say Jesus is a wonderful person, but what has he saved you from?'

Finally, he thinks it important how the church reaches out to the unchurched. In some ways he is very grateful for the fact that Margaret's family had no church connections at all, not even a Bible in the house.

In fact, when Margaret's mother realised that her daughter was going to marry a 'vicar' as she called him, she was quite horrified. Thankfully that horror eventually ceased! Some time after he and Margaret were married, Margaret's parents came to stay with them in Cheltenham one weekend and a conversation between them on the Sunday morning was overheard. Mother-in-law asked, 'What shall we do this morning? Shall we go to church with them?' Father-in-law answered, 'We had better go and hear Basil preach.' They did so and realised that their new son-in-law was not some crank or boring cleric in fancy robes, and a good and friendly relationship developed. In fact, when Margaret's mother suddenly died, her father asked Basil to conduct the funeral service.

That has helped Basil enormously in reaching the unchurched. A lot of young men today are very eager to reach the unchurched working class, which is a very noble aim and to be admired. But they have no idea how to do it. They treat the unchurched working class people as though they were ignorant fools. But they are not intellectually ignorant and many of them are very clever people. Father-in-law, though he worked all his life as a clicker in a shoe factory, was a clever man, as Basil discovered when playing Scrabble or other word games with him, and mother-in-law was a very skilled woman. The unchurched are just ignorant of the truth of the gospel, like we all were before God revealed himself to us. Basil believes we must not speak to them in a condescending way but respectfully. Preachers, with the help of the Holy Spirit, need to preach the gospel clearly, not in a roundabout way, but straightforwardly, impressing upon people their need of this glorious gospel—the same glorious gospel that saved a 'wretch' like Basil Howlett.

Chapter 2

Neville Rees

Introduction

Growing up in Evangelical Movement of Wales (EMW) circles, Neville Rees was one of the great Welsh preachers we all knew and loved. He has been to every Aberystwyth Conference, including the very first one in 1957. In fact only a global pandemic could stop him going! I remember vividly his morning addresses on the life of Joseph, when he was the main conference speaker in 1994.

There is also a great story about Luther Rees, Neville's father, who was a famous preacher in Wales in the 1950s and 1960s. He was dying and losing consciousness. His wife was holding his hand and his daughter-in-law said to him, 'Dad, you don't know who's holding your hand, do you?' 'Yes,' he said, 'and he'll never let it go!'

Neville is married to Beryl and they have three children, Tim, Matthew and Rachel, eight grandchildren and one great-grandchild.

Background

He was born in 1937 in a little village called Skewen, near Neath, in South Wales. His father worked for a firm as a master baker but had always wanted his own business. So in 1942, during the war, the family moved to Britain Ferry where Neville's father bought a bakery.

They lived there with his grandmother who had moved in with the family after she was widowed, soon after Neville's parents had married. Neville never knew his grandfather, a Cornishman who had come to work in the opencast colliery in Skewen, where he had met his wife. He had an interesting background which had greatly affected Neville's grandmother. He was of the Billy Bray type of Methodism which was largely unheard of in Skewen, but which Neville's grandfather told his family, and all those around him, all about.

As Neville's parents were so busy rebuilding the business which had run down during the war time, Neville did not see much of them during the day and was therefore more influenced by his grandmother than his parents while growing up. She was a godly woman.

The family began to worship on the Lord's day in the church in Skewen, where Neville's mother and father were married. He discovered later that the grandfather he never knew, along with his brother-in-law, were founder members of that church which had come out of Methodism. Under R. G. Campbell, Methodism was the first to fall to the new teaching of liberalism. One Sunday morning Neville's grandfather had stood up, with his wife and three children alongside him, and proclaimed to a full church, holding his Bible up, 'I'm not hearing this book declared here. I want to be assured this morning that you are going to preach this book.' But they shouted at him and told him to be patient as they were not sure whether the Bible is all true. As he heard these things he said, 'I can see that you're not going to teach this book. Well I've got to tell you, that as for me and my family, we are here for the last time and I am going to go out and form a church which will teach the Bible only. Anybody who is interested can follow me.' About thirty or forty people followed him out and that is how they formed the Free Mission Church in Denver Road, Skewen.

This was the church that Neville grew up in. His mother was involved with the singing, his father did some of the preaching, and so he sat by his grandmother who nurtured him in the Christian faith. She was constantly prodding him and put a text behind his bed from Proverbs, which said that whoever put his trust in the Lord shall be safe. She would say to him, 'When you go to bed, look at that text and remember the Lord Jesus is looking after you.'

Neville passed the scholarship, later called the 11-plus, to go to the Neath Grammar School when he was just 10 years old. It was quite an experience to go to this school a year before he should have, but when he got to the O Level class, as he was only 15 and too young to sit the exams, he had to do the Fifth form twice.

By this stage in his life he started to really listen to the ministry at the Mission and was struck with its emphasis on the Bible and the need to be converted. He also noticed at this time that his father, Luther Rees, was preaching a lot more. He had actually become the lay pastor there in 1948, some five years earlier. Luther Rees' preaching was influenced by Lionel B. Fletcher. Luther's father, who was an engineer at sea, had taken Luther to hear him preach at Wood Street Congregational Church in Cardiff when Luther was a teenager.

Conversion

1953 was a big year. It was the year of the coronation and his father was so busy baking cakes for all the tea parties, as well as preaching in the mission, that he was taken seriously ill. As Neville and his mother and grandmother watched the coronation on a black and white TV, there was a knock at the door and an ambulance outside the house. His father was carried into the house on a stretcher. The doctor said that if he carried on at this rate he would be dead within five years. His father needed a complete rest and so they went to stay with his mother's sister in America for a long break. It was a bit different from their normal annual holidays in Bournemouth!

1953 was also the year Neville sat his O Levels and, more importantly, the year he became a Christian. His history teacher, Sam Evans, who was also his form master, was a very remarkable man. As well as teaching history, he was also the Head of Mathematics. Neville remembers him walking in on the first day back to school after the Christmas break and saying, 'Now then, do any of you boys remember what we were studying before we had the Christmas break?' A boy put his hand up and said, 'What it was like to live in the eighteenth century in England, sir.' 'Well done,' said Mr Evans, 'Today I am going to talk to you about some characters we know from that time. Hands up any if you have seen the light.' There was silence and all the boys turned to look at Neville who was sitting in the corner, because by this time he was learning the Bible with his grandmother and entering Bible quizzes in the Christian Endeavour Movement. But Neville thought, 'I can't put my hand up as I have not seen the light.' The teacher went on to explain that it was a reference to Wesley's *'warming of his heart strangely'*, and then said, 'They want me to be a deacon in the church, boys, but I like having a pint too much, and you can't be a deacon and have a pint.'

It shook Neville that he couldn't put his hand up. From then on every Sunday in January, right through to March, he came under conviction of sin, and two sins in particular which had become prominent in his teenage years: being conceited and being deceitful. In front of his father, the lay pastor, he was a very good boy, always in all the church meetings. But deep down in his heart he knew he was a sinner.

The school break came for Easter and there was a week of prayer in the church, leading up to Good Friday. Neville did not go on the Monday night or the Tuesday, but decided to go to the Wednesday night prayer meeting, which was the normal one. He had never been to the prayer meeting before and he was the only one out of the large group of young people at the church who was there. In that meeting, his father opened in prayer and gave a little verse to encourage the people to pray. As the people started praying, Neville's grandmother and her friend, Mrs Morgan, broke out into song. They were singing the hymn, *'Standing somewhere in the shadows you will find Jesus'*, which repeats the line, *'and you know him by the nail prints in his hands'*. As people continued to pray, Neville wondered what on earth he was doing in this meeting. Then Mrs Morgan, in her 70s and someone the young people considered a pain as she was always correcting them, began singing a solo quietly, *'Oh how I love Him since for me He bled and died'*. At which point Neville began to weep and weep. He doesn't remember anymore of the meeting. He was just crying out to God, 'Please give me the faith of my grandmother and Mrs Morgan. I'm sorry, please take away my sin.' At one point when he did open his eyes, he said it was like he saw the Lord Jesus with his nail prints in his hands saying, 'Come to me.' The year before, the family had moved from Britain Ferry back to Skewen, so when the meeting ended, Neville was able to walk home. He couldn't wait for his father to come in through the door. When he did he immediately took his father into the front room. Neville couldn't speak because he was weeping. His father asked him what was wrong, to which he replied, 'I want to be sure that Jesus is in my life, please lead me to Him.' After explaining to his father what had happened, his father and Neville got on their knees to pray, first his father, then Neville. When Neville said, 'Oh Lord, I'm sorry for being so deceitful,' his father prodded him and said, 'Pour out your heart, my son, pour it all out to Jesus, he'll cleanse you of it all.' Neville's father then prayed and thanked God for working, and they both embraced each other.

Neville felt ten foot tall and was sorry that the school was on holiday. He was on fire and wanted to go back to Neath Grammar School to see all his year group converted, as well as his form teacher, Sam Evans.

From that moment, Neville had full assurance of salvation and never had any doubts. In fact his assurance has only become deeper and stronger.

The Call

Neville did not know what to do with his life. As his father was a baker, he was exempt from going to war because people needed bread. There were a group of men Neville remembers like that, including the butcher and the bank manager, who affectionately became known as 'Dad's Army'. Neville's father directed him towards Mr Walsh, the bank manager, and felt that banking would be a good career for him. Through Mr Walsh's influence, Neville went to Cardiff for two interviews in Lloyd's Bank and Midland. At these interviews they told Neville he was too young but that they would send for him on his seventeenth birthday. So Neville continued with his 'A' levels, waiting to see what would happen with the bank.

At the same time, the Slavic Gospel Mission visited their young people's meeting and Rev John Thomas came. The meeting was open to everybody, but when John Thomas saw about twenty young people sitting in the church, he really changed his approach and went after the young people. He challenged them that if the Lord Jesus had died for their sins and they loved Him, why not think about serving Him? He had been to Keswick where they invited people to go out to the front and give themselves to become missionaries, and he did something similar that night. They sang a hymn and, as they were singing, people were invited to go to him and give themselves to the Lord to become missionaries. Sitting next to Neville was Alan Watkins. He turned to Neville and said, 'Come on, Neville, let's go out. I'm going to serve the Lord in Spain.' As he said that, Neville thought, 'I'm not, I feel the Lord is calling me to serve Him in Wales.' Alan Watkins later became a minister in Tredegar. Not quite the Costa Brava!

When he went home that night Neville thought, 'What have I said?' And so he prayed earnestly. He waited then for an opportunity to speak with his father. Since their holiday in America, Neville had grown very close to his dad, and on that trip had already talked to him about the ministry.

Neville sent off for the prospectus of the London Bible College, but being a member of the congregational church in Neath, his father encouraged him to apply to the Congregational Theological College in Brecon. When Neville sat the entrance exam it turned out his father, Luther, was sitting it as well! He had been the lay minister at the Mission in Skewen for many years, but they had never called him to be their full time pastor. Needless to say, they both passed and it was there that they met men like Derek Swann and Malcolm Evans.

Neville then went off to study at Cardiff and it was a time of real strengthening before his theological training. He shared digs with his close friend, Keith Davies. Neville became president of the Christian Union at Cardiff and Keith was the prayer secretary. They are still good friends today.

Ministry

Neville became the minister of Libanus in Morriston, Swansea, and was the pastor there throughout the forty years of his ministry. It was a liberal, totally run-down church. It was in the congregational denomination that did not believe the gospel at all and did not want it.

Neville went there as a student pastor during the summer of 1961, and it was on the strength of him being there that they felt he was a good prospect to stay and be their pastor. They had not had a pastor since 1940. They convened a church meeting early, and in October Neville received the call to be the pastor of the church. His college principal told him not to accept the call yet as he was preaching in other churches, and there was a much loved Aunty Bessie living in Dowlais who was anxious for him to go to the congregational church there.

The new year came and he felt he should make a decision. He had a mentor who had come to take charge of the young people's work at the church. He told Neville he had to decide whether it was the Lord diverting him, or was it the devil? It made Neville sit up and he realised that he should go to Libanus, Morriston. He had a verse of scripture given to him from Acts 18, 'Do not be afraid, I have much people in this city.' He began his ministry there in July 1962, aged 25.

By this time he had married Beryl. Their great desire was to see people soundly converted and to see the church transformed from its liberalism and thinking. Beryl started up a young wives' meetings while Neville started up a children's meeting, re-started the prayer meeting and preached on the Lord's day. Bit by bit they saw conversions, but in the early days there was much opposition and there were difficulties to overcome.

Difficulties

A crucial year was 1969, by which time Neville was pushing the deacons hard. He had inherited twelve deacons, six women and six men who in reality were only figureheads. When Neville and Beryl started up things they were never asked in deacons' meetings how they were getting on with the young wives' meetings, or how was the children's meeting going. So Neville began challenging them. Only one of them went to the prayer meeting. When Neville pressed them on this they started to attack him and tell him how disappointed they were in his ministry. He would go home and say, 'I can't take any more of this.'

The church secretary came to see him because four deacons had resigned, which was a big surprise. That led to an urgent church meeting, to which every member was called, and to which every member came. The letter simply said, 'If you are anxious about the future of this church please attend this meeting.' After Neville opened the meeting, he sat down and one of the men, who had offered his resignation, started attacking him. Neville was not allowed to open his mouth but just had to sit there and wait for his opportunity. When Neville eventually stood up to speak, another man jumped up and said:

Mr Chairman, I came to this meeting not knowing what was happening. It seems to me that our deacons are not supporting our young minister. I want to make a proposition that all of them stand down. We have full confidence in our minister because sitting in front of me are my two granddaughters and their husbands and who have all been saved and their lives have been transformed.

He went on to say that it had not happened to him, but all he knew was if it has happened to them and has changed them, then let's have more of the same. Another person jumped up and seconded it and said, 'Let's put it to the vote.' Everybody voted in favour, and the deacons, who were very upset, all stood down. After an election, eight people got two-thirds of the vote and subsequently met with Neville. He told them they now had to work with him and he explained what he believed. He gave an outline of his plans, which they completely endorsed.

Blessings

Up until that point they had only known of the two young couples being converted, but there were many others throughout the 1960s and 1970s.

In 1973 Dr Martyn Lloyd-Jones came to preach at Libanus. Neville's father, who was very good friends with him, had asked him to come and preach at Neville's induction, but he was away. The occasion in 1973 was the centenary of Libanus as an English-speaking church (it was a Welsh-speaking church before that for ninety years). Dr Lloyd-Jones preached on the Saturday and the Sunday and six people professed conversion. The mother and father of the two girls had started attending church. The father was a big man, weighed about twenty stone, and had a big deep voice. He was there on the Sunday morning the Doctor preached. He usually spoke Welsh to Neville on the door, but this particular Sunday morning he just walked past him as if he was staring into space. He came back in the evening and said, 'Pastor, I was converted going home in the rain this morning.' That night Lloyd-Jones preached on, *'How shall we escape if we neglect so great a salvation?'* Neville encouraged the man to go and talk to Lloyd-Jones who was sitting down the front, but the man thought he would not want to see someone like him. So Neville pushed all twenty stone of him down there, and in Neville's own words:

What I saw moved me overwhelmingly. There was Lloyd-Jones getting out of the big seat and putting his arm around him, because he was weeping like a child, and putting him to sit by him and that arm did not leave all the time he was talking with him. I had to go out and greet other people, and then he came out to me, radiant, and said, 'Pastor, what do you think he said to me? He said, "I would have travelled the Atlantic to see you like this."'

Dr Lloyd-Jones never forgot that man, and whenever Neville went to the Puritan Conference in London he would call Neville over and ask how the big man was doing. Four years later he had a massive heart attack and died. When Neville told the Doctor, he wished Neville had told him at the time and took the family's address and wrote to them.

In 1976 Dr Lloyd-Jones went back to Libanus to preach at a Thanksgiving Service. The schoolroom next to the church building needed a lot of work done to it and some people suggested they try to raise the money for the building project. But Neville challenged them on why couldn't they all just give the money, which they did, and a party of men from within the church worked three nights each week on demolishing and rebuilding the school room. At the thanksgiving service three children were converted that night, including Alun McNabb's (see Chapter 3) daughter-in-law, Jane.

Neville was heavily involved in the ministry of EMW camps in Bala. He led them, was chaplain on them and became chairman of the camps committee in 1980. In fact, after we interviewed Mr Rees, we received several emails from people, including Jonny Dyer, saying they wished he had spoken more about his work on the camps as they were such special times and many young people were converted on them.

Advice

When asked, Neville found it difficult to give advice to young ministers but thinks it would be to love people and not to give up on them. Throughout his ministry, he chased and chased after people and never gave up on them and as a result he saw people coming unexpectedly to the church.

Morriston is four or five miles outside the city centre of Swansea, and so they saw themselves very much as a local church for local people, and that is where they directed their energies. They were not interested in attracting people from all over Swansea. Their aim was to rebuild the church which was going to be Bible-based, gospel-orientated and with born-again experience to become the entrance into membership and nothing more. He would urge young preachers to have the same approach.

He would also emphasise the need for prayer—real prayer—with other pastors. In the 1960s Neville, along with Eryl Davies (see Chapter 9), went to a prayer meeting that was convened on a Friday morning with Neville's father, Andrew Davies' (see Chapter 11) father, I. B., and pastor George Griffiths. The prayer meeting was for revival, and in those meetings Neville had a glimpse of men with an experience which he had not known before: people like John Thomas, Elwyn Davies and plenty of others; men of the Evangelical Movement of Wales, really.

Furthermore, he would encourage men in the ministry to have good friends and outlets. For him, one was the EMW ministers' conference in Bala. Neville was asked by Hugh Morgan and John Thomas to be the treasurer because he was good at maths! That resulted in Neville eventually becoming the secretary. Unbeknown to Neville, it was a conference that Lloyd-Jones had planned, so Neville had to be in touch with Lloyd-Jones. To Neville, he was someone way up there, but he became without question the man he admired and loved more than any, and Lloyd-Jones helped him immensely in every way. He took Neville through an experience once when he was being pulled away from Libanus. Lloyd-Jones asked to see Neville, and after Neville told him all about it Lloyd-Jones told him to stay in Wales as he was needed there, and that is why Neville stayed in the same place for forty years.

Alan Tovey, who became the general secretary of the Evangelical Fellowship of Congregational Churches (EFCC) was a good friend to Neville. He remembers him arriving as a first-year student to the Theological College in Swansea when Neville was in his final year. They built a friendship which never ceased until Alan was called home.

Other people who have been a big influence on Neville include Douglas MacMillan, Eric Alexander, John and Eluned Thomas, Vernon and Morwen Higham and Hugh and Mari Morgan. Neville's father, Luther, and Andrew Davies' father, I. B. Davies, had such a close relationship that Neville and Andrew were drawn together. The families would holiday together in the 1980s.

The State of the Church and the Need of the Hour

Neville felt it was very difficult to assess how things really are in the UK at the moment as, at the time, we were still in the grip of the pandemic. However, he has sensed for a while that we are beginning to lose our way in terms of preaching. He says this after decades of never missing the Aberystwyth Conference, the ministers' conference in Bala and the Banner of Truth Conference. Too often in preaching, the Lord Jesus Christ is not clearly seen. 1 Corinthians 2:2, '*I determined not to know anything among you except Jesus Christ and him crucified*', becomes sidelined a little. He also says that people often ask him if churches are becoming too middle class, a bit academic, and where today is the working man? He wondered when we spoke to him how things would look when churches came out of lockdown, but said three areas are without doubt paramount: prayer, preaching and pastoring. Neville wants to hear preaching again which is from a burning heart, not lecturing. People praying and really pleading with God, and his greatest longing is for the power of the Holy Spirit to be upon the church.

Chapter 3

Alun McNabb

Introduction

When I was at University in Aberystwyth and attended Alfred Place Baptist Church, I remember Geoff Thomas telling us that of all the men he knew, Alun McNabb was the one who had the least fear of man and was an incredibly bold open air preacher. I also remember Mr McNabb preaching a very memorable sermon in the Aberystwyth Conference in 1994 on 'Receivers and Rejecters' from John 1, and then a sermon in the Heath Evangelical Church a number of years later on Judas Iscariot. He is a tremendously clear, no nonsense preacher, and has been someone I have hugely admired and loved to listen to over the years.

Background and Conversion

He was born into a Christian home and had the privilege from his earliest days of hearing the gospel. Like many people born in Christian homes, he assumed that he was a Christian. This went on for a few years, but he soon discovered that he was a sinner who needed a Saviour. He needed to confess his sin and trust Christ. There were no dramatics, but it was real and he praises God for that.

It could have been very different because his father was born into a drunkard's home and they were very poor and hungry. His father would tell the story of when he was a boy, a cart passed him full of loaves. He went up behind it and stole one of the loaves and took it home to his sisters. There were no plates, no knives and no butter, they just pulled the loaf apart and ate it because they were so hungry.

When his father was fifteen he was on his way to work and a man he was travelling with said to him, 'What are you doing tonight, Tom?'

'Oh,' he said, 'I'm not doing anything.' 'Well,' he said, 'Why don't you come with me to the tent?' He thought he was going to a circus so asked how much it was to get in. 'Oh, it's free,' said the man. His father was on to anything that was free and agreed to go to the tent. When he got there, instead of animals the place was full of chairs and there was a line of men sitting on a platform. The service began and he didn't understand the slightest word of all that went on as never in his life had he been inside a church. It was the Brethren Assemblies who were having a gospel mission and at the end there was some kind of appeal for people to go out if they had a spiritual need. When he saw these people going forward, Alun's father thought maybe they would give him something, so he went out. When he got there, there was a counsellor who was assigned to him and told him to sit down and asked him his name. 'McNabb,' he said. 'No,' said the man, 'Not my name, your name.' It was such a strange thing as there are not many McNabbs in the world. Here was his father being spoken to by a Mr McNabb! He asked him why he had come forward. But Alun's father didn't really know. So the man pressed him: was it something he heard in the sermon, or maybe in one of the hymns, or was it the Bible reading? To which Alun's father responded each time, 'No'. He really didn't know. 'Well,' said the man, 'let's begin at the beginning,' and this faithful gospel man went through the gospel from A to Z. His father sat listening and all of a sudden the Spirit of God came upon him and he saw and understood the whole thing. He went into that tent blind, ignorant and in total darkness but he came out 'ransomed, healed, restored, forgiven'. He was a new man at 15 years of age.

He went straight home to his sisters and told them about the gospel and they got wonderfully saved. Then they said, 'We must start on our mother,' and invited her to church. She said she couldn't possibly go to church as she did not have a coat. So they clubbed together and bought her a coat and she went to church and was saved. By this time she was sixty years of age but still had a lovely voice and she used to sing in the open air. Her favourite hymn was, *'In loving kindness Jesus came, my soul in mercy to reclaim, and from the depths of sin and shame, through grace He lifted me'*. It was a wonderful work of grace. But it didn't end there.

His father's sisters had girls and two of them married ministers. His father had Alun, of course, and he became a minister. Then it went down to the grandchildren. The daughters had sons who went into the ministry, and Alun has a son, Wesley, and he is in the ministry. And so it goes on, and it all began by a man saying to Alun's father on a tram car, 'What are you doing tonight, Tom?' Who knows where the little things we do for our Saviour can lead!

The Call and Training

Alun's father married Elsie and then Alun came along. They worshipped at the AC Mitchell Memorial Hall, which was a branch of the Liverpool City Mission. The minister there was Pastor H. J. Bogle. Like most gospel preachers he got his fair share of criticism, but he was good to Alun and such an encouragement. He used to get Christian magazines from America, as there were very few in this country at the time, and pass them on to Alun. He would read about these preachers in America, and even at the age of 17 was already getting ideas about becoming a preacher. His minister encouraged him and so he started to go to different places preaching, and when he was 18 he joined the Merseyside Lay Preachers Association.

He had a very interesting experience one wet Sunday night. He was on the No.27 bus travelling to a church in the south of Liverpool. There weren't many people on the bus but he was sitting by the window on the right hand side and there was a man sitting by the window on the left-hand side. All of a sudden he leaned over to Alun and said, 'Excuse me but what's that book you've got there?' Alun told him it was his Bible. The man asked him what he would want one of those for, so Alun said he was on the way to preach. 'Oh,' he said 'you're a preacher are you? Well, have you done much reading?' By this point all Alun had read was the *Dandy* and the *Beano* and one or two other things, but he wasn't a great reader. This total stranger then said to Alun, 'If I give you the name of a book, will you read it?' A bit intimidated, he agreed. The book was, *In*

Understanding be Men by Canon T. C. Hammond. Alun bought that book and read it, which was the beginning of his serious theological education. The man in the bus was a Christian and turned out to be a lecturer at Fuller Theological Seminary in Southern California. The question is, what was a lecturer from Fuller Theological Seminary in Southern California doing on a No.27 bus in the south of Liverpool on a wet Sunday night? It was nothing other than the providence of God!

When Alun's father was 14 he got a job as an apprentice in a firm of printers. He saved and saved and saved until, when the boss retired many years later, he was able to buy the business. It was a big difference from when he was stealing a loaf of bread! Alun was the only child and so he was lined up to take over the business, but Alun felt God calling him into the ministry and his father never raised any objection and was happy that his son should do this. Even so, Alun did serve his apprenticeship at his father's printers as a compositor, and then he went for two years RAF national service.

He then went to Manchester Baptist College, the same time as Basil Howlett (see Chapter 1). On the last day of college they were all standing in the hall waiting to move out, and Professor Farr came up to Alun and said, 'Well, Mr McNabb, you have finished the course.' Alun looked him in the eye and said, 'Yes sir, but have I kept the faith?' Alun maintains that if he had believed all that that man had tried to teach him, he would have had a question mark over every chapter in the Old Testament and probably every chapter in the New Testament as well.

Nevertheless he learned a great deal at college. Two-thirds of the students were modernists and a third of them were evangelicals. He is so grateful to God for those evangelicals and for people like Peter Garner with whom he is still in touch sixty years later. He remembers them as golden times and came out of college with the great blessing of being able to smell modernism a mile away!

He left college in June and in August married Margaret Titherington. They have been married for over sixty wonderful years. The Lord gave them four children, Andrew, Wesley, Rachel and Peter, and by His grace they are all following the Lord.

Ministry

Kay Street Baptist Church, Rawtenstall, Lancashire (1961-1968)

Alun was called to the Baptist Church in Rawtenstall, which is in north-east Lancashire, on the Lancashire/Yorkshire border in the Rossendale Valley. Both Alun and Margaret were young and nervous. The church was in the Baptist Union Church, which proved difficult.

He remembers that about two weeks before the induction he and Margaret were at the manse getting a few things together. The church building was only a few yards away, and so they went down to have a look around. When they got to the church hall they discovered they were having a jumble sale and Alun quickly realised that this was going to be one of their first problems. Margaret was made the Chair of the Baptist Women's Meeting and at the first meeting, at the ripe old age of 23, she stood up before these ladies, who were all old enough to be her grandmother, and said, 'Ladies, I understand just before we arrived you had one of your jumble sales. Well, we won't be having any more; instead the church will be supported by direct giving.' Then she sat down and waited for the arrows to fly. But not an arrow flew, nor was the jumble sale matter ever mentioned again.

In the kindness of God, a few miles away lived a couple in the ministry at another church, Keith and Marjorie Maudsley. Alun and Margaret just loved going to their manse, and their coming to theirs. It was such a strengthener and a real means of grace.

During his first two years at the church, Alun saw no conversions, but after two years one of the girls, Di, said to him after the morning service that she would like to come and see him that afternoon. They arranged a time, and when Di came she said she wanted to be baptised. There were many baptised members in the church but they were little more than just big Baptists, so Alun asked her why she would want to do that. She replied, 'I have been converted to Christ and I want to be obedient to Him.' She was in the sixth form at the local grammar school and witnessed to her friends there. They started coming with her to church and it was the nearest thing that they saw to revival, as one after another of the young people were converted. They used to meet after church on Sunday nights and would share what they had been reading from the Word during the week. Alun recalls, 'It was a precious, precious time. It really was.' He was thankful to God for those days and didn't have as many blessings with conversions like that again in his other churches. Despite there being many good people there who loved what was happening among the young people and really encouraged Alun, some of the older members couldn't cope with what was happening, and one man who had been a member for many years accused Alun of turning the church into a circus.

There was also a deacon who attended church only once a month on a Sunday evening. Being a young pastor Alun thought he had to do something about this. So he went to see the deacon to speak to him about it. He went back home to Margaret and said that he felt the deacon had taken it quite well. But the following Sunday, all the deacons (the church didn't have elders) were in the vestry, and the man came in and shouted, 'Put me down in your book, you cheeky monkey, checking up on me.' Then he walked up to Alun, raised his fist and stood over him. He didn't hit him but Alun was bracing himself, if he had, to give him the other cheek!

Finaghy Baptist Church, Belfast (1968-1974)

After Alun had been at Rawtenstall for nearly seven years, he preached in Belfast at Finaghy Baptist Church. Whilst at the communion service on the Sunday morning he had an overwhelming conviction that he would be called to that church, and so it turned out. Neither Alun or Margaret had been to Ireland at all, did not know anybody there, or anything about it, but they felt that God had called them.

So over they went, in 1968, during the time of 'the troubles' as they are called. He and Margaret maintain that those seven years in Belfast were their golden years. They were unaware of any member saying a wrong word to another, nor did any of the overseers say a wrong word one to the other. It was a precious time.

For about three years he also taught part time at Belfast Bible College which he loved, particularly during the coffee time afterwards, talking to those godly people there. So, one might ask, why would you ever leave?

Priory Road Baptist Church, Dudley (1974-2003)

Alun was visiting one of his members, Mr Qua, in the Belfast City Hospital. He asked Alun to have a word with the man in the next bed who was a believer, which Alun did. The poor man was very ill and had an oxygen mask. Alun said he was sorry to see he was so ill and understood he was a believer. He was gasping, *'The sufferings of this present life are not worthy to be compared with the glory which shall be revealed.'* Alun went back to Mr Qua who now asked Alun to go and talk to the Sister who was a member of Great Victoria Street Baptist Church, which he did. He then returned to Mr Qua again, who this time pointed to a young doctor and told Alun to have a word with him as he was a member of Knox Presbyterian Church. So Alun went and had a word with him as well.

Alun had already preached at Dudley the previous summer and they had rung him afterwards and asked him if he would be interested in a call to the church. Alun had no interest. They were in the Baptist Union and he had come out of the Union when he left Rawtenstall. They also had a choir, the Baptist hymn book and who knows what else. He really didn't want to go to Dudley, but said he would pray about it for a few days. He then declined the offer.

But after visiting the Belfast City Hospital ward, he came out and stood on the pavement and said, 'Lord, I have only spoken to four people in that ward and they are all believers. I don't think that would happen in any hospital in England; maybe I made a mistake about Dudley.' Four months had elapsed but he rang the folk at Dudley and asked how things were and whether they had settled on a new minister. They had not done anything about it since Alun had last been there. Alun said, maybe he had made a mistake and perhaps God was calling him to Dudley. He went to preach there again, they called him, and he ended up being there for twenty-nine years.

While he was there, they decided to come out of the Baptist Union because of the dreadful things that were being said and done, particularly the denial of Christ's deity. But they knew of others who had come out and they had lost their building. The church building at Dudley was lovely and they worried about losing it. But they thought they had to do what was right and wrote a letter saying they were resigning from the Union. They received a letter back saying they were very sorry to lose them, wished them God's blessing in the future, and they never heard a word about the building to this day!

There were some wonderful people at Dudley and the prayer meetings were outstanding. On Alun's first Sunday he asked someone how many had been at the previous Thursday's prayer meeting. They answered that there had been about thirty or thirty-five. The church had more than a hundred members, and so on the Sunday he said to the members, 'Now I understand there were about thirty or thirty-five people at the prayer meeting last Thursday. I don't think that's good enough, is it? Now this coming Thursday I personally will put out a hundred chairs in the hall and I challenge you to fill them.' That Thursday there were about one hundred and thirty-five people there. They could hardly all fit in, and from that time onwards they had a hundred people or so at the prayer meeting. They were wonderful times.

But there were also difficult times and sixty people left, but the interesting thing about that time was that the prayer meeting did not decline and the offerings went up. There were blessings in the midst of difficulty.

Open Air Preaching

In Rawtenstall, Alun would stand with Keith Maudsley in the Open Air. There were just the two of them and none of the members would stand with them because they thought they had gone mad. In Belfast he did some open-air preaching, but when he went to Dudley he began straight away, and every other Saturday morning they were there, and that was for twenty nine years. Even since Alun has retired from the church, for the last sixteen years or so, they are still having their open air meetings. According to Alun, that is where the sinners are. Often there is a complaint that reformed men don't preach the gospel, which Alun thinks is true. He has heard sermons and there has been no word for sinners, but the sinners are outside and he fears that reformed men have become accustomed to preaching to Christians for years and years. He believes preachers should go to the marketplaces or wherever the people are. He once counted eight or nine thousand people every hour walking past the spot where they were standing preaching the gospel.

Disappointments

Alun has found that the biggest disappointments in the ministry have been when people have abandoned the faith. He had one young woman in her twenties who was saved through the open air meeting at Dudley and she was going on so well. The Sunday school children loved her, she was a great teacher, and then after a few years a non-Christian man came along and that was that. Similarly, there was another young lady, always in the front row at the prayer meeting, always sharing with Alun and Margaret scriptures that had been a blessing to her and were then a blessing to them, and then a man came along when she was in her 30s and away she went.

The Need of the Church Today

Alun thinks we could easily be discouraged if we allowed ourselves to be. In Roland Burrows' most recent book, *Our Priceless Christian Heritage*, he gives a lot of facts and figures. He says that at one time 53% of the nation's children were in Sunday school. Alun wonders if today 1% of our nation's children have ever heard of the expression, 'Sunday School', let alone been to one, and is sad that a lot of churches have given up their Sunday School work. It is too easy to use the excuse that they will not come. Alun remembers having to provide transport and go and get them, which he found hard work but worthwhile. A Sunday School of twenty became one of one hundred and fifty.

But the fundamental need of the church today is the same as her need in every age: for the Holy Spirit to come upon us in every single thing we do and grant us revival. He believes that our nation is under God's judgement, and if He doesn't grant us revival, what we need in the meantime is faithful plodding and delighting to do the work of God.

Books and Preachers

The main book that has influenced Alun, aside from the Bible, would be *The Pilgrim's Progress*. He remembers reading that Spurgeon had read it over a hundred times and, as he assumed Spurgeon knew a good book when he saw it, he thought he had better get on with it and resolved to read *The Pilgrim's Progress* three times a year—which he did for twenty-five years. He still does it once a year now.

As for preachers, there are many, but he remembers when he was a young fellow going to the Calvary Convention in Liverpool where Albert Chillington was the minister. They had an annual convention week when every night they would have a different preacher. He loved to go there and hear these great preachers. One man that always stood out to him was W. H. Davies from Blackpool Tabernacle. He would open the Word and begin to expound it, often without a note.

Legacy and Burden

Overseas Mission

Despite never feeling called to overseas work, during their time at Rawtenstall, Alun and Margaret began to have a great burden for it and wondered how they could best support missionary work. A nearby church was holding a missionary convention and Margaret went along on the first evening. She came back and said to Alun that he must go along with her the following evening to meet these godly people. He went the next night and he was enthused as well. It was the early 1960s and some of these missionaries had been present at the Congo uprising. They were mainly Worldwide Evangelisation Crusade people. Alun and Margaret travelled up to Scotland in a little van they had, sleeping in the van overnight. After reading more about these people, they really wanted to meet them and kept praying about what they should do and how they could support and help them, conscious of the sacrifice these people had made.

Alun told us something during the interview which he has never told anybody else before, and is not telling anybody else to do, but he and Margaret felt the Lord was asking them to give away every penny they had to missionary work. They counted up their money and they had just a little over £300 and they gave it away, assigning it to various missionary societies. It was their custom at that time to read the Daily Light at breakfast, apart from their quiet time. The following morning the first words their eyes lit upon were, '*As having nothing yet possessing all*', and it seemed as if God had sent a thunderbolt of confirmation to their doubtful hearts that they had done the right thing, and they praised Him for that.

All three of his churches have given thousands of pounds to mission work. Again and again, the words have come to him, '*What have you but what you have received?*' (1 Corinthians 4:7). He was also influenced by the books of Oswald J. Smith who was a staunch Arminian but who loved the Lord and loved souls, and therefore his church was a great giver to missions.

Sending Out

One of the great blessings Alun has had is that out of the three churches he has pastored, twenty nine people have gone into full-time service. The devil would come to him time and again, like he goes to all ministers, and say, 'Think of the men that went before you, those great men of God, and you have such a paltry ministry.' To which Alun would agree with him and say back, 'It is a paltry ministry, but I can praise God that my paltry ministry is being multiplied twenty nine times.'

Radio

It has never ceased to amaze Alun how wonderful a thing it is to be in the ministry, and one of the great opportunities he has had has been to preach on the radio. He did this for about eight years: four years in Rawtenstall and four years in Belfast. In Rawtenstall he was able to use the broadcasting studio of the European Christian Mission whose headquarters was about a mile up the hill from the church. In Belfast the Brethren Assemblies allowed him to use their studio and he preached over the radio to thousands of people in Africa.

Pathos

Finally, as he looks back on his ministry, he wishes he had preached with more pathos. He thinks he is right in saying that at the end of his ministry

Chapter 3

Dr Lloyd-Jones was asked, if he had his time over again, what changes would he make, to which he replied, 'I would preach with more pathos,' and Alun would say exactly the same about himself. He believes that the question people so often ask after the service, 'How many people were there?', is the wrong question. It is not how many people, rather it is how many *needs* were there? How many bereaved, how many depressed, how many broken-hearted, and how many potential for service for the Lord? He remembers preaching at a place once and a lady came to him afterwards and said, 'I am going to see my son tomorrow.' 'Oh,' he replied, 'that will be nice.' She said, 'It won't be nice at all. I dread it. He hates me, he hates himself, he hates everybody and is suicidal.' It was her duty to visit him but she said she could hardly do it. Alun thought to himself, what had he said that morning that might have helped this dear lady with a broken heart? Had he said anything that would help her? He preached at another place and asked a lady at the door, 'How are you today?' 'How am I?', she said sorrowfully, 'How would you be if your son was in prison for murder?' Again he wondered, had he said anything that day that would help that lady? His plea to young men who are not yet leaving the stage, but just coming onto it, is therefore:

Preach with passion and preach with pathos. There are broken-hearted people sitting in front of you and sometimes you would never know it. Bring them to a tender-hearted Saviour.

Chapter 4

John Blanchard

Introduction

John Blanchard really needs no introduction. Unlike all the other men we interviewed for this series, John never pastored a church but was an international evangelist. He sold over 18 million books, the most famous one probably being *Ultimate Questions*. It has been printed in over sixty different languages including, I am pleased to say, Welsh.

Less than two months after we interviewed him, on 14th May 2021, he *'left the stage'*. He was a giant of the faith and we thank God for the gift of John Blanchard. There will no doubt be quite literally thousands of people in eternity who will bless God because of him.

As you read this chapter, keep in your mind the amazing truth that John Blanchard is now in the presence of the One he spent most of his life proclaiming, together with many other Christians we love and miss. The certain hope of the gospel is that John is not dead, he has just gone on ahead.

Background

He was born on Guernsey in the Channel Islands, in 1932, to a working class family. His father was a greenhouse labourer and so was his grandfather. In fact, when his grandfather was born John's great grandfather 'signed' the declaration with a cross because he was illiterate.

John's mother died in her early twenties, when he was only five years old and his younger brother, David, was two years old. His father decided he could not take care of both young boys, so John went to live with his godly Aunty May (as they called her although her Christian name was Christine) about two miles away in the northern part of the island. His aunt attended, without fail, a local Elim Church and took John along there every Sunday for the next three years.

He had some happy memories of those very early years, but all of that changed in 1940 when the German army swept across Europe and clearly had their sights on the Channel Islands. The Guernsey newspaper that went into virtually every home on the island, published a notice to all parents of school aged children telling them to decide within twenty four hours whether their children should be evacuated or kept on the island. It was a very traumatic choice to make because if they sent them away and the war lasted fifty years they might never see them again, but if they kept them on the island and the troops cut up rough, then there was no telling what might happen. John's father decided that both the boys should be evacuated.

John went on the ship *SS Felixstowe*, with his brother, and sailed to Weymouth, and from there went by train to Scotland. He remembered sleeping on the floor of the Calvin Hall in Glasgow for a little while before being, quite literally, farmed out to the island of Isla in the Inner Hebrides. His brother was taken to north Lanarkshire, which was a hundred miles away from Isla. There was no further contact between them for the duration of the war.

Isla was quite a large island as far as the Hebrides are concerned, famous for nine distilleries and had more sheep than people. John went to live on a farm owned by John and Jesse MacGillivray. John spoke Gaelic for five years while on the farm but was educated in English. He walked three miles each way to primary school before moving on to high school, which only involved a one mile walk to the bus stop and then a mile back from the bus stop at the end of the day.

Then in 1945, victory in Europe was declared, the Channel Islands were free and so he could return home. He remembered it all very well. His father was there to meet him (and his brother, whom he met on the voyage home!) at the White Rock harbour in St Peter Port. He had with him his new wife whom he had married just one week earlier. She became his stepmother and they took John and his brother to their flat in New Street, St Peter Port.

It was a very small, second floor flat, and the only running water was down the walls! There were no taps or sinks and no electricity. They had to bring every drop of water up by bucket from the area at the back of the house. Every two or three weeks, on a Sunday night, a big tin bath was filled up by a bucket. His stepmother had the first bath, his father the second, his brother the third and John went in fourth, by which time the water was not exactly crystal clear.

John went back to Vauvert School on Guernsey but soon realised that the standard of education in Scotland was better. In a very short time he was in the top class and there was nothing more for him there. He had ambitions to leave school at 14, but his father was having none of it. Despite having never written a letter or used a telephone in his life, his father somehow got in touch with the Education Secretary for the state of Guernsey and arranged for John to go to the intermediate school as it was then, which later became the grammar school, to meet the headmaster. John had to write an essay, and as a result the headmaster agreed to accept him at the school, which John attended for two years. After this, his father encouraged him to apply through the school to the Guernsey Civil Service, which he did, and joined at the end of 1948.

John's father was not a Christian, and as far as John knew never darkened the door of a church except, as they say, for births, marriages and deaths. His stepmother was a firm, consistent member at an Anglican Church on the island, called Holy Trinity Church. She asked John and his brother if they would like to go to church with her. At the time there was nothing else to do on the island, and so they went along with her.

John found himself at morning service, evening service, choir practice and eventually teaching in Sunday School and a member of the church's youth club. He had all the religion he could handle, but to him it was like driving a car that had no engine in it. His Christianity was a performance and not an experience. If somebody had asked whether John Blanchard was a Christian, the instant reply would be, 'Of course he is, he practically lives at Holy Trinity Church; how could you think he isn't a Christian?' But his Christianity wasn't real. However, that was to change through two people in particular.

Chapter 4

Conversion

The first was the Reverend Arthur Geary Stevens who became the new vicar at Holy Trinity. The church at that point was mildly evangelical but Geary Stevens was a very strong conservative evangelical vicar and hearing him preach got John's attention. It was almost as if he had read John's life story and could see into his heart, and John began to be quite struck by what he was saying.

The second person was a really lovely young lady called Joyce. John began his Civil Service work in the Registrar General's Office and then, to his great delight, they transferred him to the Attorney General's Office where he found himself sitting in the same office as this absolutely delightful young lady. John thought all his Christmases and birthdays had come at once! However, his opinion soon changed when he discovered that on Monday mornings in particular, when coffee time came, she and the senior clerk, Michael John Langlois, talked over coffee about the church services the previous day: who was there, who was the preacher, what did he preach on? John wanted nothing to do with that. He had all the religion he could handle on a Sunday and certainly didn't want it during the week.

Joyce attended one of the three Elim churches on the island. Not long after John had started working at the Attorney General's Office, these churches organised an evangelistic campaign on the island, led by a Canadian man who had American citizenship, called Paul Cantelon (who, incidentally, was related to Walt Disney). The campaign was held at the Candie Gardens auditorium and Joyce asked John if he would like to go. He said no, but she kept on inviting him and John finally agreed when she said that they could go together. For all the wrong reasons, John agreed to go.

It was very different to the formal liturgical Church of England services that John was used to. Paul's wife played the piano, his daughter sang, and it was just not the kind of thing that he was used to. But he heard what Paul said and John remembered it was like having seen all the pieces in a jigsaw, the corner pieces and then the different colours, meeting with each other and everything fitting into place. One night, at the end of the service, he found himself singing words from one of Frances Jane van Alstyne's hymns, *'Pass me not oh gentle Saviour, hear my humble cry, while on others you are calling do not pass me by.'* John recalled, 'I sang the first verse as a religious hypocrite but sang the last verse as a born-again Christian.'

His stepmother, who was not very expressive about the Christian faith but read her Bible and prayed every day, was thrilled that John had come to faith, and so was his Aunty May.

There are two postscripts to the story. The first is that he married the girl! The second came twenty six years later. John was preaching in the United States and one of the invitations he had was from Paul Cantelon, who by then was the pastor of a church in Bellingham, Washington, on the west coast. It was just an unspeakable joy for John to preach for him and on one of the early nights of his time with him, John became assured that he should be baptised as a believer and so Paul baptised him.

National Young Life Campaign

Very soon after he became a Christian he met two other young people on the island, George and Molly Raby. They were very interested in the work of the National Young Life Campaign (NYLC) and needed six members to form a new branch. So, along with another two people, George and Molly and Joyce and John formed the Guernsey branch, and within eight or nine years there were a hundred members.

They began to meet two nights a week: one to study the Bible together and the other to have some kind of evangelistic event. They were seven or eight years that John never forgot and were never matched again throughout his entire life. As strange as it seems today, there was no internet, no mobile phones, no Twitter, no Facebook or anything like that, but remarkably, within seven years there were twenty members in full time Christian work in various parts of the world. As John put it, 'It was all wonderfully simple, and simply wonderful.'

Within four years they organised an evangelistic event, grandly named 'Guernsey for God Campaign'. They hired the largest church on the island, that seated a thousand, which they filled several times. Nearly sixty churches gave at least some measure of support to it and at the end of the two-week campaign they had written to forty churches to tell them of people who had responded in some kind of way and needed to be counselled and followed up.

John was the secretary to the campaign and the evangelists concerned were Frank Farley and Raymond Castro who were on the staff of NYLC. They had with them the gospel witness trio, Reg and Grace Tomlinson and a blind pianist by the name of Peter Jackson. Like John, they are all now with the Lord. Reg and Grace Tomlinson were actually murdered sometime later in Canada. But they were amazing days and very much the work of the Holy Spirit.

The Call

Frank Farley came back to preach on Guernsey in 1961 when John was still in secular employment. At one of the services John felt suddenly and powerfully constrained to offer himself for full-time Christian service. By then he and Joyce were married and had begun a family, which meant he was at the church service without her. He got back rather late and said to her, 'I'm sorry I'm late, I've been talking to Frank Farley,' to which she replied, 'About full time Christian service?' She was absolutely right, and in their tiny little flat, which was really part of a house in Hauteville near where Victor Hugo lived many moons ago, they talked into the night.

John got up late the following morning and had to get to work. He normally used Scripture Union notes with his daily Bible readings but did not have time to read a passage. However, he quickly opened the study notes and at the top of the page was the verse of the week: Exodus 4:12. As he was turning to the verse he prayed it would have some relevance to what he was feeling about the call. Just then, a voice as clear as if a human being had been standing behind him said to him, 'You will never be able to be involved in full-time Christian service. So you give an epilogue now and then and help a little bit in various small informal meetings, but you would never be able to preach once a day.' He came to realise whose voice that was, but by the time he had processed those words in his mind, he came to Exodus 4:12 and read the words of Someone far greater, '*Now therefore go and I will be with your mouth and teach you what you should say.'* And that was that!

Ministry

In early 1962 John applied for a full time post with NYLC. At the time the family were very much living hand to mouth and so they made the booking for the boat journey provisionally with no funds to pay for it. They were due to leave on 5th March and a few days before this date an envelope with £50 in it was pushed under the door. This paid the fare to get the whole family from Guernsey to Weymouth and then on to Weston-super-Mare, where Frank Farley himself lived.

Their first home was a tiny flat, up fifty-seven steps. They had to carry their necessary food and other items up, carry the trash down and, when John was away, Joyce had to negotiate those fifty-seven steps alone with three young children and all the equipment that went with them. Despite the landlord telling them they were safe there and he would not ask them to leave, within a year he had evicted them. Someone who could only have heard John preach once or twice at this stage, and later became a dear friend, somehow discovered that the family had a housing problem and bought a house for them in Clifton Road, Weston-Super-Mare, which they rented from him.

The Lord had wonderfully provided for them and continued to do so in so many ways. The only heating in the house was a pot boiler in one room and on one occasion they were running out of coal. John phoned a coal company and ordered a supply of coal which came very quickly. As the man was walking around the side of the house with a sack of coal on his shoulders and pouring it over the wall into the little area at the back of the house, John said to Joyce, 'I've got good news and bad news. The good news is the coal has come so we can stay warm. The bad news is we don't have any money to pay for it!' As they were discussing that little problem, the postman delivered an envelope with cash in it that exactly, to the penny, matched the money the coal-man was asking for.

After three years with NYLC John was invited to join Movement for World Evangelisation (MWE). This involved preaching overseas and he spent the next thirteen years with them. In December 1966 he got a telegram from Greece which simply said, Acts 16:9. He didn't have a clue what that was but when he looked it up it said, *'Come over into Macedonia and help us.'* So on New Year's Eve he was on a plane to Thessaloniki and was met there and taken to the town of Katerini in the middle of the country to do a week's preaching.

While he was there he began to feel quite unwell. His hosts took him to a lovely Christian doctor who ran a little clinic in Katerini who discovered that John had neurosis of the heart. However, he was due to have a week of preaching in Athens and so got a train down to Athens and preached in the first Greek evangelical church there. After he had preached for two nights the pastor said that John needed to return home because he wasn't fit to carry on. John agreed with them, but he asked if he could stay one more day and if possible, be taken to Corinth, which was a drivable journey from Athens. This was agreed, and on the way there the driver asked John if he had ever been to the Banner of Truth offices in London, which John had not. The man went on to say that he had been to college with one of the leading members of staff there and encouraged John to go there and introduce himself. This turned out to be a hugely important meeting which led to all kinds of opportunities, including the Banner of Truth publishing one of his book titles.

In 1968, Dave Foster invited John to preach in what was then Czechoslovakia. He was the founder of a remarkable work called Eurovangelism, now called Transform Europe Network, which does an amazing work in Eastern Europe. John found himself in a service that lasted many hours and had five sermons in it, including two from John. He preached and thought that was the end of it until a couple of hours later somebody asked him to preach again! That was his introduction to Eastern Europe, which led to many other visits in the future.

On his next visit he took with him his colleague Peter Anderson and another very good friend of theirs, Eric Clark, a singer from Northern Ireland, who was also on the MWE staff. They drove through Poland and down into Czechoslovakia. The man who had arranged their tour and accompanied them on their travels was one of the most remarkable and unforgettable men that John had ever met. His name was Milos Solc, who on one occasion took them into a bank to change some travellers cheques. He asked the teller if they had a microphone that he could use because one of friends was a singer and he would like to sing to the bank. They didn't have one but Milos told Eric to stand in the corner and sing anyway! Eric had prepared some songs in the Czech language and in a loud voice sang, *'Burdens are lifted at Calvary'*. Everybody in the bank stopped, nobody did any work and the president of the bank came down from upstairs to listen. So Eric sang another song, after which the president invited them up to his office for a cup of coffee. It was one of the happiest, most delightful memories John ever had of his time in Eastern Europe and could never imagine it happening in NatWest or Barclays!

Westminster Chapel

In 1975 John was invited to preach at Westminster Chapel. He could only manage an evening because he was preaching in Hertfordshire in the morning. He was immediately invited to go there again and thought it was nothing other than that they did not have a minister and needed to fill the pulpit fifty-two weeks a year. So he went and preached there again. He remembered it well as it was on 4th July in 1976, the 200th anniversary of the American Declaration of Independence. He preached from Galatians on the subject of Christian liberty. When he had finished preaching, the elders, led by Sir Fred Catherwood, took him behind to the little room where the retired minister Dr Lloyd-Jones used to speak to people after a service. They asked if he would consider his name being put forward to become their next minister. John clearly remembered his reply. He simply said, 'You're crazy', which they thought was a rather unusual response! The next day he went to the secretary's house to meet the deacons. They had a long conversation. John had spent the day drawing up at least six reasons why it was the wrong thing to ask him. He told them he had no formal theological education, to which the flattening reply came back, neither did Martyn Lloyd-Jones or Campbell Morgan. The men opened the door as wide as it could be opened for him.

Some weeks later Lloyd-Jones himself called John to his manse in Ealing. They had a long session together and the Doctor told him that he must be the only person in the country who did not think he was the right person to go there. He asked John to be sure he was the first to know when John had taken his place. It took John months to make up his mind that it was not the right place for him, especially as, when his name went forward, 93% of the church were in favour of him becoming their pastor. The main reason John turned it down was simply that he did not believe he had the gifts to be the pastor of that church, or indeed of any church. According to John, 'My heroes today are pastors of churches who remain faithful to the Word and to the church to which they are called. I'm thinking especially of pastors who are the under shepherds of fifty members or twenty members or even fewer than that. Week by week they pray and prepare and preach to those people and pastor them and love them. I think they are heroes. They have gifts and abilities and graces that I simply don't have.'

In 1980, along with Peter Anderson and Derek Cleave, John left MWE and founded Christian Ministries, working throughout the United Kingdom and in many overseas countries. They spent twenty-three years together, 'years of delightful fellowship and the same vision for taking God's Word to today's world', before John went back to being an independent evangelist.

Writings

Read Mark Learn

In 1966 it occurred to John that when a person became a Christian they would be given a whole Bible or the Gospel of John and told, 'God bless you as you read it.' Not doubting the Holy Spirit's enabling to help them understand it, John nevertheless thought that was a strange thing to do; to give them the most theological gospel of all, give them no help to understand it and just let them get on with it. At the time he decided to read the Gospel of Mark in his own personal devotions, and after a very long time he prepared a little book with forty five devotional studies going through the Gospel of Mark. This was called *Read Mark Learn* and was deliberately intended for people who had just become Christians. It was turned down by the first publisher to whom it was offered, but eventually it was accepted and has now gone into about thirty printings. It has been translated into several languages, including Bulgarian by a man called Georgi Markov, who is better known for being murdered, allegedly by an operative connected to the KGB and the Bulgarian secret police, as he was walking across Waterloo Bridge, having been jabbed with a poisoned umbrella.

At this time, theologically John would have been Arminian. He remembered being given a copy of *Redemption Accomplished and Applied* by John Murray and, after reading a few pages, he threw it away and said, 'I don't want that.' Things did change a little later. Helped by reading C. H. Spurgeon's *The Early Years* he became fully persuaded of the Reformed position.

Right with God

In 1971 he wrote a book called *Right with God*, published by the Banner of Truth. There have been wonderful stories over the years about people who have come to faith by reading this book. One of the most remarkable was that of a man who stole a car and when he took it home discovered it had a copy of *Right with God* in the back window. He read the book, came to faith and, you'll be glad to know, took the car back!

Ultimate Questions

Ultimate Questions was first published in 1987. John did not have the remotest idea at the time that it would be translated into more than sixty different languages. It was published on 5th March, the twenty-fifth anniversary of the day John and his family came from Guernsey to England. The original order, so he was told by Evangelical Press (EP), was a hundred thousand copies, and it had sold out by the time it arrived in the publisher's office. So a quarter of a million were ordered, and so it went on. A shipment of 400,000 was sent to Russia and EP received tens of thousands of responses from people who wanted to know more about the

Christian faith. On another occasion there were 15,000 copies distributed to American soldiers in Iraq. John felt the book almost 'had a life of its own' and none of his other publications matched up to it.

Whatever Happened to Hell?

In 1993 he wrote quite a large book called *Whatever Happened to Hell?* In the course of his research John asked a minister in England who had a very, very large library, how many books he had on the subject of hell. He told John that he had one but had mislaid it. When John was preaching in Australia he went to a large Christian bookshop and asked how many books they had on hell. He was told they once had one but nobody wanted it and so they gave it away. That encouraged him even more to write his book on hell. He believed that the doctrine of hell is one of the 'Cinderella' doctrines of the Christian church today and said, 'We are very big on calling people to be saved, but unless hell is preached firmly and clearly in all of its horror it seems to me that the gospel has much less impact, because people will want to know what they're being saved from.'

Does God Believe in Atheists

Back in the 1970s he was on a team mission in Torquay and was asked to speak at a men's gathering. He spoke on the problems of being an atheist and it had such an interesting reception that he felt he needed to keep speaking on that. Over the next ten years he must have spoken on it nearly a hundred times. He began to be more and more convinced that the rising tide of atheism and agnosticism in our land and elsewhere needed to be addressed. Eventually he wrote a very large book called, *Does God Believe in Atheists?* which was published in 2000. Originally intended to be 150 pages, it eventually became 850. It is a masterful and comprehensive defence of belief in God, written with devastating logic yet with a compassionate heart.

Popular Christian Apologetics

As well as writing the book, he began a project called Popular Christian Apologetics (PCAP). He wanted to speak on the subject of *Does God believe in atheists?* in every county in the nation, which was just over seventy. He would set himself up in one area of the county and then commute from there to various other towns in the area. A dear friend of his, Howard Williams, from the north-west of England, began to go with him and do all the hard work. He did all the driving, the setting up of things and all the book sales. According to John, 'All I did was stand up every night and tell the truth.'

Within four years John had delivered a presentation in every county in the UK. This also incorporated universities and colleges including Oxford, Cambridge and Eton. He was inundated with invitations from around the globe to widen the scope of the project. Despite being past retirement age, he dedicated the rest of his life to this huge task, which was to include the delivery of many hundreds of international presentations and the publication of a further twenty-seven books.

As well as Howard Williams being integral to John's ministry, so too was his wife Marlene who became John's unofficial editor. By the time any of his book titles ever reached the publishers they had been so brilliantly edited by Marlene there was nothing much else for the publishers to do.

As well as being an author himself, John was influenced by other authors. These include some who are no longer with us like the Puritan Thomas Watson, J. C. Ryle, C. S. Lewis, Jim Packer, John Stott and R. C. Sproul, as well as authors today like John Lennox, Alistair McGrath and Sinclair Ferguson. John loved to read books written by these men and benefited a great deal from them.

Being Widowed and Remarrying

In 2010, after nearly fifty-three years together, his wife Joyce died. Much earlier in their marriage Joyce had suffered from a great deal of depression. At that point in her life, John was asked to preach at Keswick in Greece. She was in a very poor condition. They both agreed, along with their doctor, that he would fulfil this engagement in Greece and then, if she was no better when he returned after a couple of weeks, he would give up the ministry. He was preaching in Leptokarya, Macedonia which was literally on the Aegean coast. John said he could lob a tennis ball out of his accommodation onto the sand. He got up early one morning and saw a group of Greek ladies clothed in black from top to bottom on the beach praying. After their meeting they came to John and told him that by the time he got home his wife would be better. John thought, 'Well you've obviously got no idea how deep this depression is.' When he got back to the UK he telephoned Joyce from Heathrow. When he spoke to her, he didn't recognise her voice. It had changed so much and she had been completely rescued from that horrible situation.

In 2008 she contracted colorectal cancer which had spread elsewhere in her body and she eventually died. They laid her body to rest on 5th March 2010, the 28th anniversary of their leaving Guernsey to come to England. It was just a remarkable coincidence. In those two very difficult times, not least of course the last one, John was upheld by God's enabling grace and by hundreds of people who were praying for him. According to John, 'It was wonderful to be at the cemetery in Epsom and look down into the grave and to assure myself, "Joyce is not here; her body is here but she is in the presence of the Lord whom she loved so dearly and served so faithfully." That assurance of her presence in the Lord's glory overcame all the grief that was naturally mine. We do grieve, the Bible tells us that, but not as those who have no hope. In the New Testament the word "hope" always means absolute certainty and we rejoice in the certainty of what lies ahead.'

In April 2015, John married Pamela Robertson. He had known her for many years. She had prayed for him every day for fifty years. Here was someone who in her life was never in full-time Christian service, nevertheless was absolutely committed to sharing the gospel, especially in Eastern Europe, which was one of John's passions too. For the last six years of John's life they were together; blissfully happy, loving each other, loving the Lord and seeking to serve Him.

The Need of the Hour

When the Lord Jesus told his disciples that the harvest was plentiful, the one direction he gave them was to pray that the Lord would send labourers into the harvest. John dearly wished that a great deal more of that was done today. John was over 70 years of age when he started the PCAP project, and his strap line was, 'As much as I can, as well as I can, for as long as I can'—happily put into the plural when he married Pam. People would often say to him how wonderful it was for someone at John's late stage in life to say that. John's response was, 'Why shouldn't the person in the middle of life, why shouldn't the teenager say that? I don't consider that to be a ceiling that we must somehow strive to reach. I think that's the floor. That's where we ought to begin.' His longing was that today there would be a generation of young people willing to ask themselves, 'Is there a possibility that the Lord would call me into full-time service? Am I willing to be called into full-time Christian service, willing to leave whatever I am earning, whatever my present situation is, whatever my commercial or other prospects might be, and be willing to go wherever the Lord would call me?' He concluded, 'I would love there to be a new generation of young people putting themselves in that position and called by the Lord to serve Him.'

Chapter 5

Teify Ebenezer

Introduction

All the men we interviewed in this series are among my heroes, but the fifth one we interviewed just about edges it as my absolute favourite. He's my dad and I couldn't have had a better one. Hard working, un-selfish, faithful and strong. There are lots of things my sisters and I love about him, but one of the things we love about him the most was the way he loved Mam. And while for some preachers, the world is their parish, for dad, as you will see, the parish has been his world.

Background

His testimony can be summed up in 1 Corinthians 15:10 which says, *'By the grace of God I am what I am.'* As he looks back over his life he can see God's provision, God's providence and God's presence. God provided a Saviour for him and, as Romans 8:32 says, *'has freely given him all things'*. He has seen God's providence throughout his life in all things, even in the times He has said 'no' when Teify wanted the answer to be 'yes', and can agree wholeheartedly with what Paul said in Romans 8:28, *'All things work together for good to those who love God, to those who are the called according to His purpose.'* He has also known God's presence. God has never left him nor forsaken him (Hebrews 13:5).

When he was born, his father was pastor of a Forward Movement church called Radcliffe Hall in Pendaran, Merthyr Tydfil. The Forward Movement was the evangelistic arm of the Presbyterian Church of Wales.

When he was born in 1944, the NHS had not come into being and so his mother went home to her mother to have him. He was born with a clot in his throat and reportedly the doctor threw him to the bottom of the bed and said, 'He's no good.' But his grandmother kept a small bottle of whiskey in the cupboard because her husband, Teify's grandfather, was a miner and she used to put a little drop of whiskey in his tea in the morning to help with the coal dust. She put her finger on the top of the whiskey bottle and put it on Teify's tongue and apparently he coughed the clot up. His grandmother then picked him up and nursed him for a week. Understandably, the bond between him and his grandmother was very precious.

There was no electricity in the Duffryn Rhondda, the little village where his grandmother lived, between Neath and Maesteg, but he remembers the family Bible being on the table at all times. In the village there was a little flat roofed chapel that the Forward Movement had built, and when he was on holiday at his grandparents', he would go there to Sunday School. At the age of five he can remember one of the evangelists who was part of the Forward Movement team, a man by the name of Philip Jones, saying to him, 'Teify, you must be saved.' Fifteen years later, when he was saved, he went to Alice Road in Neath and knocked on the door and said, 'Mr Jones, I've come to tell you that I've been saved.' He was so delighted and then said, 'Never promise the Lord anything you don't intend to fulfil.'

In 1947, when he was three-and-a-half, his mother and father moved to Ebbw Vale because his dad became the minister of Mount Pleasant Presbyterian Church. The following year, his sister Mair was born. His home was very disciplined, but it was full of love and full of care. Sunday was the Lord's day, papers and comics were put under the cushion not to be seen, and on that day scripture had to be committed to memory. At bedtime his dad would kneel by the bed and put his one arm around Teify and the other arm around his sister and lead them in prayer.

The elders in the church at that time stick out in his memory. They had come out of the 1904 revival and there was something about them. In the Sunday school there were 320 children which meant there were two schools, one from 2–3 pm and another from 3–4 pm. That led to his father approaching the Forward Movement to ask them to build another little chapel on the housing estate that was above them in Ebbw Vale. Ieuan Phillips, who was the superintendent of the Forward Movement at the

time, had a sister called Bethan Lloyd-Jones. The Forward Movement had
ladies who were called Sisters of the People, including Morwen Higham
and Joan Davies. They had a Sister named May Markey attached to them.

At the end of the Sunday evening service they held what was called
the second meeting. The children had to stand up, turn around, face the
congregation and repeat their memory verses. They had to have a different
verse every week and there was no reading their verses—they had to learn
them off by heart. The Ebbw Vale Sunday School Union held annual
Scripture exams. It involved learning Bible passages and then writing them
out for the exam.

When his sister was five years of age she contracted tuberculosis. In
those days that was extremely dangerous, so for six months she had to
rest at home. She then went to Sully hospital for two and a half months
and there she had major lung surgery. Teify's parents were told to take her
home and spoil her because she wouldn't live beyond the age of twelve.
They prayed hard and when she was sixteen years of age her parents took
her back to the hospital and the consultant discharged her. Her father was
weeping with joy. God had overruled the medical profession and today
she is still here in her 70s.

Conversion and The Call

At the age of 14, he became a volunteer nurse in the Ebbw Vale hospital
and it was there that he heard one of the male patients saying that he didn't
believe in God. The impact was phenomenal because up until then he had
never met anybody who didn't believe in God.

But at the age of sixteen, he went on to work in the local steel company
which at that time employed 10,500 people. He became an apprentice and
the attraction of the world became very powerful and he became friendly
with a young lady of whom his mother did not approve. His mother had
a nose like a bloodhound and when he got home and had been drinking,
there would be a row in the house. By now he was 19 and fed up with all
the aggravation and vowed he would never go back to chapel. In February
1964 he went into the chapel saying it was the last time he would ever be
going to that place.

He cannot remember anything his father said or preached on, but remembers that he gave out the last hymn, 'Today Thy mercy calls us to wash away our sins'. The last verse begins, '*O all embracing mercy! O ever open door!*' His mother called him 'the ever open door', which had something to do with his appetite, and it was then that God stopped him in his tracks. He left the meeting and went straight to see the young lady he was friendly with to say he was sorry but they had to end their relationship. He wasn't converted that night but God had begun a good work in him.

Later on that year he met a young man from the Salvation Army by the name of Jeff Davies. Together they were concerned about young people on a Sunday night having nothing to do after chapel. So they formed what was called the Ebbw Vale After Church Fellowship. It was at this point that Jeff Davies introduced him to a young lady called Beryl Penny. He fancied her straight away but she thought he was bigoted and full of himself. Her dad was the secretary of Zoar Baptist Church in Beaufort. They held preaching services every Autumn and every Spring, and that particular Autumn, in October of 1964, they had invited the Reverend Hywel Griffiths to preach. He was then the pastor of Litchard Mission in Bridgend. He had come out of the revival and the impact he had on many, including Stuart Olyott was phenomenal. Teify has precious memories of him and on that particular October night after he had preached, Teify went out of the meeting realising that this man knew as a reality in his heart what he himself knew only in his head. In Teify's own words:

I sat in the driver's seat of the car and I remember the registration, it is the only car registration number I remember, DEU 512. It was there in the driving seat I realised what the cross was all about. It was there that I understood that Jesus had died for me. I was given an assurance that if I had died there and then, I was going to heaven, but if I lived another fifty, sixty or seventy years, I was still going to heaven, and that has never left me. I was willing to do anything for the Lord and to go anywhere for Him.

A little while later, he was in the after church fellowship and someone came to speak on Isaiah 6:8, '*I heard the voice of the Lord saying: "Whom*

shall I send, and who will go for Us?" Then I said, "Here am I! Send me."'
He knew at that point that the Lord wanted him to go out for Him.

Training

He finished his apprenticeship in 1965 and went to the Theological College
in Aberystwyth. His time at Aberystwyth was hard. There were thirty-
five students in total. Eighteen were evangelicals and seventeen were
modernists. They were taught that the Bible was like a jigsaw puzzle
with different pieces coming to it from different places. He remembers a
fellow student of his from the Heath Evangelical Church, Michael Hayes,
tentatively putting his hand up and asking the lecturer, 'Please sir, what
about inspiration?' The professor just exploded, so much so his glasses
came off, as he shouted, 'You fundamentalists!' By September of that
year he had had enough and in October he left—the same October 1966
that Dr Martyn Lloyd-Jones was calling for evangelicals to leave their
denominations, which led to his disagreement with John Stott.

It was also in 1966 that he and Beryl got married. The late Reverend
Owen Milton who had baptised him, officiated at their wedding. In the
meantime he found a secular job in the retail trade, but then in the Spring
of 1967 Zoar Baptist Church held another series of preaching meetings.
Hywel Griffiths was invited to preach on the Monday and the Thursday
and the Rev Paul Tucker from the East London Tabernacle preached on
the Tuesday and Wednesday. The lady who was giving him hospitality
asked Teify if he would do her a favour and come and talk to him because
she didn't know what to say. So he spent the Wednesday afternoon with
Paul Tucker. In the course of conversation, he asked Teify if he had ever
heard of the South Wales Bible College in Barry and then proceeded to
encourage him to approach them.

Teify sent in an application and was invited for an interview with
the college council. Teify remembers John Dart, who was the vice-
principal at that time, coming into the common room and, typical of
the fatherly figure that he was, putting his arm around his shoulder
and saying, 'We're not going to eat you, you know.' When the door
opened to the Principal's study, who should be sat in the chair but the

Reverend Paul Tucker! Unbeknown to Teify, he was the chairman of the college council.

He was accepted but then wrestled for a little while about what to do because the company he was working for offered him the manager's job. However, as Teify puts it, 'I had to go because God was calling me.' God provided for him and Beryl, and not long after he had gone to college in Barry their first daughter Sarah was born.

It was easy to remember his lecturers' names because the principal was John Waite, the vice-principal was John Dart, the tutor was John Cook and the visiting pastoring lecturer was John Thomas who was pastor at the time in Sandfields. John Thomas would always say, 'When revival comes'—never 'if', but always 'when'. The difference between his time at Aberystwyth and Barry was stark. Now the emphasis was upon knowing what God had said in his Word rather than what men were saying in their books.

During his time in college they had to do door-to-door visitation. He remembers going to one door with a fellow student in Cadoxton on a Wednesday and spending an hour talking to a man. The man fired question after question at them and each time they answered his questions, but he remembers walking away from the door thinking that unless God changed his heart he would never be saved.

While he was there, one of the students came to him one night after a study period at 9.30 pm saying she was concerned because she didn't have sufficient funds to pay her fees. They prayed together, and the following morning as she was going into the dining room she picked up her mail and in the envelope there was a cheque to cover her fees. The interesting thing was that the envelope was already on its way before they prayed, and so they proved Isaiah 65:24 to be true, *'Before they call, I will answer.'*

Preaching in the open air was great. They would go to the square in Barry in the winter months and on the beach in the summer. He remembers hearing John Dart preaching and then a young student who came behind him by the name of Mike Mellor. These men preached with a longing that people would be saved.

He also remembers Al Martin coming to preach at the college and impressing upon them the need of pathos in their preaching (a point stressed by Alun McNabb, see Chapter 3). Al Martin warned them against becoming 'professional word machines grinding out reformed theology'.

In 1969 they went on a mission to Port Talbot with the college. Three evangelical churches in the area got together and it had been arranged by John Thomas before he died so suddenly. He remembers, along with one of the female students, picking up a young lady and taking her to one of the meetings. Gareth Davies was preaching, and on the way back from the meeting the lady said, 'Who told the preacher about me?' They hadn't said a word, but God had spoken clearly to her.

Bethany Baptist Chapel

In his final year in college, he was invited to Bethany Baptist Church in Pontypridd with a view to becoming their pastor. He remembers going into the room with the church officers, putting his Bible on the table and saying to them, 'Brethren, this is the source of my faith and my practice.'

He started at the church in 1970 and remembers with fondness the young people, many of whom are still there, including Marilyn Hyde who was the first person he baptised, Diane Parry the second person he baptised, along with Ann Barrot and Lyn Young. The night he baptised Lyn Young, by now their second daughter Bethan had been born. She had gone upstairs with her mother to watch the baptism. Suddenly her little voice resounded around the church, 'Why is daddy bathing Mrs Young?'

Three weeks after he had been in Bethany as the pastor, they experienced tragedy. A young boy, nine years of age, from Sunday school, had gone into his bathroom at home where there was a problem with the geyser and he died of carbon monoxide poisoning. His was the first funeral Teify ever conducted. It coloured his ministry and impressed upon him the need to reach out to children as well as adults.

At Bethany they really proved God. He remembers a time when his father-in-law was coming to stay and they had no coal. Beryl asked him to go out to the coal cot and see if he could scrape together any bits of coal, only to find when he got there that the cot was full. The father-in-law of one of their neighbours had died and they had to clear his coal cot, so they dumped it into Beryl and Teify's.

Another occasion when they had no meat for Sunday, they remember opening the front door and finding that someone had left a big bag of food. If his wife Beryl was still alive she could tell you exactly how many chicken pieces and lamb chops were there.

There was also the time when, on his way to East Glamorgan Hospital to visit one of his members, as he was driving through Church Village there was a big bang and his car came to a sudden halt. He looked across the road and, lo and behold, it had broken down in front of a garage. The garage owner came over and they pushed the car into the forecourt. The mechanic took a look at the car and said he needed a new gearbox and it would cost £49. That was four times Teify's weekly stipend at the time and he and Beryl had promised each other they would never ask anybody for anything but they would always take everything to God in prayer. Later that afternoon, a lady came to visit them. After she left, Beryl went back into the front room and on the piano was an envelope. She picked up the envelope and inside was £50.

There were also times they saw God's healing hand. Two weeks after their third child Alun was born they had to take him back to hospital. He was in an oxygen tent and in those days the tent was literally over the cot. He was gasping for breath and they remember the consultant coming to the bed and saying, 'The next hour is critical, he can go either one way or the other.' That was the longest hour of their lives, but God answered their prayers and spared him. Then another lady from the church was taken seriously ill with a tumour on the brain. Her daughter phoned Teify and he went down to the Heath hospital in Cardiff to visit her. Mr Weeks was a consultant in Heath at the time and J.P.R. Williams, the great Welsh rugby fullback, was a registrar. The prognosis was horrendous and she was almost definitely going to die, but they said they would operate anyway. They prayed all night and the following morning, when she went into the operating theatre, they opened her up and incredibly the tumour that was fastened to her brain had frozen up and it was like a prune. They put the forceps in and took it out and she's still alive today, fifty years later.

Chapter 5

Zion Baptist Chapel, Brynmawr

In 1975 they returned to Beaufort to live and for a year Teify did itinerant preaching around South Wales and England, as far afield as Royton in Manchester to the north and Poole in Dorset to the south. During this time he went to Bury St Edmunds and had an experience there he has never forgotten. There was a spiritual bond between himself and the church secretary which was phenomenal. Within twenty-four hours they invited him to go as their pastor and Teify really wanted to go. But God had other plans. There were family circumstances that prevailed which made it impossible for him to leave Beaufort at that time and God made it clear to him, in a way that is better 'felt than telt', that he was not to go. It coincided with Reverend Jeffrey Fewkes leaving Zion Baptist Chapel in Brynmawr and going to Hay Hill in Bath. Two of the deacons came to Teify's house and gave him a 'Macedonia' type call. They said, 'Come over to Brynmawr and help us.' He agreed to go for three months which turned out to be the longest three months of his life because, forty-five years later, he is still there.

Over the last nearly five decades, they have enjoyed great blessings in Zion. The church had the reputation of being a caring church which had nothing to do with Teify—it was like that before he arrived. He remembers preaching one Sunday morning and the door bursting open and a young man appearing at the door and saying, 'Can anybody help me?' Teify had never seen him before but it turned out that his grandfather had been a deacon in Zion before his day.

On another occasion, Teify was going to preach on a Sunday night at six o'clock. At quarter past five he was prompted to write an extra sentence into his notes. The sentence read something like this: 'You can work for God and yet not be a Christian.' The day before, they were doing some practical work on the church and a few men had come to help them. That Sunday evening a man whose wife was a member in Zion said to her, 'I'm coming to chapel with you tonight', and it was that sentence that hit him and led to his being converted.

The church was greatly blessed during the 1980s when almost every week for a period people were converted. On one Sunday night, Teify baptised seventeen people. God also wonderfully provided for them when the chapel building had to be completely renovated because of dry rot. But the church also suffered a painful split when a large part of the church left to join the charismatic movement.

Open Air Preaching

Every Saturday he would stand in the open-air and preach on the market square in Brynmawr. It used to be a big market and hundreds of people would pass by. He would play hymns on an old cassette player and preach in between the hymns. A lady with some difficulties was fascinated by the singing and so one of the ladies from the church, Chris Kivell, befriended her, as a result of which she began attending the church.

Then one afternoon he had a phone call from one of the local undertakers saying a gentleman had died in Nantyglo, a little village below Brynmawr, and the family wanted Teify to take his funeral. Teify had no idea who he was but the undertaker said the family insisted he took the funeral. So he went to see the family. Apparently this man had been disabled for a number of years and his son used to drive up to the market on a Saturday and park his car across the road from where Teify was preaching. His father would stay in the car, wind down the window and listen to him.

Gypsies

In 1989 the church was blessed with an influx of gypsies. Margaret, the queen of the gypsies, was a believer and, when she died, providentially arrangements were made for Teify to bury her. Gypsies came from all over the country to the funeral and the church was so full that people were hanging from the rafters. As a result of that service several of her family were converted and have been members of the church ever since.

Margaret's husband, Eddy, was a hard man, a big drinker and quite cruel to his children. While he had respect for Teify, he kept him at arm's length. Teify and Beryl were on their way to the Aberystwyth when they had a message to say that Eddy was seriously ill in the Prince Charles hospital in Merthyr and he didn't have long to live. They took a detour and went to see him. He didn't want Teify to pray with him but Teify insisted. When they returned from Aberystwyth they had a call to say that

Eddy had deteriorated and now had just hours to live. Teify went in to see him and said, 'Eddy, you are about to go into eternity and meet your Maker and you are not fit to die.' As Teify put his hand on the bed rails, Eddy clasped it and said, 'I believe, Boss. I believe!' Incredibly Eddy lived another twenty two days and returned home. His children said he was like a completely different man.

Chaplain to the Mayor

Teify was Chaplain to the mayor on five separate occasions. On one occasion he preached on the verse, *'Render to Caesar the things that are Caesar's, and to God the things that are God's'* (Mark 12:17). The late Labour leader, Michael Foot, was the MP for Blaenau Gwent at the time and was in the service. As he was going out he said to Teify, 'You intended to make me think, and you have.' Michael Foot related that story at another function some time later.

Funerals

Over the last forty five years, being well known in the Blaenau Gwent area, Teify has conducted on average an incredible two or three funerals a week. This has provided opportunities to preach the gospel to people who would not otherwise darken the door of a place of worship.

Sermons, Books and Friends

Three sermons stand out in his mind. The first was preached by a young Eryl Davis at the South Wales Bible College in 1968. He preached on 2 Chronicles and Jehoshaphat saying, *'We know not what to do, but our eyes are upon You.'* It introduced him to revival, and he remembers Dr Davies being reduced to tears and before he finished saying, 'Does anybody care?' The second was Dr Lloyd-Jones at the Heath in 1969 preaching from Acts 4:12. He analysed the company of people who were opposed to Peter and John at the time and, in a typical Dr Lloyd-Jones manner, showed that these people, who had nothing in common with each other naturally, united in their opposition to the gospel. The third was Alun Mc Nabb's sermon, again in the Heath, in 2004 preaching from Matthew 26 on Judas Iscariot, one of the twelve. It was a ten point sermon showing a person's gospel privileges yet how one can be so near and yet so far and at the end not being saved?

As for books, there have been many, but three stood out in his memory during the interview. First of all a book that originally came out as Andrew Woolsey's biography of Duncan Campbell, which is now called *Channel of Revival*. He learned a lot from that in the 1970s. Then Basil Howlett's book *1966 and all that*, which he would recommend heartily to young people as it is so helpful in succinctly explaining what happened at that time. The book he has read more recently and found helpful is Kevin DeYoung's little book, *Amaze them with God*. The titles of each chapter in themselves are compelling: 'Grab them with passion', 'Win them with love, 'Hold them with holiness', and 'Challenge them with truth'.

Friends he has greatly appreciated include the late Rev Vernon Higham who was a tremendous mentor to him and, along with his wife Morwen, were great friends to him and Beryl over the years. Then there was Fouzi Ayoub and his widow Wendy who have been a huge encouragement to them.

Beryl

The death of his wife Beryl has been an enormous loss to him. At her funeral he realised the impact she had had on the lives of so many people, as on that last Friday in August in 2019 around six hundred people came to her funeral, with many others sending messages as they were away on holiday. She was one of those people who wanted to mother people. She was a mother and a grandmother to her own children and grandchildren, but also a mother in Israel, at the heart of the church and the local community. They opened their home to all kinds of people, even had them to stay with them for a while, including ex-convicts, alcoholics and drug addicts.

He well remembers those days leading up to her death in the hospital in Newport, and Sarah, Bethan and Alun reading and praying with their mother; and then the four of them would all sing hymns together and, even though she was struck down with a stroke, there was this awareness that she was very much part of it with them.

The day she died Teify said he lost his prayer partner, because every morning after breakfast they would spend time praying for the family, the church, the community, the nation and the world. He also lost his confidant because he could share literally everything with Beryl, things he could not share with anybody else. She had been by his side throughout his ministry, including accompanying him on fourteen of his twenty trips to Croatia in the 1990s where he preached and delivered aid to refugee camps.

It was an enormous loss and still is, but, as he said in her funeral, he does not dwell upon the parting but rather on the future meeting. The love of the fellowship in Zion is precious to him and he feels like the richest man on the planet because his three children are Christians, his three in-laws are Christians and he has six grandchildren who are Christians, including one grandson who is in the ministry.

Advice and the Need of the Hour

His advice to young people is to give God the days of your strength because you will never lose out. He would add, in this present environment, to give God your mind, because our minds are being bombarded by so much today. We need to bow in the presence of God, and as Philippians 4:8 puts it,

'Whatever is true, whatever is honourable, whatever is just, whatever is pure, whatever is lovely, whatever is commendable, if there is any excellence, if there is anything worthy of praise, think on these things.'

His advice to young men going into the ministry is to avoid gimmicks and, for example, thinking that if you change the translation of the Bible people are suddenly going to understand. The need is for the eyes of their understanding to be enlightened, which is a work that only God can do. Preachers need to be utterly dependent upon Him, not their own cleverness. Teify's great longing is for revival. In his own words:

As much as I am overwhelmed by modern technology and everything else, it will be the Spirit of God alone who will change the hearts of men and women and boys and girls. We need the Spirit of God to descend, and my prayer always is that, before the Lord sends His Son again, He will send his Spirit and that we should see many crying out, 'What must I do to be saved?'

Chapter 6

Ian Hamilton

Introduction

Ian Hamilton is the president of the Westminster Presbyterian Theological Seminary in Newcastle as well as a trustee and editor of the Banner of Truth. It has been my privilege over the last few years to get to know Mr Hamilton and remember fondly when he visited The Fulham Boys School and spoke to all the boys and staff at a whole school assembly. My first memory of him is from the Aberystwyth Conference back in 2003. He preached a really powerful sermon which has stuck with me ever since from Ezekiel 33:11 on a pleading God: *'I have no pleasure in the death of the wicked, but that the wicked turn from his way and live. Turn, turn from your evil ways! For why should you die, O house of Israel?'*

Background and Conversion

He was brought up in the east end of Glasgow in a housing scheme which later became somewhat notorious as the murder capital of Western Europe. He was not raised in a Christian family. His mother's family were devout Irish Roman Catholics who were poor but were always very kind to Ian, and he remembers growing up just thinking how lovely they were. By background his mother was therefore a Roman Catholic but his father did not profess to be anything, and they never went to church. His parents did send him to Sunday School, as many parents did in the mid to late 1950s, but he soon gave that up.

His parents, especially his mother, encouraged him to work hard at school. He was the bright little boy in the class, but as his parents could not afford for him to go to a grammar school or a private school he was destined to go to the local comprehensive school, which did not have a great reputation. However, his primary school teacher was from the Island of Lewis and told him that if he studied Gaelic he would get him to a good school in the centre of Glasgow, near the university. Ian wanted to learn and so he travelled across the length of the city, east to west, each day for six years.

He did not know anyone who was a Christian or anyone who really went to church, but when he was in lower sixth, a boy started witnessing to him. Ian does not really remember him actually witnessing to him, but the boy later told him he was doing it all the time. He does, however, remember the impact this boy's life had on him. He was very different from Ian. Ian was in the academic stream, he wasn't; Ian was in the sports stream, he wasn't; Ian was into girls, he did not seem too fussed. He played in a gospel band, not that Ian really knew what that was, but his life said something to Ian.

Late one Saturday Ian had been out on the town with a friend and bumped into him in the middle of Glasgow. He invited Ian and his friend to a Sunday afternoon Bible class and, to the boy's astonishment, they said they would go. So on a wet Sunday afternoon Ian went to this young people's Bible class. There were about twenty-five to thirty young people there from the ages of 15 to 25. He discovered later this boy had told the Bible study leader that there would be two unconverted boys attending on that afternoon, so he preached on John 3:16. Ian did not possess a Bible, and while he may have heard of John's Gospel he had never heard of John 3:16. As the man preached, he became engrossed and two thoughts impacted him. The first was that God loved him and that God loved sinners. Ian could not get his head around this. It really puzzled him: why would God love people who didn't love him? Ian didn't question that there was a God, but when he heard that this God sent his Son to take the punishment for his sin, he couldn't understand it. He sat there thinking, 'Why would God do that for me?' Ian was seventeen years old and aware there were girls around, but it was all he could do not to cry. The meeting ended and, being a polite boy, Ian went to thank the speaker. He cannot remember what he said to the man, but he could clearly see that Ian was somewhat distressed and simply said, 'Would you like me to explain more to you?' Ian said yes and he very simply led him to Christ. Other than having memorised David's lament over Saul on Mount Gilboa because his primary teacher said it was beautiful language, John 3:16 was the only verse in the Bible that he knew. But he left that meeting knowing he had become a Christian and he wanted to tell the world about the Lord Jesus.

It changed everything for him really. He went into school on Monday morning and immediately began to tell people what happened to him. They all just thought he was being a little bit weird, but the Lord was merciful to him. He probably lost all the friends he had, but he gained other friends and shortly after that he went to university, which was very unusual for someone from the area of Glasgow where he lived.

University and Training

At university he immediately joined the Christian Union and the Socialist society. His father was a left-wing trade unionist and his background was very left-wing. He was elected to the socialist executive in university by a Marxist clique who had infiltrated the socialist society. After that the Christian Union asked him to become evangelism secretary and he thought evangelism was probably more important than socialism, so he resigned from the socialist society. The person who took his place became the first Marxist student president in a university in Britain.

By that time he realised there was only one thing his heart longed to do, and that was to preach. When people ask him when he was called to the ministry, he has two answers. The first is that he was called at the same time he was converted, but that may be him romanticising it—he doesn't think so, but is conscious it could be. Certainly over the next two or three years after he was converted there was a war in him if he did not preach the gospel. He realised there were a lot of things he could do but only one thing he wanted to do. It was important, though, that the church where he was a member validated his call. He spent four years at university in Glasgow and then the church that he attended shortly after becoming a Christian increasingly believed that God was calling him into the ministry.

He went on to Edinburgh University and studied there for three years and then became an assistant for a year. Edinburgh kindly offered him a scholarship to go back and study for another three years, which he did. God was exceedingly kind to him when he was in Edinburgh and he attended Hollywood Abbey, where James Philip ministered. In six years he missed only one prayer meeting and one service. He had never experienced such quiet, gentle, passionate, rich expository preaching. James Philip was a shy man, but his passion for the Lord just oozed out of him when he preached and those six years were very significant for Ian. Along with Eric Alexander, he was probably the greatest preacher and one of the finest men he has ever had the privilege of knowing. He had a huge impact on Ian and has shaped his life as a Christian.

Newmilns

Then, aged 29, after studying more or less for ten years, Ian was called to a parish church in the Church of Scotland, in a small town called Newmilns, about twenty-five miles south of Glasgow. The church had 1,100 notional members and forty-two elders but realistically they probably had five elders and thirty members.

He spent twenty years at the church and, on the advice of James Philip, he thought he would keep his head down for the first ten years. It was only halfway through the tenth year that things changed significantly. People had been converted in dribs and drabs, but probably for a period of six months in the tenth year the whole complexion of the church changed.

Having started with forty-two elders, they ended up with eleven. The previous minister averaged forty-four baptisms a year, Ian averaged four as he only baptised the children of believers. It created problems, so much so that television cameras and newspapers turned up because he was causing ructions in the church by not admitting people to membership nor baptising their children. The Lord was very kind to Ian, though, and he had the support of five very good men who stood by him through thick and thin.

The latter ten years were profoundly different from the first ten years and, while not spectacular, it was a time of encouragement. People came to faith and the Lord added to the church. The evening service, as well as the midweek meeting for Bible study and prayer, grew. Between Glasgow and the English border, about a hundred miles, they were the only congregation with no women elders and the only congregation with an evening service and prayer meeting, and so people started coming from all over, as far as from twenty-five to thirty miles away. The congregation became the best giving congregation in the Presbytery, which got the attention of worldly-minded religious people. They were keen to know how the congregation gave so much and what appeals they had!

In the church he had one elder who was a very fine preaching elder and he would preach regularly. Ian was keen that preaching should not just be by one man, but if the Lord had gifted elders they should use their gifts in preaching and leading in prayer. There were no female elders or deacons but they appointed a woman to each elder's district for the elder to use as he thought wise, as some visits are very sensitive, especially with females. Then they appointed a lady pastoral visitor to visit widows.

He was the only minister in the town as there was no Roman Catholic church, no Baptist church, no Methodist church, just Ian and a small Gospel Brethren hall that they got on well with. He therefore got to know the people in the town very well, and in the twenty years he was there he took 701 funerals.

Cambridge

In 1999 Ian was called to Cambridge. Whereas when he went to Newmilns his first question he was asked was, 'What is your view on fundraising?', when he went to Cambridge the first question he was asked was, 'What are your views on the hypothetical universalism of the seventeenth century Carolinian divines?' People have often asked him if he was a bit intimidated by Cambridge, to which he would reply, 'Wherever you go in the world whether it's Cardiff, Glasgow or Timbuktu, you'll only meet two kinds of people: they need either saving or sanctifying.' He actually found that he was disappointed in most of the students he encountered because they didn't think very much. They were all very accepting of what others thought and consequently didn't really make each other think.

When he got there, the church was a very small congregation that had not long begun. But the membership grew and the Lord added to the church. He had had opportunities to go to other places but in Cambridge there just seemed to be a rightness about it.

There were just a small number of elders, excellent men, so different from when he began in Scotland. The Christian Union in Cambridge kindly gave him many, many opportunities—he thinks probably because they liked the accent! Altogether, he had seventeen very happy years in Cambridge, which he loved and it was a very fruitful time.

Teaching

After seventeen years in Cambridge, Ian thought it was perhaps time for a younger man to take over. He was in his mid 60s by then and had always enjoyed theological teaching. As he was thinking about leaving Cambridge a couple of seminaries approached him. Having previously taught for almost three years at Edinburgh Theological Seminary, he now teaches at Westminster Presbyterian Seminary in Newcastle, mainly teaching historical theology and one or two other things. He also teaches Puritan spirituality at Greenville Presbyterian Seminary in South Carolina.

Banner of Truth

Prior to going to Cambridge he had been asked to become a trustee at the Banner of Truth. So for the last twenty-four years he has been on the board of the Banner. That has been a huge privilege because the first substantial Christian book he recollects reading was John G. Paton's missionary autobiography to the New Hebrides. The second was Robert Haldane's commentary on Romans and the third, John Murray's *Redemption Accomplished and Applied*. To him that is the finest and richest exposition of the atonement and he recommends it to people wherever he goes.

Good Books and the Importance of Reading

From the Banner of Truth monthly magazine it is clear that Ian is very fond of John Owen, something he confirmed when we interviewed him, and he said it went back a long way. The first volume he read of John Owen's works was volume 10, *The Death of Deaths in the Death of Christ*, and the reason for that was his professor at college, T. F. Torrance, was a godly man but was passionately against the doctrine of limited atonement. So Ian read Owen and loved it. He then read Volume 6, *The Mortification of Sin*, not realising he should have begun with volume one, volume two and volume 3. Owen's volume 2, *Communion with God*, is probably one of the most influential books he has ever read. Calvin's *Institutes* has shaped his Christian life in terms of his view of the grandeur of God and the holy Trinity, but he found Owen's *Communion with God* the most profound. People often say that Owen is very latinate and his long coordinate sentences can go on forever, but Ian maintains that once you get into a rhythm with Owen he can be very lyrical and incredibly moving and leaves you stunned at times. When Ian teaches Puritan spirituality and the Reformed Pastor at Greenville, he uses Owen a lot and says his writings are experiential divinity at its purest. He also recalls Sinclair Ferguson saying that once you've read John Owen you wonder why you should bother reading anyone else.

When asked whether he thought younger generations read enough and did he think that they are reading the right kind of books (lots of books published today are very small because the assumption is that people cannot read big books), he said that, while he is sure there are a lot of good modern books, he is saddened by how little young men preparing for the ministry read. When he was teaching in a seminary for a while, the students were very kind about his teaching, but he got two complaints at the end of the year. The first complaint was that Dr Hamilton doesn't always translate the Latin, to which he replied, 'I always translate it, but you don't always listen.' The second complaint was, 'He expects us to read too much,' to which he just gave a three-word response: 'Get a life!' He was astonished that in a class of twenty-five not one student had read John Murray's *Redemption Accomplished and Applied*, not one student had read anything by B. B. Warfield, and he didn't even get to John Owen. As far as Ian is concerned, if you are not reading the classics of church history, Augustine's *Confessions* (which should be a must-read for any theological student) Calvin's *Institutes*, Owen volumes one, two, three, six and seven, ten, thirteen; Thomas Goodwin, Jonathan

Edwards, Spurgeon and Gresham Machen, then the weight of Christian literature and Christian thought, and the richness of insight that God has so signally used and blessed throughout the centuries, will be lost to us. Ian maintains that ministry is like an iceberg and seven eighths of your ministry is beneath the surface, hidden away, and it is what ministers put into those hidden days and years that people don't see that really will sustain ministry.

He would want to say to any young men thinking of Christian ministry, or even beginning to prepare for Christian ministry: read well, read thoughtfully, take your time and digest, ponder, meditate on what you read. He wishes he had thought more and read less as a young man. Reading has never been a problem because he grew up in an era when they didn't have computers and so they went to the library every week with their three tickets and they would get books of all kinds. He has always loved books but wishes he had pondered more, and thinks he rushed through books.

He would encourage young people to cultivate the art of thoughtful pondering as they read, and to go back to the ancients, knowing that you don't need to agree with all the church fathers because they got something spectacularly wrong, but the things they got right they got gloriously right. He would encourage them to go back in history which is what Calvin did, who quoted Augustine over four hundred times in his *Institutes*. He quoted Bernard of Clairvaux not because he agreed with everything, but because he knew that he was standing on the shoulders of the great masters of the spiritual life. The great Reformers and Puritans loved the church fathers. Ian urges us to likewise read these great Christians of the past, adding, 'Sola scriptura never meant *nuda scriptura*. Sola scriptura does not mean you neglect the tradition of the church. It means you bring everything to the touchstone of holy Scripture.'

He clearly feels passionate about this and went on to say that people are intimidated by literature today and believes it is because we live in a visual society where people blog and tweet and do all sorts of things. But it is never too late to start, and a good place would be to read Robert Letham's book on the Holy Trinity. It is a compelling read.

The State of the Church Today

He thinks there are some things that are very heartening, one of which is the desire for church planting that he increasingly sees in the little denomination of which he is a part, the Evangelical Presbyterian Church in England and Wales International Presbyterian Church.

However, he is troubled by the lack of reverence and awe in worship. When he was preaching through Nehemiah for a church in Glasgow and looked at Nehemiah's opening prayer, *'the great and the awesome God'*, it was not just the language, but you could almost feel the pulse beat of reverence that permeates the language, something Ian thinks is present in all the great prayers and times of blessing. People want to engage with modernity and that's a good thing, but we can become overly familiar and we forget that our God is a consuming fire. He is our Father, but he is our Father in heaven and the unfallen angels veil their faces. The opening prayer in a service is so important. William Still could pray for twenty minutes and at times you just wanted to go home after that because it was as if you had been taken into the heights. James Philip did not pray as long (and Ian is not suggesting you have to pray for twenty minutes), but when he prayed you were also caught up into something grand and glorious. It seems that this was something similar to what Basil Howlett (see Chapter 1) experienced when he heard Dr Martyn Lloyd-Jones preach. Ian also remembers the one time he heard Lloyd-Jones preach. He was 19 and someone took him along to the centenary of the YMCA in the east end of Glasgow. He had heard people mention Lloyd-Jones once or twice, and when he got there saw a row of old men with black coats and this little fellow got up to preach. He looked so unimpressive, but for the next hour Ian sat on the edge of his seat and didn't move. It was absolutely compelling.

So a recovery of who the Lord God is in his triune majesty, that would be the one thing Ian would love to see recovered.

Advice

Ian thought a lot about what advice he would give to a young Ian Hamilton and consequently young ministers today. He would simply say this: do better than you've tried to do, all the subsequent years of your life. He was shaped in a church that said the heart of Christian ministry is preaching, prayer and pastoring the people. He wishes he had preached better and wishes people had helped him to preach better. He wishes he had given himself more to prayer and is ashamed of how poorly he has given himself to prayer. He has always had a high commitment to pastoral visitation. He visited four afternoons and three evenings every week for thirty-seven years as a pastor in Scotland and Cambridge, and so he would be visiting people all the time. But looking back he wishes he had been a little bolder in challenging people than he was.

Moreover, he has been profoundly privileged and wishes he had been better and done better with the privileges. God has been so faithful, so forbearing, so patient, so gentle and so generous to him. He surrounded him with examples that are wonderful and gave him fellow elders who were real godly, faithful men of God. He doesn't think there's a young minister who had better examples than he did: James Philip, Eric Alexander, and William Still whom he knew quite well but never sat much under his ministry. Quoting John Owen, 'Unacquaintedness with our privileges is our sin as well as our trouble.' Ian believes that could be said very much about him.

If he was to say anything to any young man going into the ministry, he would tell him to keep it simple because the Bible does. God promises to honour those who honour Him. Preach the Word in all its richness and all its fullness, never forgetting that Jesus Christ is the beginning, the centre and the end of it. Pray and pray and pray, and pastor the people.

And, perhaps above all, in the goodness of God, marry well like he did.

Chapter 7

Geoff Thomas

Introduction

Geoff Thomas is one of my fathers in the faith. I remember as a young boy going to the Aberystwyth conference and on the Sunday we always flocked with hundreds of others to listen to him preach.

As a student in Aberystwyth I went to Alfred Place for three years where he was my pastor. I have happy memories of being in the manse every Sunday night with all the other students, eating salted popcorn, discussing various issues and the house being full of laughter, joy and happiness. Now we are in London together and members at Amyand Park Chapel. I have to say back in the day I never thought I would be a guest at Geoff and Barbara's wedding. That really is like 'schoolboys' own stuff!'

His autobiography has recently been published, called *In the Shadow of the Rock*. On the back of it I wrote, 'Geoff Thomas is one of Wales' best-known preachers during the twentieth and early twenty-first centuries. And now his life story is print. It is everything I was expecting and more. The story is fascinating, and the way it is written, a real page turner. It deserves a wide audience.' I recommend it warmly to you and, if you haven't read the book, I hope that this chapter will whet your appetite.

Background

Geoff is a Merthyr boy. His father was a twin and he and his brother, Bryn, were born on 30th October, 1904. They went to Bethania Chapel in Dowlais, which at the time was one of the largest congregational chapels in the world. It was Welsh annibynwyr (Independent). Somebody once told Geoff's father that he was born on the day that the 1904 revival started. However, it is very difficult to say exactly when that was. Evan

Phillips, the grandfather of Bethan Lloyd-Jones, was from Newcastle Emlyn, where the Spirit of God was moving. He had preached in the church on that particular Sunday, with great power, taking as his text, 'The time has come.'

Peter Price, who had arrived at the church a few months before Geoff's father was born, baptised Geoff's father and brother in December 1904, and in January 1905 Evan Roberts came and preached at Bethania. Two thousand people filled the church and its Sunday School room, as well as reporters from the press. Evan Roberts walked up the aisles and challenged people to put their faith in Christ and confess Him as their Lord and Saviour, but the absence of preaching was disappointing.

A week later Peter Price wrote a very long letter which was given great prominence in the *Western Mail*. It was very critical of Evan Roberts. Geoff's grandfather had to make some sort of choice at that time. Was he going with Peter Price and his criticism, or was he going to agree with the methods that Evan Roberts was using? Geoff's grandfather supported Peter Price and from then on he stayed a Welsh Congregationalist. Geoff's Father, Harry, became a deacon in his 20s and the church treasurer. He and his father witnessed the steady decline in the church as well as a moral and cultural decline in the nation. His grandfather was an unhappy man; Geoff cannot remember hearing him laugh. He even observed the closure of Bethania.

Geoff's father's sister married a minister, his twin brother also became a congregational minister and, of course, so did Geoff, his only child. But Geoff's father was a station master. He was very moral, always in church twice on Sundays and always at the prayer meeting, but Geoff never witnessed him reading the Bible, and rarely saw him reading a book.

That was one side of Geoff's family. His mother Elizabeth's father was Jack Francis, from the southern end of Merthyr. He was a Marxist, although a member of High Street Baptist Church. He worked as a railwayman. His great heroes were Keir Hardie, Gandhi and George Bernard Shaw. His wife's brother, Oliver Bown, was enormously different and that brought gospel Christianity into Geoff's family. He was converted around the time of the 1904 revival. He went to Tabernacle Baptist Church

Porth, where R. B. Jones was his minister. He loved him and experienced first-hand gospel preaching that changed the lives of men and women in the Rhondda. For the next sixty years he was zealous in evangelism. He was by trade a very successful antiques dealer while his shop was under the railway arches in Pontypridd, but he also opened an antiques shop in Cardiff. He would carry a text around Pontypridd and spoke at any opportunity. They might go on a bus trip with the family to Mumbles, and he couldn't resist getting up and facing all the people sitting on the beach. He would start preaching to them and say, 'Oh, ladies and gentlemen, isn't this a wonderful day? You see this world around you? Our heavenly Father made all this and He sent his Son into this world to be our Lord and Saviour.' He would preach at the fountain at the bottom of Merthyr on a Saturday night. He was unashamed of the gospel. He would walk with Geoff's cousin, Bobi Jones, then stop and say to the boy, 'Look at this piece of ground here, look at these little flowers, our Lord and Saviour made all this.' Bobi said it was very powerful.

He started children's meetings at half past six on a Friday night in Merthyr and he wrote words and music for the children. Geoff's mother professed faith around 1920. She went to these meetings and to old people's homes and spoke and gave her testimony. Dr Lloyd-Jones knew Geoff's Uncle Oliver. He remembered he had a distinctive 'Amen', and followed the Doctor wherever he preached in the Rhondda.

Conversion

Geoff's father became station master in Nelson and the family moved to Hengoed and lived in the station house there. There was an evangelical Baptist church called Tabernacle where Geoff attended three times on a Sunday and to Christian Endeavour on Friday nights. It had started well with its core of saved people from the 1904 revival. The minister in 1951 came as a student from Cardiff and initially preached the gospel. His mother had been converted in the 1904 revival and had prayed for him all his life. He went to a liberal theological college and changed, but while Geoff was there he was preaching for a decision. Geoff remembers walking to church in 1954 thinking, 'I wonder, will God call me to Himself tonight? I wonder if I will have an inner witness tonight that He has loved me and sent His Son to die for me?'

One night that happened. There was always a second meeting after the main service on a Sunday evening to test the meeting. Everyone would stand up, and if anyone had come to profess faith in Christ they were to remain seated. Geoff remained seated and this minister came up the aisle and shook his hand and said, 'God bless you.' Geoff was baptised, joined the church and took communion. He was 15 years of age. Along with another boy converted at the church he started a Christian Union in school. He later went to camp in Llanmadoc in the Gower which was a great help. There he heard the young officers talking about Dr Martyn Lloyd-Jones.

Training

Geoff went to Cardiff university to do Biblical Studies in 1958. A friend in school gave him J. I. Packer's, *Fundamentalism and the Word of God* to read. He read it and thought, 'Ah, I can trust the Bible.' None of the lecturers at the college believed the Bible was all truth, but the Lord kept him. He was then given Dr Lloyd-Jones's *Studies in the Sermon on the Mount*, which was life-changing. It showed him the beauty of the Christian life. He wanted to live like that and wanted to hear preaching like that.

He then found in the local library a copy of J. C. Ryle's *Holiness* and that just shaped and confirmed these convictions. While he was a student in Cardiff he occasionally worshipped in the Heath. In 1959 he preached for the first time for a godly woman known affectionately by us all as 'Aunty Bessie', in Elizabeth Street Presbyterian Church in Dowlais. She would always encourage him to consider the ministry. He read Inter-Varsity Press (IVP) publications there and started to read the Banner of Truth magazine. I. B. Davis gave a copy of the 17th edition of the magazine to his son Andrew (see Chapter 11) and Andrew passed it on to his wife-to-be, Pam, who gave it in turn to fellow Biblical Studies student Geoff. He took out a subscription to the magazine and started his lifelong pursuit of reading Banner of Truth and IVP books. These publishers were printing books from professors at a place called Westminster Seminary in Philadelphia, authors like John Murray, Ned Stonehouse, Edward

J. Young and Edmund Clowney. Geoff thought that sounded the right place to study, so he providentially came across its address and began to write and he was accepted.

In 1961, he took a cargo boat from Liverpool docks and sailed for eleven days across the Atlantic to America, where he stayed for the next three years. It was an enormous privilege to sit under men like Cornelius van Til, and John Murray especially whom he dubbed the man most full of God that he has ever met. He owes a great debt to those men.

But the preaching in Philadelphia churches was poor. The city was the same size as Wales, three million people, but there was no awakening ministry there at all. He looked back and thought of the men had met and had influenced him in Wales, whom he had loved, Elwyn Davies, John Thomas, Hugh Morgan, Eifion Evans, I. B. Davis, Omri Jenkins, T. J. Russell-Jones, Vernon Higham, Gareth Davis and Luther Rees; and then the friends of his own age he admired like Neville Rees (see Chapter 2), Peter Jones, Geraint Fielder, Tony Horne and Keith Lewis. He missed spiritual friends and the preaching back home, and as soon as he graduated, within a week he was back in Wales, but the grumbles he had about Philadelphia when he was there soon became grumbles about Wales now that he was back.

Evangelicalism in England and Wales had the air of a big village. When, in a couple of years from returning, Dr Martyn Lloyd-Jones announced his retirement from the pulpit of Westminster Chapel, the Doctor had written in his letter to the church that one task before him was to speak and lecture about preaching. So Geoff sent that information to the Principal of Westminster, Edmund P. Clowney, urging him to invite the Doctor to come to Philadelphia and lecture there. He wrote immediately to Lloyd-Jones to invite him to come to the Seminary to lecture. Out of the invitation, subsequently accepted by Lloyd-Jones, came that magnificent book *Preaching and Preachers*.

Alfred Place, Aberystwyth

Geoff got married to Iola in 1964 and they were married for fifty-two years. They lived in Swansea for a year. Iola was a teacher in Gowerton

Grammar School for Girls, and then their first baby was coming the following year. He had a call from Aberystwyth to become the pastor in Alfred Place English language Baptist church. In many ways it was a typical Baptist Union Church. There were about a hundred names on the church membership; a third of them never attended, a third just came once, and then a third that was the heartbeat of the church. These were the people who prayed in the prayer meeting and taught Sunday school and worked with the young people and prayed for Geoff and encouraged him in his preaching. There were also still some students there whom he knew from the time when he was a student in Cardiff, and they came and they brought their friends along too.

He had been in academic circles for nine years: three years in Form 6, three years at Cardiff university and three years in Westminster. He was 25 or so years of age and looking back feels in those early days an inadequacy from almost a decade of study; in other words, that he was too cerebral and too academic in his inclination. This was compounded by his decision to launch into preaching through Genesis in the mornings and preaching through Matthew in the nights. Looking back, he should have done what Lloyd-Jones did in the mornings, which was expository systematic preaching, and preached on the big texts in the evening, similar to Spurgeon and what Vernon Higham did at the Heath. He was still learning his trade and how to minister to the affections of people as well as to their minds. There were bursts of pathos in some of the more effective sermons from the Calvinistic Methodist ethos that had nurtured him.

The church was supportive of him, though. Even the people who were spiritually immature, while they grumbled a bit, were impressed because the building was full and the giving went up. The chairman of the deacons, who was a lecturer in the philosophy department at the university, resigned as he was a Unitarian. He had apparently been asked to resist the direction that Geoff was leading the congregation but felt that that would have been just a political act. He left the church and he and Geoff got on well for the rest of their lives.

In total, Geoff was the pastor of Alfred Place for fifty years. In his dry-witted way he muttered, 'I never had a call anyway, and no one wanted me, so I stayed in Aberystwyth all those years!'

Encouragements

Geoff's greatest encouragement and blessings come from his family. He has three daughters of whom he stands in awe. They are fun to be around, intelligent, all teachers, but they are mighty serious concerning the kingdom of God. They counsel, they help, they raise their children to know and love the Lord. His grandchildren are also a blessing to him and his one grandson followed in his footsteps as the pastor at Alfred Place. He has another grandson in Cardiff, waiting for a call, while another is working for the Universities and Colleges Christian Fellowship (UCCF) in Wales, evangelising among students.

Then there is the encouragement from all the men that have gone into the ministry who sat in Alfred Place while they were students or members of the congregation. Forty-six in total, including James Allan from the Heath who is now pastor at Hebron in Dowlais, as well as his brother in law, Dan Peters, who is in Newcastle, and refers to the Alfred Place as a 'conveyor belt of preachers'. Others went on the mission field, to Kenya, Ecuador, Germany, France and America. They were not all converted under Geoff's ministry. Some came from godly homes and from fine churches, but they all sat under the Alfred Place pulpit and were helped and influenced by him. Geoff thinks that Dr Derek Thomas is one who has achieved much in his preaching and writing. He is in America, preaching in Thornwell's old pulpit and a professor at Reformed Theological Seminary. He has written many fine books and is a most helpful preacher.

Geoff has also been greatly encouraged by Muslims who have been converted over the years. A man phoned Geoff and asked if he could visit his aunt who was dying. He went to see her, prayed and read with her, and then some years later with her niece who developed Alzheimer's, and Geoff would sing to her, and finally with her husband who had cancer. His niece and her husband, a nominal Muslim, came to stay for months in Aberystwyth, caring for him. Geoff would speak to this older man and would read to him and preach to him. The week after he died, the Muslim gentleman asked if he could see Geoff. He assumed it was about the funeral arrangements but he asked Geoff if he would baptise him. Geoff asked him to write out his testimony, and when Geoff read it, it was full of Christ. He was baptised and now he lives in Wolverhampton and is going on well with the Lord. Another girl was brought along to church and she was saved, and then her husband was saved. They now live in Oxfordshire.

Then there was this encouraging event: when Geoff had been in Aberystwyth for just six weeks and was going through Matthew's Gospel, he came to Matthew 3 and the preaching of John the Baptist. He preached a sermon he called 'The Preaching God Blesses to Awaken Sinners' on the words, 'the axe is laid to the root of the tree … do not say that we have Abraham for our father, for God can raise up out of these stones children for Abraham'. The cassette of that preaching went everywhere. There were two brothers in the Philippines whose father had the biggest protestant church in the Philippines. But he left his wife and moved in with a Philippino girl. As a result, the younger boy gave up his faith, but his brother got hold of this tape somehow and sent it to him. He heard it and listened to it and it washed him; his life changed. Geoff has visited him in the USA, and he has been to Aberystwyth and London. He is now a professor and an elder in a Presbyterian Church. That was such an encouragement to Geoff, a counterpoise to his self-criticism concerning his early years of preaching.

There was then a man in prison who went to a warden to ask for help, asking this Christian whether there was anyone he could recommend to whom he could write. The warden knew Geoff and so they began writing to one another and Geoff also visited him in prison. As soon as he came out of prison, Geoff got him a place to stay. He married a Christian girl and is still in Aberystwyth. He would today hew wood and draw water for God.

Geoff did some open air preaching in Aberystwyth and heard a report of some encouragement from that. One evening, preaching on the promenade in Aberystwyth to far more seagulls than people, he felt the Spirit of God was on him and that there would be fruit from this message. He was preaching in the Dudley convention the following year and a man talked to him saying that he had been preaching in a place nearby earlier that year and had met a Christian woman. He asked her when she was converted and she said, 'On the promenade in Aberystwyth'. God's sovereignty is real. Faithfulness is rewarded, and very occasionally we are given the knowledge of how and when and where.

Geoff is frequently encouraged by his friends in the ministry: Gary Brady his son-in-law, Iain Murray (see Chapter 16), Al Martin, Steven Rees, Paul Washer, Ian Parry, Chris Rees, Ted Donnelly, and especially Gerard Hemmings who is his minister now. He also fondly remembers Douglas MacMillan.

Prayer

When asked what advice he would give a young Geoff Thomas and the things he wishes he could have done better, he acknowledges that he has found praying and the disciplines of personal devotions tough going. He said, 'If you want to humble a minister, you ask him about his prayer life.' The 'quiet time' has been an enormous challenge for him. He has been encouraged by having a praying wife. Every day Iola would go to the front room and read her Welsh Bible and go through her prayer list. Geoff wouldn't see her for half an hour. Geoff's daughter, Catrin, said she saw her mother coming out of the room once and she had a mark on her forehead because she had been leaning on her forehead while she was praying. A few years after her death he married Barbara from Germany, and she reads her German Bible each day, but they both read the daily passage from Tabletalk before breakfast and pray. He was also blessed by the examples of praying elders, deacons and church members in valuable meetings each Wednesday evening.

Geoff was asked to pray once at the Banner of Truth ministers conference and recalls: 'I don't think I prayed like it before and I don't believe that I've prayed like it since. I was given a prayer of much authority and beseeching and earnestness without breaking down. I kept my self-control but I was enabled by God to pray that prayer that people have remembered since that time. I wish there were many more like that.'

The State of the Church Today

Geoff thinks there are many encouragements. When he came back to Wales in the 1960s there were not many solid evangelical preachers he felt he could ask to occupy the pulpit. His yearning at first was that there would be a free grace gospel pulpit in every university town, and that has come about in Newport, Wrexham, Pontypridd, Bangor, Swansea, Cardiff, Carmarthen and Aberystwyth. And then, one by one, the smaller towns also have preachers in them faithfully opening up the Bible. In saying that, though, he grieves that there are not many men going into the ministry and only a few in Wales with an awakening ministry. He is thankful that there are people like Stuart Olyott who has a special gift of helping young men to preach. The books he has written about preaching are appreciated all over the world. When Geoff lectures in Kenya he gives to the theological students Stuart's books. They are indispensable and he would love to see some of his booklets and shorter books brought out in one useful volume.

He is thrilled by the sheer number of publishing houses and of books appearing, something like two new book each day across the world. And now on the web there are many of the works of the reformers and Puritan made available, and via Zoom one can hear men from across the UK, North America and Australia.

He thinks the greatest honour he was ever given was when the Evangelical Movement of Wales asked him to give the conference addresses in Aberystwyth. He preached four messages on Daniel and felt that in three out of the four he had experienced some divine help. Those addresses came out as a book that has now sold out. I was there for those addresses, and found all four superb!

Geoff has a sense that he has betrayed Wales in coming to London, but he came to the English metropolis because Alfred Place called his grandson Rhodri Brady as their minister and he didn't want to get under his feet. After Iola died he got friendly with Barbara Homrighausen. He had known Barbara for over forty years and she was very precious to all his family. They spoke together and got married and Geoff is now a member at Amyand Park Chapel.

The Need of the Hour

According to Geoff:

It must be Jesus Christ. The challenge of the ministry is to show men the loveliness and his omni-competence to meet the needs of the most helpless and guilty. When one day I see Him, I will just plead 'Mercy. Mercy, mercy.' I think in preaching today, pathos is missing. Too much emphasis has been placed on correct exegesis and the history of redemption insights. It is too cerebral an approach to the ministry of the Word of God.

He wants to urge people to return again to the gospel of our Lord Jesus Christ, calling people to a decision to follow the Lord, the Lamb of God who takes away our sin and as the Good Shepherd who protects us.

To Geoff, as he looks back, what is wonderful is that he has kept the faith. He heard Ernest Kevan, the former principal of London Bible College, speak once on Good Friday in Neath mission for I. B. Davies. Geoff had tea with him afterwards. Mr Kevan said that his father's last words were these, 'I have believed all the great truths of the gospel since I became a Christian. I believe them yet.' By the grace of God, Geoff is able to say the same. When Iola died, the three girls came and joined him at her bedside at four o'clock in the morning; they wept and hugged one another in Bronglais Hospital. He read from 2 Timothy 4, *'I have fought the good fight, I have finished the race, I have kept the faith. Finally, there is laid up for me the crown of righteousness, which the Lord, the righteous Judge, will give to me on that Day, and not to me only but also to all who have loved His appearing.'*

Chapter 8

Bill Hughes

Introduction

I first came across Bill Hughes when he preached in the Aberystwyth conference. He preached a memorable sermon on, 'Choose you this day, Jesus or Barabbas.' When I was a student in Aberystwyth, he came to preach at Geoff Thomas' thirty-year anniversary at Alfred Place, which was one of the highlights of my time at Aber. He more recently came to preach at Amyand Park Chapel in London, and once again preached so powerfully.

Whenever he is asked to say anything about himself and his life he always quotes Psalm 34:6 which seems to sum up his life: *'This poor man cried out, and the LORD heard him, and saved him out of all his troubles'*, and then verse 3 of that psalm, *'Oh, magnify the LORD with me, and let us exalt His name together.'* In fact, he and his wife had that text in their wedding rings. He was married to Alma for forty-nine years. She was as easy to stay in love with as she was to fall in love with. He does not know whether he would have been able to do anything in the pastoral ministry without her support. He has three children. His eldest daughter Caroline is married to a Welshman, Dyfan Williams, who is a pastor. He has a daughter, Helen, who is in Manchester, and he has a son, Jonathan, who is in Denver in Colorado. As he looks back over his life, he repeatedly finds the providence of God prominent.

Background

He was born in Liverpool in the year that war broke out, 1939, in a part which many people then, and even today, would know as the Holy Land. The street where he lived was a main street and opposite the street were other streets: Moses Street, Isaac Street, Jacob Street, David Street, and Grace Street ran through the middle.

He was evacuated as a child with his mother, brother and sister to a village named Tarporley in Cheshire before returning to Liverpool a couple of years later. His mother was a single mother. His father was in the merchant navy and he jumped ship in New Zealand when Bill was five years of age and they never heard from him again. So his mother was left with three children.

She either had to put her three children into an orphanage or else she had to go out to work, and she chose to go out to work. Every day she would leave the house at 7.30 in the morning and come in at about 6.30 at night. So until he was about 15 he does not remember ever coming home and his mother being there.

He went to a Church of England primary school, the same primary school that his future wife went to, but they didn't know one another back then. Then he took the 11-plus exam and went to St Margaret's, Anfield, another Church of England school. It was a grammar school and while he was there he was confirmed in the Anglican Church. He sometimes says to people that the Bishop of Chester put his empty hands on his empty head and it meant nothing. But he did have one thing that he benefited from going there, and that was he had to learn the Apostles' Creed which has stayed with him throughout his life.

When he left school at 15 he saw another providence in his life. In those days when you left school a medical doctor would come to examine you. The doctor came to examine Bill, and just as Bill was walking out of the room he called him back again and asked him if he could listen again. When he did he discovered a defect in his heart. So Bill had to have open heart surgery, which in those days was pioneering, and because of that he was restricted from doing anything for a year.

Conversion

He eventually got a job and started work in the local council in Liverpool, and then he got a job in the atomic energy authority near Warrington. At that time, in his mid teens, he was extremely lonely. He found a book of poetry entitled Palgrave's *Golden Treasury*, and he used to go to the park and read poetry. In order to break out of this loneliness he joined a youth club for young men in Liverpool and there he met a young fellow and they became friends.

His friend's mother was the first real Christian he had ever met and they worshipped at a little mission church, called The Sailors' Chapel, in the Dingle in Liverpool. In order to retain this friendship he used to go to this chapel on a Sunday evening and that is where he began to hear the gospel. He was conscious that his life was going in the wrong direction. A group of men from the Methodist Cliff College in Derbyshire came to take a series of evangelistic meetings and during one of those meetings he was deeply convicted and he responded to what the Americans would call 'the altar call'. He went forward at the meeting and knelt at what they called the penitent form and he asked God to save him, and believes that He did.

He was 19 years of age and remembers going home and his mother asking where he had been. He told her that he had been converted and she told him it was just a phase that young people go through and it would pass. She changed her mind a week later when he got up at six o'clock on a Sunday morning so he could go down to this little church for a seven o'clock prayer meeting. He went into a side room at 7 am that morning and there were about eight people there. He doesn't think one of them was under 80 years of age and he was 19. He was welcomed and he was told that it was a prayer meeting and they would read the Bible and then they would all kneel to pray. According to Bill, 'I shall never ever forget those prayer meetings, because when I listened to these people praying they really knew God, and that's where I cut my teeth on prayer.'

He got involved in the life of that church and he started a youth fellowship. He also engaged in open air preaching. In those days there was no television, and so people would gather at an open-air meeting on a street corner on a Sunday evening after church. He had to preach and give his testimony.

There were also some Youth for Christ meetings in Liverpool at that time on a Saturday evening and he started going to them. That is when he first took notice of the person who was to be his future wife and they went to those meetings together. They also went to an after-church meeting on a Sunday evening in somebody's house where they got to know one another.

The Call and Training

Bill began to have a burden to become a full-time worker. He wanted to be a missionary in Brazil. He decided that he would go to the Bible Training Institute in Glasgow.

He went to the Bible Training Institute in Glasgow. Then, through the providence of God he met a number of men and women who have remained constant friends throughout his life, including Peter Brumby and others who have gone on to serve the Lord as pastors and missionaries. It was at college he first heard Eric Alexander giving pastoralia lectures.

During his time there his views began to change as to where the Lord would have him to serve. In Glasgow he sat under the ministry of George Philip who was the minister of Sandyford Henderson Church of Scotland.

The Saturday evening Bible studies, where George Philip engaged in a consecutive Biblical teaching ministry, had a profound impact upon him.

Ministry

Liverpool

Towards the end of his time in Glasgow, thinking that he might now go into the pastoral ministry, he applied to go to the Baptist College in Belfast where David Kingdon was the principal at that time. But just as he was about to do that, he received an invitation from the small mission church where he had been converted, asking if he would go and be their full-time pastor. He believed this was how God was leading him and that is what he did.

He was in Liverpool for five years and from the outset he saw great blessing there. He would never advise any young man to do what he did because he didn't know any Greek or Hebrew, yet despite that he felt God was guiding him there.

Chapter 8

Cumnock

In 1970 he received an invitation to go to south-west Scotland, to Ayrshire, a small town called Cumnock. It had a population of about 10,000 as well as outlying villages. Bill had been reluctant to go into a Baptist Union church because of the ecumenical issues, but on the day they were going to decide whether to call Bill, they had also decided to leave the Baptist Union in Scotland, and he took that as a further indication that he should go.

Cumnock is in the middle of Covenanting country. Alexander Peden's grave was immediately opposite the church and Richard Cameron's was just a few miles away. The town was mainly a mining and farming community and was the home of the Labour party.

When he got there, there were about twenty-five people in the congregation. For five years he saw no growth, but he remembered that before he left Glasgow to go to Liverpool, George Philip took him to one side and gave him some advice which was to be prepared to preach the Word for ten years before starting to look for results.

He started a monthly series of Bible rallies on a Friday evening and an annual Bible convention to which he invited a number of men to come to preach, including Sinclair Ferguson, Douglas MacMillan, Eric Alexander, Derek Prime, Alistair Begg, W. H. Davis, Geoff Thomas, John Blanchard and others.

Then around 1975 there was an unusual increase in the number of people that were coming to the church and being converted. It grew so much that they had to expand the church in order to get people seated.

It was a remarkable time, and from listening to other ministers he believes that the time between 1975 into the early 1980s was a time of great blessing in different churches throughout the country.

He started attending the Banner of Truth conferences at that time and these were a great help and blessing to him, from all the men he met there, to the preaching he heard and the friendships that developed.

It was during his time in Cumnock that he met Ted Donnelly at one of the Covenanting conventions in the Solway Firth and they became lifelong friends.

It was also at this time that he and his wife developed an interest in a mission in India, the Ramabai Mukti Mission, and were involved in it together.

At that time he was reading the life of Samuel Chadwick, a Methodist pastor, who, when he went to a mill town in Lancashire, asked the people to pray for a 'Lazarus' to be converted. They did, and a Lazarus was converted. Bill was relaying this story to the prayer meeting and encouraging them to pray for Lazaruses to be converted in their town. Well it wasn't a man, it was a woman, the worst woman in the town, who arrived at one of their ladies' meetings. She had committed every sin in the book. She also had what they called in those days a club foot and had her leg in a calliper. Her husband, in order to stop her going down to the town to get drunk, would hide the calliper. But she would strap a yard brush on for a calliper and would hobble down to the pub and hobble home drunk. Many a morning she was found frozen on the ground in their garden.

The ladies, when they saw her come into their meeting, were all concerned that she might disturb things, but she listened. The speaker, who was a converted Roman Catholic nun, gave her remarkable testimony and Bessie Bates was wonderfully converted. She was eventually baptised and became a really wonderful Christian witness and the talk of the town.

A number of people were converted at that time, including her husband who also came to faith. He was the complete opposite to his wife, with a very quiet, gentle demeanour, and he started attending the church with her.

Almost a year later, at the end of the evening service he remained seated in the church and Bill went up to him and asked him if he was all right. He said, 'Mr Hughes, I think I've been converted,' and went on to say that what really spoke to him was the benediction that Bill had pronounced: '*The grace of the Lord Jesus, the love of God.*'

Glasgow

In the early eighties Bill started to notice some small groups of visitors coming into church each week and he later discovered they belonged to a church in Glasgow. They were what they called their 'vacancy committee' who were coming to observe Bill as a prospective pastor, and he then received an invitation to go and meet with these people. They had written to him a number of times and Bill had kept saying no, but eventually he thought he would just go up in person and tell them all the reasons why he would not be involved in this church. There were sixteen deacons in the church and Bill would have been the sole elder. When he met with them and went through a whole list of things he thought would put them off asking him to be their pastor, they answered every one and said that they really felt that they wanted the kind of ministry that Bill had. He was eventually convinced that he should go to Glasgow. Eric Alexander also encouraged him to come to the city, and so after thirteen years in Cumnock he went to Glasgow to the Harper Memorial Baptist Church. The church was named after John Harper who had established the church and had a reputation as an outstanding preacher. His wife died giving birth to their first child and he was invited to go to Moody's Church in Chicago. He went there and preached and they then invited him back, and he and his young daughter with their housemaid sailed on the *Titanic* which sank in mid-ocean. So the church was named after him.

When Bill went there the church was in decline. There were people only on the ground floor, nobody in the galleries. Being the sole elder it was difficult, but he started to preach and gradually people were coming in—not necessarily unconverted people but people of a Baptist position who were wanting to have this kind of ministry. The Lord blessed them and the prayer meeting regularly had about a hundred and twenty in attendance each week.

However, after about six years, there was a vocal minority who were unhappy about the kind of ministry they were getting and they began to agitate. Bill was in the unusual position of being the most loved and the most disliked person in the church at one and the same time. Some people would have given him their kidney if he needed it, others would have packed his bags right away, but he struggled on.

Then, having never been really ill throughout his entire ministry, he was starting to get some palpitations, and because of his heart condition he visited the doctor who made him take two months off. After the two months all the medical tests were fine and he was told to avoid situations of stress.

He went back on a Monday, conducted a funeral, and in the evening he had a deacons' meeting that lasted until nearly midnight. It was a difficult meeting and it all came to a head when he confronted his deacons and asked each one of them what their view concerning his ministry was. Some of them said they no longer wanted his kind of ministry and others remained silent. Bill thinks if he had taken the matter to a church meeting he would have carried the vote, but these men said if he did that they would resign from the diaconate. If they had told him they would have left the church, he would have done it, but they didn't, and he would have had sixteen disaffected men with some of their families, and to him that was intolerable.

Therefore, he decided to leave. It was difficult because he was living in the church manse. About forty people left the church, and Bill deliberately kept his distance from them because he didn't want it to appear that he had brought them out. He spent a whole year thinking that his ministry was finished. But at that time he was greatly encouraged by Eric Alexander and Sinclair Ferguson who were ministering at St George's Tron church.

The group that had left Harper after Bill did had been meeting in each other's homes on Sundays, and they eventually formed themselves into a Reformed Baptist Church and asked if he would be their pastor.

At that time he went with Eric Alexander and Sinclair Ferguson to Douglas MacMillan's funeral in Edinburgh and afterwards they took him for dinner and really encouraged him to stay with this group whom they believed they were his flock.

The new church met in a school in another part of the city. It was very inconvenient and they had to clean the school every Saturday because it was filthy dirty, but for nearly ten years they had great blessing.

Towards the end of that time he felt that the work needed a younger man to take the work forward. He had also at this time had been attending pastors' conferences in the United States of America. He was invited to go to South Florida to see if he would be willing to help out in a church where the pastor was struggling.

Florida

He and his wife left Scotland with the blessing and support of the church in Glasgow. He originally planned to go to America for three years, but that eventually turned into ten. The pastor he was helping did not have good health and had to move, and Bill didn't feel he could return to the UK and leave them without a pastor. It took a long time to get another man to come on board and when they finally did, again Bill didn't feel he could leave straight away.

Looking back he can see God's providence in all that had happened. They returned by sea to the UK in 2012 and it was wonderful seeing all their family waiting for them as they sailed into Southampton. At that time his wife was struggling with a bad foot as a result of a bad fall she had when they were in Florida. It eventually turned out to be motor neurone disease and they were told she would probably have just two years to live, which turned out to be correct. After two years of fighting it valiantly she was promoted to glory.

When they had returned from America they decided to settle near their family in Cheshire and they eventually joined a church in Deeside, where Bill still worships.

Advice

On reflection, Bill thinks George Philip's advice to him was very good and he would pass it on to younger ministers today: to be prepared to preach, and to have a biblical, expository ministry that is applied to the different age groups in your congregation, one that will encourage people; to be prepared to plod on and pray to God for results. There is a verse in Isaiah 30:18 which has been a great help to him: '*Therefore the LORD will wait, that He may be gracious to you.*' There are delays in God's providence and we may wonder why things are not happening, but they are happening. We should never doubt in the dark what we believe to be true in the light. The devil will tempt us to doubt whether what we are doing is right, or whether we are in the right place. Bill would stress to young men, that as much as they possibly can, to be sure that they are in the place where God wants them to be. There will be times when some people will say they think that your ministry is being wasted where you are and you would be far better somewhere else. At which point the question must be asked, 'Whose strategies am I going to live by, their strategy or God's strategy?' When the Lord Jesus sent out his disciples He had a clear strategy for His disciples (Matthew 10:5). In the same way, God has a strategy for each one of our lives. We must trust in the sovereignty of God, that He knows the end from the beginning.

Books and People

Shortly after he was converted he was at a meeting in a church in Liverpool where they had a bookstall, and there was a book by a man he had never heard of before. It was the *Revival Year Sermons* by Charles Haddon Spurgeon. When Bill began to read those sermons he felt as if he had been converted all over again. He said Spurgeon really became his 'paper pastor'. At one point he had all 66 volumes of Spurgeon's sermons and he used to read one a day for his own benefit.

He thinks it is a wonderful thing that in his lifetime there is the availability of so many tremendous books. The Banner of Truth has done a wonderful job and he reads anything by Iain Murray. He loves biographies and has read the Lloyd-Jones biographies by Iain Murray, Spurgeon's biography and Whitefield's biographies by Arnold Dallimore. He found *Power through Prayer* very helpful early in his pastoral life, along with J. C. Ryle's *Charges and Addresses for a Pastor*, and of course Lloyd-Jones on Romans, Ephesians, and *Preaching and Preachers*. More recently he read Dr Lloyd-Jones' Westminster Conference addresses which he found absolutely wonderful. The letters of Samuel Rutherford became very precious to him and something Rutherford said he found particularly helpful at one point. It was at the time he was about to go to Liverpool and somebody said to him that he was making a mistake. He had just read in one of Rutherford's letters that *'Our dear Lord Jesus will overlook and pardon our honest mistakes if they are made with a mind for His glory.'* He also found *Knowing God* by J. I. Packer a great help, as well as the writings of Stuart Olyott.

He loves poetry, and at the risk of being controversial really misses the hymn book which is often replaced these days by a screen. He thinks young people today could be missing out on a tremendous heritage of great hymnody.

The State of the Church and the Need of the Hour

Bill believes that we all know what the need of the hour is, it is prayer and preaching, and so it is just a matter of doing it. God has promised to bless the preaching of His Word but we are living in days where increasingly the ministry of the Word is being edged out in many places by other things. When he was first converted it would not be unusual for most pastors to preach for forty-five to fifty minutes, even an hour, and nobody complained, but today we are being told not to make it more than thirty minutes. He is thankful that he is now in a church where they have faithful expository preaching and caring elders and a wonderful praying congregation.

When we interviewed Mr Hughes, it was during the pandemic and he said that his heart was breaking at the thought that millions of people were going into a lost eternity, to a fate that is worse than COVID-19 that will never end. We need to pray earnestly for these people and pray that God will raise up missionaries to go out into the world.

He believes there are positives in our generation too. As well as good books, he is thankful for technology, particularly during lockdown. He thinks it is wonderful the way he can find a verse of scripture on Google faster than he could by going to the concordance. He is thankful for all of this technology but it can also bring with it certain dangers. Young people need to be careful not to get led astray by social media. It can do a great deal of damage as well as doing a great deal of good.

To Bill, the wonder of the Christian life is that there is always more to gain and there are always heights yet to be attained. In some ways he enjoyed lockdown because it did his spiritual life the world of good. He had more time to pray and more time to read. He has had more time to be on his own, and in solitude there is great blessing.

At the time of the interview, he was 81 and did not know how much longer he would have left on this earth, but he is still learning things all the time. He is thankful for the men who have been such good friends to him and he would really encourage young men to develop friendships with men that they can trust.

Finally, he thinks sometimes the emphasis today is focused too much on getting the people in the world inside the church, instead of focusing upon the people who are in the church going out into the world.

Throughout his life he has seen more people come under the sound of the gospel through the personal witness of believers in their homes and in their places of work than he has through any other outside activity. He and his wife visited every door in Cumnock when they were there, he has engaged in open-air preaching, and while he is not undermining those efforts or discounting them he thinks the emphasis should be more upon people's characters being changed by the Word of God. As they are nurtured in the church under the preaching ministry, they then go out and gossip the gospel.

Finally, Bill mentions two little volumes by William Still on the work of the pastor, and in those volumes, he says:

The pastor is called to feed the sheep, even if the sheep do not want to be fed. He is certainly not to become an entertainer of goats. Let the goats, entertain goats and let them do it out in goat-land. You will certainly not turn goats into sheep by pandering to their goatishness.

Chapter 9

Eryl Davies

Introduction

When I was a member of the Heath Evangelical Church I used to look forward to my termly chats with Dr Davies over a cup of tea. I would also recommend listening to his talks on the way God worked in the 1960s and 1970s in Wales. They were very special and available on the Heath Church website.

He is unable to look back over his life without talking about God's providence, because it really has been quite unexpected as far as he was concerned. Eryl Davies had his own ambitions, but the Lord ordered otherwise. He can testify that the sovereign grace and love towards him in Christ has been quite remarkable, not just for himself but for his whole family, his wife Magwen and her family, and his brother John and his family.

Background

Eryl is from North Wales and was born in Old Colwyn on the edge of the lovely coastal resort, Colwyn Bay. His grandparents on his mother's side were Welsh Congregationalists and attended the chapel that still stands on the main street in Old Colwyn. At 14 his mother became a member, though not converted, while his father was from a Welsh Baptist family in Abergele. His father was one of seven and his mother was one of eight, so there was quite a big extended family. When my mother was 15, her mother died giving birth to the youngest child, which had a huge impact upon her and the rest of the family. Not long after her mother died, her father also died. Losing both her parents so young meant that Eryl's mother took care of most of her sisters and some of her brothers, and after she got married some of them came to live with her. Therefore, Eryl grew up in a home full of uncles and aunts and remembers it was a very loving, warm, secure childhood.

Eryl's mother and father married quite young. His father was a brilliant footballer and could have turned professional. But there was no money in it back then and so Eryl's parents got married on the condition that he gave it up and got a permanent job. He got a job with the London Midlands Scottish Railway and he moved around quite a lot. Eryl had a younger brother, John, who was born in Malpas in Cheshire, where his father at the time was a signalman and porter, before getting a job in Chester station as a guard on the railway passenger and goods trains. It was all very exciting for Eryl and John because they could have free travel, or reduced travel costs, and go with him on some of the trains.

His childhood was very happy and he benefited enormously from having a secure, loving family. It reminds Eryl of the inter-Trinitarian relationships: Father, Son, Holy Spirit; their unity, their love, their intimacy and purpose; and that we are made in the image of God and social creatures and that the Lord appointed marriage as a divine institution at creation.

His childhood was also exciting. One of his uncles who lived with them had a bread round with the Co-op and Eryl would go with him on Saturdays and in the holidays because his uncle was colour-blind and never knew the traffic signals, when to go and when to stop. Eryl also learned to drive at the age of 8 without anyone knowing. All in all, growing up he had a whale of a time.

His parents sent Eryl and his brother to the local Presbyterian Church just a couple of minutes' walk away, but he can't say he learned the Bible there. The people at Sunday School were all very friendly and helpful but they mainly discussed sports.

He found school boring and saw it just as an interference with childhood, which meant it was no surprise when he failed the 11-plus. His mother was distressed over it and some of the mothers in the village gloated over his failure. He remembers the teacher, after the results came out, reading a small essay Eryl had written and saying, 'Eryl Davies, this is very good but it's too late now,' which remained with Eryl for some time. He showed no interest at senior school either and would be 37th out of 38 in the class and quite proud of that as he was not bottom.

At the age of 14 he decided he wanted to be a policeman and also a footballer. So his father made enquiries with the police who welcomed the thought of having a 15-year-old as a police cadet. They said he should read some books on police law and then in school switch courses so that he would have a mastery of shorthand and typing, which he did. At 15 he left school with great joy and assumed he would be in the police for a long time, until the chief constable, an elderly and tough military type with no interest in education, called Eryl in and told him, amongst other things, that if he really wanted to give more of his free time to education, then go and come back in five years' time. Eryl was bitterly disappointed and couldn't really understand it, and even though by now he had started going to evening classes at college, he got a job with Home Pride Flour and enjoyed his time there.

The Call

The family were going to the Presbyterian Church of Wales which was socially very good but very liberal. There was no Bible teaching and they didn't have a minister. But at 15 he and his brother needed to be baptised, by sprinkling, and an interim moderator came to do it. He had been a missionary in India and told a remarkable story. Eryl cannot remember the text he took but realised that there was something very different about him. Christ was real, the gospel was important, and to be a Christian he told them, was very exciting. Something happened which Eryl cannot explain, but he was aware that Christianity was more than just a nominal religion.

A few weeks later he was cycling home from work and unexpectedly felt a call from God that was quite overwhelming, calling him to the ministry, even though he was still unconverted. He did not know the Bible but he knew the direction of his life would change and he would never join the police or become a professional footballer. It was daunting, and not really understanding what was happening he shared it with his parents and then with the church secretary.

Things moved very, very quickly—too quickly in one sense, because the church was informed and the presbytery was told and Eryl had to preach before the church. Then the presbytery arranged for him to preach in six of their churches. Eryl found their supervision of a candidate for the ministry was superb and speaks very highly of the care they took of him, and in each church where he went there was a good congregation. Midweek the minister was there and the report would be sent into the presbytery which would be assessed. He was sent to the candidates' board with a warning: 'You don't know the Bible, Eryl Davies.' They arranged for one minister to teach him the Bible, which he really didn't know, and he made a real mess of the Scripture exam. He could not answer some of the questions, but the candidates' board providentially accepted him. For a few months he had to prepare in one of their preparatory colleges to learn classical Greek and get some A-level subjects.

Conversion and Training

He was still only seventeen when he went into the preparatory college, so the Presbyterian Church took a risk on him, which they told him, but they believed that there was something genuinely going on in his life. Instead of going on to university after he had finished his A Levels and his studies in Greek, he asked the presbytery if he could go to the Theological College. It was not the usual custom, but he told them that he really did not know the Bible, and so they agreed. That again was providential because he met some Christians there like Vernon Higham, who was in his last year, and Gareth Davies and Eifion Evans. They witnessed to him, but at that point he still didn't understand.

In the middle of the second term, from his own feelings, aware of sin, far from God and not knowing the gospel, Eryl just poured out his heart before God in his study and cried to the Lord to save him, and it was immediate. He knew the Lord had forgiven him and accepted him. He knew joy, the gospel became very precious to him and he rejoices in God's providence in the timing of his conversion.

The student body in the college was very liberal; there were only a few evangelicals and there was a lot of animosity towards the evangelical students. Eryl changed sides and suffered as a result of that. He joined the Christian Union and the theological students' fellowship.

Even though the teaching was liberal, the principal was kind to him and he found the three years there a help. The evangelical students had to work harder to counter much of the liberal teaching, but God was good and it was there he met for the first time Elwyn Davies who had started travelling for the UCCF at that time.

The principal tried to persuade Eryl to go on to Oxford and said he had a place ready for him and he could get better results from going there. But he decided he wanted to stay in Aberystwyth. He had met Magwen by this time, who was still in college, and he felt he needed to support the Christian Union. So he stayed in Aberystwyth to study Philosophy for three years and he benefited enormously during that time.

One of the great benefits of being in the denomination was that there was a system of summer pastorates for students, whereby churches without pastors would use a student during training. Eryl did one for four weeks in Morriston and then did two in the village of Nantyffyllon in the Maesteg valley. At Nantyffyllon, even though there were three elders, for two summers Eryl was given free reign. He preached every Sunday, led Bible studies, prayer meetings and youth meetings, as well as visiting. He learned so much at that time about how important it was to be relational, to love people and to draw alongside them.

But at the end of his second student pastorate there he went up near the golf course, not to play golf but to prepare his messages for Sunday. It was a beautiful summer day and as he was reading the Word, preparing and praying, he had an overwhelming conviction that God would call him to Maesteg. This was remarkable because the Maesteg church was a big congregation of two hundred and the church where he was, in Nantyffyllon, had about fifty members. He had never been there and the two churches had nothing really to do with one another. But the conviction grew and he developed a real love for the people and the valley.

As he entered his final months in university and having to choose between research and a call and going to different churches, out of the blue came this invitation from the Maesteg church to preach with a view. The story behind it was that Presbytery had given them permission to call a minister because, despite the fact they had been ten years without a minister, the church had grown enormously. It was crowded with young people and young married couples, but they could only call a student and one of the few students available that summer was Eryl Davies. He preached and they gave him the call. It was a joint pastorate with Nantyffyllon. That summer he and Magwen got married and then in September 1959 he started what would be a tough period of ministry in Maesteg. But the Lord was good.

Maesteg

Maesteg had a large congregation but not many Christians. The Sunday School was huge with about 180 children. Eryl had lots of requests for baptism of their babies which created openings into people's homes and families. There were twelve elders, three of them were women who were better than the men. The elders ruled the church and for two years Eryl was not allowed to hold a Bible Study. After the evening service, the senior elder would have a second meeting where he would recap Eryl's sermon, but in reality contradicted it. In God's providence what that really did was make the congregation even more sympathetic towards him as they felt sorry that what he had preached was being denied by this elder. Not surprisingly, when he was invited to stop one thing, it was the second meeting. When Eryl announced the benediction it was the end of the service. It was brave but definitely the right thing to do.

For Eryl, there were lots of things happening in the church which were wrong, but he realised that the big issue was not so much, for example, the jazz evenings the young people held, the big issue was the gospel. The congregation by and large were unconverted. Out of maybe 220, only about five had a testimony to the grace of God. It was really a mission field.

Eryl would have to admit that it was the Lord who kept him there in the first five or six years, as he and Magwen found it so difficult. The middle-aged people were tough, especially the women. They disliked gospel preaching, especially if it went over twenty minutes, but one or two were converted.

Then around 1965/66 he became much more desperate. He felt the gospel is powerful, the gospel is being preached, so why is it having such little impact on the congregation?

He attended a very helpful minister's fraternal in Sandfields, Port Talbot, just eight or nine miles away. He went there monthly and John Thomas usually hosted it. Neville Rees (see Chapter 2) and lots of other good men were there. He remembers I. B. Davies before he left for New Zealand, in one fraternal looking around and saying and weeping at the same time, 'God has been good. I remember a time in Glamorgan when I could count evangelical ministers on one hand, and now look at you young men. The Lord has raised up young men into the ministry.'

That fellowship was a real support and on one occasion they decided to extend it into the afternoon. They had a prayer time recognising that they needed the Lord desperately. He went back to the Nantyffyllon church that Monday evening to the prayer meeting. The meeting was dead but he read Luke 11:1–13 and the words gripped him. Later that evening a minister phoned him to ask him to pray with him for the next day, which they did, and the Lord really met with them both, which was precious and powerful. Eryl then went to the Maesteg church's prayer meeting which wasn't much better than the one in Nantyffyllon. He tried to tell them what had happened but couldn't, so Magwen had to take over for a minute or so. The prayer meeting was very ordinary and nothing happened, but at the end, these middle-aged women and men, some of them miners, were walking out quietly, when one of the tough women turned to Eryl and said, 'I feel dirty, pastor.' She was under conviction of sin. Others said similar things and some of the miners were in tears, and that began a period of probably about nine months where a lot of people were converted, not dramatically but quietly, sometimes at home and sometimes in the service.

Before that period, Eryl had started an over-21 group because they had lots of young people who had got married and had children. They met fortnightly for a Bible study and discussion. One by one they saw quite a number of them being converted and Eryl began to realise the importance of young people and young families being converted and forming the church of tomorrow. Some of them now have died, but they were the backbone of the church in Maesteg for a long time.

Eryl became burdened for the young people in the valley. He estimated there were two thousand living there and he wanted to reach them. They saw a public house nearby for sale. The price was prohibitive for them but they began to pray and Eryl couldn't forget this public house. One day he went to see the agent and said we would like to buy it and told him he could offer £500. The agent just laughed his head off and ridiculed Eryl. He told him he would not handle it but urged Eryl to write to the brewery, which he did. Weeks later they accepted his offer of £500 provided he used it for the youth and wouldn't sell beer, which was no problem.

Over a three-year period all the teenagers and the early twenties heard the gospel in that place in the coffee bar. Sunday nights there would often be two to three hundred young people packed in there, and people like John Thomas and Colin Leyshon would come and preach, as well as Eryl. There were some conversions although Eryl is not sure how many. All he knows is, he was able to say that he was free of the blood of teenagers and early 20s in that valley.

While he was at Maesteg, he would go to preach at Barry Bible College. For one day every year the college would have a quiet day where staff and students spent the day in prayer and invite a preacher in to preach morning and afternoon. As Teify (Chapter 5) mentioned, on one occasion Eryl preached a powerful sermon from 2 Chronicles 20. Driving there, it was verse 3 that really gripped Eryl, particularly Jehoshaphat's personal response to the crisis which he couldn't manage himself and so he set himself to seek the Lord. It really struck Eryl, as well as Jehoshaphat's awareness of the glory of God in verses 5 and 6. He preached quite normally, but towards the end it was obvious that the Lord was speaking very powerfully. There was great freedom during the prayer time with much weeping and repentance. Lunchtime was a quiet occasion and the afternoon meeting was less spectacular but the Lord met with them and it was a very precious time.

Chapter 9

Bangor

In 1970, he preached for the Bangor church when they bought an old Welsh Congregational building. He preached the first Sunday they were in the building. It was an ordinary Sunday, but on the way to his car after the evening service and driving home, he had once again had this direct overwhelming call that he would be the pastor there one day, which shook him. Apart from Magwen he told no one for several years. He believed he would go there as the second pastor not the first. The students had done a good job in witnessing throughout the area in English and Welsh and then in setting up the church. But the Bangor Church invited him to be their first pastor and Dr Lloyd-Jones, Arthur Neil and others told him he must go. Eryl knew he had to go but, like Paul in Philippians 1:8, where he says that, 'as much as I have you in my heart', there was a deep bond between the pastor and the people which Eryl felt deeply. To leave Maesteg and go to Bangor was so hard and he delayed it as long as possible. He remembers Arthur Neil telling the Bangor church, 'If you don't get him quickly he won't come at all,' and that was true.

It wasn't an easy first five years in Bangor. It was a preaching station where people came from a radius of twenty-five miles, from the north in Anglesey down to the Betws-y-Coed area. It was very hard to build a local church in the community and there was a need to establish churches in other areas, which they eventually did. They also established a separate Welsh Church and English Church, which Eryl is pleased about. When he was in Bangor he was learning to preach in Welsh as he went along and remembers doing a series on the 23rd Psalm. Lots of students came, some who are now pastors, and they wanted to publish the sermons. Eryl was horrified as they were so simple and the Welsh was so basic, so he destroyed all his notes, forgetting that they were on tape anyway. They did listen to him, though, and it showed that those students from denominational churches had never had consecutive expository ministry and this was their first taste of it.

As he looks back, he is so grateful in the Lord's providence that he was able to minister, not just in English where they had lots of students, but also on the Welsh side, and to see many of them go into the Christian ministry.

Bryntirion

In 1984, Eryl chaired the EMW Conference in Aberystwyth. Rev Vernon Higham was the main speaker and spoke on revival. Eryl and Magwen stayed at the Richmond Hotel along with other pastors and their wives, including the late Hugh Morgan. He remembers on the Monday morning Hugh Morgan questioning him very closely at the end of the breakfast about whether he would like to work in the new theological college in Bridgend. Eryl said no and that he was very happy and settled. They had sorted out a lot of the pastoral problems, as well as the bilingual issues, and felt they were on course to do major gospel work in the area. Hugh Morgan made Eryl promise that if the situation changed he would tell him.

On the Friday morning, around about four o'clock, Eryl woke up alarmed, feeling darkness, and depressed, knowing that the call had come to go to the college and he was unwilling. He felt like a Jonah. He told Magwen, and Mr Higham asked him what was wrong. He didn't tell him, but some weeks later he did contact Hugh Morgan to tell him and discussions followed. There were one or two issues that made it impossible for Eryl to go, but the Lord overruled them in a remarkable way. It was difficult to leave Bangor and, though he left physically, he left his heart behind.

Bringing together two colleges, a new one, and the old Barry Bible College, was difficult, but the Lord gave grace and they saw the Lord bless in different ways.

Advice

When asked what advice he would give a young Eryl Davies now, and therefore young men going into the ministry, it was to pray more. There is always so much for a young pastor to do that it can interfere with his prayer time, in particular over preparing messages. He remembers Douglas MacMillan telling ministers in the Bala conference, and Lloyd-Jones says something similar, that if you had a five-minutes warning about preaching, what would you do, and both men said, 'You pray.' You don't go to your desk, you just pray and ask the Lord to help you because you know your Bible, you know the gospel, but pray well and to look for the Lord to intervene. Eryl has seen the Lord step in unexpectedly and powerfully. He remembers one Sunday night in Maesteg where he hadn't had time to prepare for the evening service, but as he was going to church 1 John 1:3–4 came to his mind, *'God is light',* and he preached it and there was remarkable freedom. But, he adds, ministers can't live like that or cannot preach like that normally. Those are the exceptions. Ministers must study hard and delight in the Word. They must feed their people, but keep the gospel central and preach it as simply and clearly as they can as well as to pastor their people well and really listen to them.

People and Books

He has benefited hugely from Dr Lloyd-Jones although he disagreed with him at times and did not always do what he said. He advised Eryl not to do a PhD and at the end of it he congratulated him. Eryl reminded him that he had told him not to do it, which the Doctor remembered but said in the end he was glad that he did. He was humble enough to admit when he got things wrong. The Doctor prayed and preached at Eryl's induction in Bangor.

Elwyn Davies was a mentor to him when he was a student and a young pastor and it was he who introduced Eryl to the dimensions of prayer. When he was travelling secretary for the student work in Wales, at the end of term he invited Eryl to go home with him to Eryl-Aran, the first conference centre in Bala. On the Thursday night Eryl spent time in prayer with Elwyn's family and then on the Friday he spent the day in prayer with Elwyn. It was such an education for Eryl to be with Elwyn Davies and Gwilym Humphreys praying. Eryl wondered beforehand, 'How on earth do you pray for such a long time?' but he soon found out. In Eryl's own words:

You do it when you're on your knees, when you're seeking the Lord and when you have encouragement with another older, more experienced Christian. So I thank God for that and for Elwyn's continuing influence in that way.

Eryl does not think there is one particular book that has influenced him other than maybe, Calvin's *Institutes*. His second year professor told them to read the *Institutes* and they had to summarise the opening chapters. When Eryl, recently converted, came to the end of chapter one in book one and the statement that *'no one will appreciate their insignificance until they can trust themselves to the holy majesty and transcendence of God'* it burned in on him. Again in Eryl's own words, 'I realised the importance of preaching the glory of God, the holiness of God, this transcendence and the awareness of sin comes as a result of that and proclaiming the cross.'

The State of Church and the Need of the Hour

Eryl believes there are some encouraging things happening and there are certainly better training and resources for the ministry. He wishes that some of the resources, like commentaries, had been available when he started. It was much more basic in the 1960s but commentaries, including Henriksen's, were coming out and John Murray's *Redemption Accomplished and Applied* was so helpful.

There is more talk about prayer and he thinks there is more openness among younger men to what the Lord did in the past. He felt in the 1980s and 1990s there was a rejection of the whole concept of revival but thinks we may be over that. He does, however, believe we need to restate a biblical theology of revival, not just recounting stories of revivals.

As for the challenge today, Eryl's view is that 2 Chronicles 7:14 is a key covenant principle running right through the Bible. He does not believe that promise is confined to the Old Testament but runs through the New Testament as well. He thinks as a church we are nowhere near fulfilling 2 Chronicles 7:14. We must humble ourselves, pray, turn from our wicked ways and seek Him. Then He will hear and forgive. Eryl feels we are too proud and we think too much of ourselves. The test of whether we trust God and depend upon him is the extent to which we pray. Most of us fall short and do not do what Jehoshaphat did in verse 3 of 2 Chronicles 20, in which he *'set himself to seek the LORD and proclaimed a fast throughout all Judah'*. Like him, we need to recognise our helplessness today against this great enemy that has come against us in the secularised society. We are powerless.

It saddens Eryl that young people today, including his own children and nieces and nephews, have not known some of the divine encounters that his generation knew in services in the late 1950s. He was converted in the wake of a powerful movement of the Holy Spirit in North Wales, if you can call it that, in the late 1940s and early 1950s and some of those leaders were speaking and encouraging them and mentoring them. They were in meetings where God was there, and not just a vague feeling, but God powerfully there. According to Eryl:

You couldn't speak, there were tears, there was repentance and I long that our younger people and younger pastors will know such times. I would encourage them to seek the living God. He hasn't changed. He's the same and He's the God of our fathers, and the God of Elwyn Davies and the God of Whitefield is our God today.

Chapter 10

Bruce Powell

Introduction

Mr Powell played a big part in my childhood.
The church where he was a pastor, Castle
Street, Tredegar, was just a few miles from my home church and so our
young people had a lot to do with each other. I have always had huge
respect for him and have fond memories of him as the secretary of the
Aberystwyth Conference for many years.

Background

Bruce was born in the autumn of 1941 in Newport. His parents were
faithful members of Malpas Road Church, which in those days was
known as the Malpas Hall because it was a Forward Movement Hall,
like the Heath in Cardiff and many other churches in South Wales. He
was baptised at three weeks old and, along with his older brother, grew
up in the church and in a God-fearing home. His parents, though faithful
church members, like many other faithful church members at that time
were unconverted. The gospel was not clearly preached week by week but
the chapel was very much part of his life in those early days.

His early memories were of bombs falling and air raid shelters and
barrage balloons in the air. One very pleasant memory was of American
soldiers passing the chapel in their open-top trucks on a Sunday afternoon,
making their way to an American air base just up the road from where
the chapel was situated. They would throw oranges, which were quite
scarce at the time, to the children as they stood outside the chapel after
Sunday school.

As for his early spiritual influences, he can distinctly remember at
the age of six being convicted of sins; not conviction of sin, but he was

certainly convicted of sins. He was very much aware of when he had done wrong and it troubled him. He remembers a teacher in school, whom he thinks must have been a Christian, telling them about the conscience and telling them that if they were very sinful they would lose the use of the conscience. He was convinced there and then that he had lost the use of his conscience because he was so sinful.

Another influence upon him in the very early days was in Sunday school. The Sunday school superintendent was obviously a converted man and before they went to their classes he used to pray at some considerable length, and always in his prayer he would pray that God would unstop their ears and open their eyes so that they might hear and see the truth. Unfortunately there was very little truth spoken in the classes, but that prayer stayed with Bruce and just made him realise as he was growing up that something really needed to happen to him spiritually.

Then when he was twelve years old, Dr Martyn Lloyd-Jones made a visit to the chapel. It was midweek and Bruce was at the time in the Boys' Brigade. The boys were all marched into the packed chapel seats which had been kept for them. The chapel was absolutely heaving with people and Lloyd-Jones preached on the Rich Fool from Luke 12. It made a colossal impression upon Bruce, so much so that the next day he told the boys in school about it. The Doctor stressed the need to be ready to die and face God. Bruce asked the boys in school if they were ready to die and face God, not in any way thinking that he himself wasn't ready because he wasn't.

Then they also had a Boys' Brigade captain at that time who was a converted man and he spoke from time to time about knowing the Lord Jesus; while another influence in those early days was when he was about 15 and he was on holiday with his family in the Mumbles. On one of the beaches there was a Beach Mission and he remembers seeing this young lady, about 17 or 18 years of age, leading these children in the singing of choruses and he thought how beautiful she was. It wasn't just the physical, for there was a purity about her and it seemed as if her face was shining, and within himself he thought that is what he wanted to be, he wanted to be pure like that, because he felt dirty.

Conversion and The Call

But for all that, in those teenage years he was a typical Pharisee. He became a church member at 14, a youth leader at 17 and became a local preacher at 19, even though he was unconverted. He preached the law and urged people to obey the law and be good so that they could please God.

He loved every aspect of church life. He had no interest whatsoever in dancing or alcohol or smoking and could not understand how anyone could be so stupid as to spend money on these things. He was a typical Pharisee and he can even remember thanking God when he was in school that he was not like other boys.

What really dominated Bruce, though, was money and wealth. As he was growing up in those teenage years he was consumed with ambition to do well, to make lots of money as quickly as possible, and to be somebody. So for that reason he left school at 16 in order to make as much money in as short a time as possible. He wanted to train to be a civil engineer because there were huge opportunities in rebuilding programmes after the war and he thought if he went into civil engineering, he could very quickly do very well. His minister at the time asked him what he planned on doing and then said to Bruce, 'Oh, I always thought that you would become a minister. I can just see it now, I can just see it, the Reverend Bruce Powell.' Bruce didn't say it but thought, 'Perish the thought, that's the worst paid job in the world; I'll never be a minister, never.' But his words just sunk deep within Bruce. Whatever he did from then on, from time to time those words would come back to him. That is why Bruce says that he was called to the ministry at 16. It was something very real and powerful, and although he rejected it and suppressed it and really didn't want it, he couldn't get away from it.

He started to train as a civil engineer and was consumed with ambition, so much so that he refused to follow the normal route of part-time study at technical college. He thought he could tackle the professional exams directly and get qualified more quickly, and so he did a correspondence course. However, despite hours and hours of work he was very quickly way out of his depth and failure of exams ensued. This was very humbling. He wasn't used to failing, but looking back he could see that God was obviously in it. It was the beginning of a humbling process, and then after a few years, when he was about 19, for some reason he could not account for, he had an overwhelming desire to seriously read the Bible.

Up until then he had never seriously read the Bible, even though he was a Sunday school teacher and preacher. He had only just dipped into it. But now, every evening at about half past nine, after engineering studies, he would put the studies aside and he would take his Bible and he began reading the New Testament. He came very quickly to Matthew 7:21, *'Not everyone who says to me, "Lord, Lord," shall enter the kingdom of heaven.'* He was quietly shattered by those words. All his life he had been saying, 'Lord, Lord,' and here it was, *'Not everyone who says to me, "Lord, Lord," shall enter the kingdom of heaven.'* The bottom dropped out of his world and he became very subdued—some might say depressed. Whereas previously Bruce had been convicted of sins, this was the beginning of conviction of sin; not just the awareness that he had done certain things that he shouldn't have done but the awareness of being altogether wrong and altogether in a wrong relationship with God.

The men in the office where Bruce worked began to ask him what was the matter. Also, at the same time, the name of Christ became precious to him, which he could not understand. When men blasphemed up to that time in the office it didn't bother him at all, but now when they blasphemed he felt cut to the quick.

This went on for months and Bruce was approaching 20 years of age. He was in town one day and thought he had to buy something that was going to help him. He went into WH Smith, to the religious section, and saw a little paperback, *Letters to Young Churches* by J.B. Phillips. It was brightly coloured and a paraphrase of the New Testament letters, so he bought it. Bruce would read it on the bus on the way to and from work, and it was not long before he came to Romans 8:9 which J.B. Phillips paraphrased, *'You cannot be a Christian at all unless you have something of the Spirit of Christ within you.'* As Bruce read those words he thought:

That's it, that's what's happened to me. I've become a Christian; all that's been going on these past months, I've become a Christian. The Spirit of God has come to dwell within me and I've become a Christian. I knew beyond any shadow of doubt, I mean I was vague on the person of Christ, I was vague on the atonement, I was vague on justification by faith alone, I was vague on the person of God Himself even. But I knew I'd become a Christian.

He jumped off the bus at the appropriate stop, ran into the office, ran up the stairs and wanted to shout, 'I have became a Christian.' But he didn't have the courage, so he rejoiced quietly. Then the thoughts of the ministry returned to him powerfully. That which he had been suppressing, he now welcomed.

The next year was 1962, which was very significant in Malpas Road. It was the year that Hugh Morgan came to be their new pastor. He was a man on fire and had an amazing, remarkable ministry. The first year was very significant for Bruce's own family. His father, who by that time was an elder but still unconverted, was converted through Mr Morgan's ministry. Bruce's brother and wife were also converted during that first year and his mother a year or so later.

Bruce soon went to see him and explained his doctrinal ignorance. Although he knew he was a Christian, he just knew nothing, so Hugh Morgan immediately gave him a copy of the Westminster Confession. As he began reading it, he was bowled over and thought it was absolutely wonderful. It is what he believed and he felt it in his bones. He felt it so deeply and so strongly that he began reading parts of it during the coffee break to the men in the office, much to their consternation. But they were very patient with Bruce. One of them was a Jehovah's Witness and as soon as Bruce began to read the Westminster Confession he went berserk. He was so angry he went red in the face and was very resistant. It just confirmed to Bruce he was reading the truth, and so he carried on.

A couple months later he went to see Hugh Morgan and told him again that he felt called to the ministry. Mr Morgan told him to go away and forget it, but to go back to him in three months if he could not forget about it. Bruce did exactly as he said and three months later he went back to him and said, 'I can't forget it.' He said, 'No, I know. I'm sure that you are called to the ministry and have felt that for some time.'

Bruce did not want to go through the denominational channels because he knew that they would require seven years of liberal studies. He was so ignorant of the Bible and wanted rather to go to Bible college for a few years and then apply to the denomination. Hugh Morgan agreed and said that they would say nothing about him being a candidate for the ministry in case the denomination reacted and played up, and he would just go to Bible College.

Training and an Experience of God

He went to the London Bible College in 1963. The big attraction of London was that he could sit under the ministry of Dr Martyn Lloyd-Jones at Westminster Chapel. During his first year, something very significant happened to him and has been significant in the whole of his life since. On 1st May 1964 he was in a prayer meeting in central London and about 3.30 in the afternoon God came down. Bruce recalls:

God came down, the Holy Spirit came down. I was aware of something happening to me personally. The Lord Jesus Christ was more real. There was nothing new as far as truth was concerned, but there was a totally new dimension. The deity of Christ was absolutely certain. I knew that He is the One. Obviously by then I was believing strongly that He is God, but that time when God came I knew beyond any shadow of doubt that He is God, the one true and living God. I found my whole being going out to Him and praising Him and worshipping Him, glorifying Him as I beheld Him by faith upon His throne in glory. His blood was more real than ever before. I knew that my sins were forgiven. I knew that He was Lord of all. There was overflowing joy, there was liberty and freedom in my spirit. The freedom of the sons of God. It was just an overwhelming experience of God.

Not everyone in the meeting had an experience like this, but some did. Bruce believes that God spoke to him clearly at that time and he could not get away from these words: *'Hold fast to that which you heard from the beginning.'* He could only interpret that in the sense that what he had read in the Westminster Confession, at the beginning of his Christian life, was the truth. Bruce is convinced that God was being very gracious to him, and in effect was saying to him that though he had this experience, he was not to live off experiences; he must live on truth as personified in Christ, feed on the bread of life, not feed on experiences. That has been a tremendous help to Bruce. He had heard of revival, believed in revival, prayed for revival, read Eifion Evans' book on the 1859 revival, but it was something distant. Now it was something seemingly within him. He felt that he knew at least in some little way what revival was all about. It increased Bruce's longing for revival tremendously; there was more liberty in personal witness and more liberty in living the Christian life. He went to see Dr Lloyd-Jones as soon as possible to tell him about what had happened. Theologically, Bruce didn't really understand what had happened to him, but the Doctor explained to him that the Spirit had been poured out upon him. In Bruce's naivety he said, 'Well, if that's the case, why am I not like Howell Harris and Daniel Roland?' So the Doctor went on to say that it was a matter of measure. They had known the Spirit coming upon them in a time of revival.

Bruce worked hard and pushed himself. During the summer, at the end of the first year, he engaged in evangelism and preaching. By the time he returned for his second year he was totally exhausted. He was only there a couple of weeks and he collapsed and had to have a break. The Principal kindly sent him down to some friends of his in Brighton. He was walking one day near the sea and this reference came powerfully into his mind, Deuteronomy 10:16. When Bruce looked it up in his pocket Bible, it shocked him: '*Circumcise therefore the foreskin of your heart and be no longer stiff-necked.*' He was given grace to see that what was happening through this difficulty, was that he was being humbled. It was painful and lasted another two years, but Bruce was being taught that there is no usefulness without brokenness, and Bruce could see that. Also, in his weak state, his understanding of people broadened enormously. He went on a regular basis, at least twice a term, to see Dr Lloyd-Jones and he was so helpful. Bruce recalls:

He was so kind and so generous with his time and he used to talk to me as if I was the only friend he had. It was quite ridiculous from that point of view, but that was his kindness and his generosity and it was such a tremendous help.

Then in 1965 Dr Lloyd-Jones spoke at the Puritan conference and showed that the idea of having to be in the denomination to win it was not a New Testament teaching. Bruce became convinced that he should not go into the denomination. In the spring of 1966, he told the Doctor that that was his thinking, and he said, 'Quite right, the great division is coming and you will be on the right side.' He then told Bruce to go and see David Mingard in the FIEC and to tell him he had sent him. Bruce also asked him whether he should have further training because he felt so unprepared and so inadequate. The Doctor said to him, 'You've got the Word, you've got the Spirit, now get out and preach the gospel.'

Ministry

David Mingard in the FIEC was very helpful. He had just been to a congregational church in Hertfordshire who had applied to join the FIEC because they had seceded from the old denomination and they were looking for a pastor. He had a hundred men on his books looking for pastorates but they were all baptists. Bruce told him that his background was Calvinistic Methodism and so Bruce's name was sent to the church. Within three weeks he was preaching at Braughing and Puckeridge Congregational Church. Three weeks later they invited him back and then shortly after that they invited him to become their pastor. After accepting the call, he was on the train back to London in a compartment on his own. He felt so dejected and thought, 'What have I done? I have accepted this pastorate in this remote village in Hertfordshire. I always felt that I was called to the industrial valleys of Wales and here I am accepting the pastorate in the remote villages of Hertfordshire.' He worried about how he was going to manage there and that his nearest friends would be twenty miles away. He had no transport and it all seemed too much to bear. Then suddenly in that railway carriage, there was an overwhelming sense of God and the last verse in the hymn, '*Fight the good fight*', came flooding into his mind:

Faint not nor fear, his arms are near,
He changeth not and Thou art dear;
Only believe and thou shalt see
that Christ is all in all to thee.

Bruce knew that God was with him and he would be able to go forward. On 25th September 1966 he began his ministry at Braughing and Puckeridge Congregational Church.

The Hertfordshire Congregational Union (a liberal body) were still the Trustees of the church and were sending interest on invested capital for the payment of Bruce's stipend each month. When they realised he was evangelical and had not been to one of their colleges they stopped sending the interest. The church was soon bankrupt practically, though quite wealthy on paper. He had to move on, and providentially the way was opened for him to accept a call from Castle Street Congregational Church, Tredegar, which had been founded in 1850.

Castle Street, Tredegar

He began his ministry in Tredegar in April 1969. He had a congregation of approximately forty, most of whom were unconverted church members. In the first few weeks he had a clear assurance that the Lord was going to work in saving power. There were early encouragements with a few church members being converted.

Then after a few years a burden came upon the women who attended the Monday night prayer meeting to pray for men. The congregation was predominantly female. The burden continued for two-and-a-half years, during which time a number of younger women were converted. Then, over a period of eighteen months, fifteen men and boys were converted. Three of them are now pastors and several of them are church officers. The Lord continued to work, but after twenty-one years he was exhausted and began to suffer burnout. Reluctantly he had to finish in 1990 and have a break. Through a series of personal contacts he eventually received a call from Holywell Church, Loughborough and began his ministry there in the Autumn of 1991.

Chapter 10

Loughborough

Loughborough was vastly different from Tredegar. The church was fairly new (founded in 1968) and had had only one previous minister. The membership was disciplined and there was an excellent eldership and diaconate. The congregation was international and included many Chinese. During his time there he baptised more Chinese than British folk. Students (International and British) made up about 15% of the congregation each week. Members in the main were very committed and worked faithfully and diligently in the various ministries of the church, which the Lord was pleased to bless.

After fifteen very happy years he retired from pastoral ministry on his 65th birthday. But a few weeks before he retired he had a stroke which meant that he could not move from Loughborough as he had intended. He stayed in Loughborough for another four years before moving back to South Wales. It took the church over three years to call the next pastor and so he was not in the way, which had been Bruce's concern.

His retirement years have been very active in itinerant preaching in the UK and also in Cyprus, in connection with the ministry of Middle East Reformed Fellowship (MERF).

Blessings and Difficulties

There were very early encouragements in the first pastorate. Just a couple of weeks after he started, the terrible Aberfan disaster took place. As a consequence of that, two young women around 30 years of age came to the chapel on a Sunday evening. One was a local prostitute who had a daughter who came to the Sunday school, and the other one was a real character who worked in a local factory. They said that when they had seen the terrible disaster and the children killed, they had to come to chapel. Within quite a short time God began to work. On the second or third Sunday the factory worker stormed out of the chapel and walked down the high street shouting on the top of her voice, 'Who does that man think he is, telling me I'm a sinner? I'm never going there again.' But she was there the next Sunday and continued to come with the prostitute, who was soon to be the ex-prostitute. They were both converted and became church members.

Then there was a Welsh-speaking lady who would attend the chapel on one Sunday evening and then the other at the Bingo hall, alternating between the two. But she started attending church more often and stopped Bruce one day in the village and said, 'I never knew I had to be justified by faith.' Bruce had started going through Galatians, and slowly but surely she came through.

Bruce learned three lessons in particular in that first pastorate.

One was the reality of the devil and his opposition to ministry. Quite early on he was beset by a terrible fear. He became so fearful that he eventually borrowed a car and went to his nearest friends in north London and shared with them. They called a few people together and they prayed and discerned that he was troubled by this satanic onslaught. This was the devil trying to destroy his ministry. But God met with them again in that meeting in a very powerful way and he was wonderfully delivered. There were still many attacks afterwards but never to the degree of that initial one.

The second lesson Bruce learned was how the Lord provides. He felt prompted to send a gift to somebody who was still in college whom he knew had no grant. Bruce argued within himself and took it to the Lord that he only had a little savings to buy a car which he needed in order to go around the villages. Anyway, he was so compelled within himself to send this gift which was about half his savings, which wasn't very much.

The very next day he was visiting one home and a door opened on the opposite side of the street and an old lady, a member of the church, told Bruce to go and see her after he had finished visiting. When Bruce went to see her, she told him that a man down the street was selling his car and she was going to buy it for Bruce and she was going to give him ten shillings a week to help him run it. For the first five years in the ministry his stipend never covered his essential expenses, but he never lacked. The Lord always provided through friends and gifts. He never had to ask anybody for anything.

The third thing was, 'Leave all righting of wrongs to God.' Do not try to play God. Bruce remembers a time when he was being greatly misunderstood and, he believed, criticised unjustly, and wanted to do something about it. But one morning Psalm 103:6 jumped out of the page, *'The Lord executes righteousness and judgement for all who are oppressed.'* He knew he had to leave matters in the Lord's hands. It was not long before He intervened and matters were dealt with.

Books and Men

As well as Dr Martyn Lloyd-Jones and Hugh Morgan, another man who influenced Bruce was Elwyn Davies. As for books, he found the Doctor's sermons on Christian Warfare a tremendous help and has read it several times since. *Spiritual Depression* also made a colossal impression on Bruce and he thinks that *Preaching and Preachers* is essential reading for ministers. He has been helped by Berknof's *Systematic Theology* and as, already mentioned, the Westminster Confession and the Calvinistic Methodist Confession of Faith. He would urge, particularly ministers, to always be reading one of the great confessions of faith on a regular basis, just to keep themselves reminded of the overall system and doctrine taught in the Scriptures. As for biographies and Church history, he loved reading about John Paton, the missionary to the New Hebrides, and William Carey by Pierce Carey; likewise Methodist Fathers and Eifion Evans' book on the 1904 revival. Bruce also mentioned *More than Notion*, Jonathan Edwards' *Religious Affections* and said that Iain Murray's (see Chapter 16) books have had a huge influence upon him. He thinks the two-volume biography of Dr Martyn Lloyd-Jones, must be the greatest twentieth century Christian biography.

Advice

Bruce believes that in the ministry you need the strength of youth and the wisdom of old age, but of course they never come together, and so there is always that frustration. Looking back, he wishes he had been more humble. He wishes he had known greater brokenness, and that he had possessed a greater servant spirit when he was younger. Looking back, he thinks at times he could be quite ruthless and failed to encourage people on a personal level as much as he should have done. Some people are great encouragers. Stuart Olyott (see Chapter 13) is one. Bruce was in college with him and he was outstanding then and he has been outstanding ever since. Whenever you speak to Stuart he has always got a word of encouragement.

In terms of advice, he thinks that Jonathan Edwards' great statement is always relevant, that the church's business in any generation is to know in which way the Sovereign Redeemer is moving and to move in that direction. Seek to know what God is doing in your generation and move with Him. This requires a close walk with God and keeping in touch with God. We should give ourselves to prayer and the ministry of the Word, and in that order. The priority is prayer.

Bruce would also say to remember the devil and never forget him. He will always be seeking to hinder you, he will always be seeking to trip you up, he will always be seeking to cause you to fall to fierce temptations. So many good men have fallen into the devil's traps of money, power and sex. We must watch and pray and be on our guard.

Bruce went on to say that preachers need to make sure that they are preaching the gospel and not just preaching about the gospel. According to Bruce:

Don't be afraid. Preach the incarnation, the life, the ministry, the death, the resurrection of Christ; spell it out; the atonement, the propitiation, price of our propitiation, and then confront people with their sin. That seems to be missing. These things confront people and show them that they are sinners. Explain what the law of God requires in detail and make it clear; spell it out, don't hold back.

He believes Christians should be sharing the gospel regularly and that Christians also need to hear the gospel. There needs to be the call to repentance to Christians as well as to the unconverted. Bruce believes we need to confess our sins on a regular basis; we need to keep short accounts with God, but that happens when the gospel is faithfully preached and there is a faithful, strong call to repentance on a regular basis. Bruce maintains that means if ministers are preaching twice on a Sunday, then in one of those services you should preach as if everybody in front of you was unconverted. It is hard work to do that, you have to really work at it, and vary it, but it can be done and must be done.

Finally, Bruce believes that ministers must have a message. It is not enough just to expound a passage. He remembers a 91-year-old Christian phoning him, whom he has known for nearly fifty years. She said in regard to some of the preaching she had been hearing, 'Any one of us can buy the commentary and know what the text says, or know what the passage is teaching, but what we want is a message.' Bruce thought that was spot on. There is so much modern preaching that is more Bible study than actual preaching. In his own words:

There's a big difference, or there can be, between the knowledge of the Bible and the knowledge of God. You can know the Bible, but that doesn't automatically mean you know God. The business of the preachers is to bring people to know God. I know it's through the preaching of the Word of God, but it is more than just knowledge of the content of the Bible. There has got to be a message: a message that informs the mind, moves the heart and motivates the will. That is what preaching is all about.

Chapter 11

Andrew Davies

Introduction

Growing up I was very good friends with Andrew Davies' son, John Paul. John was so proud of his father that he would always introduce himself as, 'John Paul Davies, Andrew Davies' son'. After our GCSE exams we went to London for a holiday. We went to Downing Street but the gates were shut so we couldn't go up the street. John Paul said, 'Leave this to me.' He went to the policeman and said, 'My name is John Paul Davies, Andrew Davies' son, any chance we can come in?' The next thing we knew we were having a cup of tea and a biscuit with John Major in his flat! That last bit is not true but gives you an idea of how much John, and the rest of us, loved and respected Mr Davies. Somebody has said, of all the ministers in the UK, Gerard Hemmings has the best speaking voice of English preachers and Andrew Davies of Welsh preachers.

It has been my privilege to know him, hear him preach and serve on camps with him. I have so much love and affection for him and Mrs Davies.

Background

Andrew's mother and father were from Maesteg at the top of the Llynfi valley. Like many people in those days they were brought up as chapel goers but were not true Christians. The family were very musical and all the men played rugby. Both his grandfathers were coal miners and his father, I. B. Davies, at the age of 14 went into the pits. There were three pits in the Maesteg area but in the 1920s there was a huge recession and no work, so his father was sent to Yeovil, in Somerset, for a crash course in carpentry. Andrew's parents by now were married and lived in a tiny flat with Andrew's older brother, Wynford, who was a baby.

They became friendly with a Brethren couple, the husband of whom was actually Andrew's father's employer. They invited his father along one evening to a gospel service in the Brethren assembly. He heard a very powerful message on hell and left the meeting with the resolve: 'Well, I'm not going there.' He meant to hell, and a few weeks later the Lord saved him.

They eventually returned to South Wales, to Aberavon, where his mother and father lived in a flat above the bookshop, on the main road from London to Swansea. Andrew's mother helped to manage a local shoe shop and his father became an insurance collector. They settled down under the ministry of Dr Martyn Lloyd-Jones and had the privilege of being under his ministry for most of the time he was there.

During that time his father felt a call to the ministry to become a pastor and a preacher. He went to see Dr Lloyd-Jones who said to him, 'Well, Mr Davies, you have no real education. I'm going to give you a Greek grammar book and I want you to study it and come back and talk to me about it.' Months later he saw Andrew's father with a book sticking out of his pocket and asked him, 'Mr Davies, what's that book?' He said, 'It is the Greek grammar book you asked me to read, and I've been studying it.' 'Oh,' said the Doctor, 'then you had better come and see me.' Everything changed from then on. The Doctor supported him, encouraged him and tested his call.

He had no real secondary education to speak of, and so he went to Trefecca and then to Bala to gain some education and some biblical studies. During that time he travelled back and forth to Port Talbot and then eventually to Maesteg where they began to live with the family. He was eventually accepted as a minister of the denomination and ordained in 1940. His first pastorate belonged to the Forward Movement of the Presbyterian Church of Wales. It was a dual pastorate in Pontypridd, one church in Maes-y-Coed, the other in Trefforest.

In 1941 they had a shock because Andrew was born, fifteen years after their first son, Wynford. Wynford was a very able rugby player, captained the Welsh schoolboys, who were unbeaten, and was capped for Wales, playing scrum half alongside Glyn Davies at outside half. He was also very ardent in his concern to serve the Lord, so he went away to university, continued with his rugby, became president of the Christian Union in Cardiff, before going to Aberystwyth to do a BD. He was the minister of a dual pastorate in Tonypandy and Williamstown until 1960 when he emigrated to New Zealand and had a very rich and fine ministry there. He is now in heaven.

Andrew grew up as an infant in Pontypridd. He does not remember much about the war apart from the gas masks and the ration books. The ration books continued for quite some time after the war. His father moved in 1945 to Grangetown in Cardiff, to Saltmead Hall. It was a tough area, but wherever he went people were converted. He had an evangelistic zeal, a very direct way of preaching which really troubled your conscience. Lots of people were converted both in Pontypridd and in Cardiff.

Then in 1950 he was called to the Mission Hall in Neath. Like the previous churches, it was a Forward Movement church of the Presbyterian Church in Wales. It was one of the biggest churches in Wales. Previously in the early 1900s, Frank and Seth Joshua had been the ministers there. Seth Joshua was greatly used in the 1904 revival, but by early 1950 the Mission Hall had developed a tradition of evangelicalism that was neither theological nor authentic. Andrew's father really ruffled their feathers. He preached directly to people who were obviously antagonistic to the gospel. A choir used to sit behind the pulpit, and on one occasion he turned his back on the congregation in front of him and preached to the choir. He was very bold and outspoken. But at the same time he was also a most loving, tender and gracious father and pastor. Andrew's mother was also a character in her own right. When 'I.B.' told Dr Lloyd-Jones of his call to the ministry he replied, 'You will do well, Mr Davies, but I am not sure about your wife!' In the event she turned out to be a fine minister's wife and both father and mother left a profound impact upon Andrew's life in different ways.

Conversion

Andrew's father realised that Andrew, even though he was a member of the congregation and used to go to the prayer meeting and most of the things that happened in the life of the church, was not a true Christian, and he made it clear to him that he needed to be converted.

One Friday night in the young people's meeting, his father asked if anyone knew the Apostles Creed. Because Andrew had been to a Church of Wales school in Neath he had learned the Creed and was able to recite it. The following Saturday he was involved in the Welsh athletics championships and missed the Saturday evening prayer meeting. The following Sunday evening his father preached on Ananias and Sapphira. They were hypocrites, and he talked about people who know the Apostles Creed, are very involved in sport, but they can't be bothered to come to the prayer meeting. Andrew realised who he was talking about (!) and at first he was very angry. When he went home he realised what his father had said was true. He was going behind the scenes to Andrew's real problem which was that he believed because he ought to believe, not because he really believed. Andrew knew his father loved him and had said what he said because he loved him. Some weeks later on a Saturday night in his bedroom, Andrew fell on his knees before the Lord and asked Him for mercy, told Him how proud he was and how he needed His saving grace. He thanked Him for the cross and for the work of the Lord Jesus Christ, committed his life to Him and trusted Him as his Lord and Saviour.

It was a custom in the church to hold a second meeting at the conclusion of the first in order to 'test' the meeting to see if anyone wished to confess Christ as their Saviour. A lot of people stayed behind and Andrew's father would ask people to put their hands up if they'd been converted. Andrew put his hand up, and old Harry Thomas, one of the most saintly men Andrew has ever known shouted, 'Hallelujah', to which Andrew's father replied, 'I can shout it louder than you, Harry.' It was an unforgettable evening.

Even so, Andrew still had no assurance. That came later on under the preaching of Omri Jenkins. He will never forget Mr Jenkins talking about the words on Spurgeon's grave, *'Ere since by faith I saw the stream Thy flowing wounds supply, Redeeming love has been my theme and shall be till I die.'* Andrew was broken and his heart just melted with love. He knew that the Lord had saved him. Over the following months as his understanding developed, assurance grew and deepened.

Family and Training

At the same time of his conversion, in his mid teens, he met Pam, who at the time of the interview had been his wife for fifty-seven years. A lovely Christian lady, she has exercised a truly prayerful ministry and they have been very blessed with four children, twelve grandchildren and one great grandson.

They married in 1963 when Andrew was doing his second degree. He went away to university in 1959 having attended Neath Grammar School where he had been heavily involved in athletics and rugby and had received a good all-round education. He went to Kings College, London to read History and then on to Hertford College, Oxford to read Theology. At the end of the Oxford degree he was accepted and obtained a scholarship to do a PhD in Federal (Covenant) Theology under Professor Basil Hall at Cambridge. But their first child was on the way and so, although the scholarship would have supported Andrew, it would not have supported them as a family. The door to Cambridge closed.

In the meantime he was accepted by the Presbyterian denomination as a candidate for the ministry, and after going through all the necessary preparations, attended Aberystwyth Theological College for a year, ostensibly to do a Pastoralia year, although he spent some of the time as a supply teacher at Ardwyn Grammar School.

Ministry

In 1965, after that period in Aberystwyth had ended, he was called to a Presbyterian church in Abergavenny. They had about 220 members, but the denomination had a rule that a church must have at least 250, so they blocked the call. Meanwhile his brother had given his name to the Riversdale-Waikaia parish in New Zealand and they eventually left for the South Island in 1965 and stayed there until 1968. Thereafter he went on to Kenton Evangelical Church in Middlesex, then to Chessington Evangelical Church in Surrey, then to Lonlas Gospel Mission in Skewen, then to Free School Court Evangelical Church in Bridgend, then to Smithfield Baptist Church in Sydney Australia, and finally to Kensit Evangelical Church in London. He retired in 2006. Since then he has been living in

Chapter 11

Wales, first of all for a couple of years in Ystradgynlais, and at the time of interview, eleven years in Newport where he and Pam attend Malpas Road Evangelical Church.

Times of Blessing

Andrew can testify of many wonderful things that have happened in his life which illustrate what Pascal called 'motions of grace', God moving out toward us in love and mercy.

The first, of course, was his own conversion, but as he looks back he remembers some exceptional prayer meetings in a period of six months at the Mission Hall in Neath. In those prayer meetings they were lifted up into a new dimension, a new plane of reality. In Andrew's own words:

We lost all consciousness of time, people prayed in a way they'd never prayed before. People were afraid to come into the meeting in case they disturbed it. It would often go on until 11 o'clock in the night without any weariness. They were unusually pivotal moments in our spiritual pilgrimage and we were conscious of the presence of God. We sensed not only our own unworthiness but the wonder of God's grace.

He remembers another occasion when he was at a communion service at an IVF conference when they were overwhelmed, all of them, by the love of God and the wonder of the Cross. They sat in awed and total silence for three quarters of an hour. Nobody moved. It was an amazing experience of communion with the Father and the Son through the Holy Spirit.

He has also heard some powerful preaching when he was in London. He went to some unforgettable meetings in Westminster Chapel when the Doctor was preaching. So gripping were the evening evangelistic sermons that Andrew wanted to take everybody with him. He remembers taking Ted Rowlands, the former MP for Merthyr Tydfil, along with him, and there were others. He wanted everybody to hear this message of good news. The sense of God's presence was sometimes quite extraordinary, not only during the ministry of Dr Lloyd-Jones but also through the ministry of other men whom his father invited to preach at Neath. These included Professor R. A. Finlayson, Iain Murray (see Chapter 16), Omri Jenkins, Bill Davies, Dr Kevan (Principal of London Bible College) and Dr J. I. Packer. They all stayed at the family home and their lives and ministries left an indelible impression on him. His heart was deeply moved and his mind stimulated.

There was also a special time in New Zealand at his induction in 1965 when he felt the Holy Spirit coming upon him. They sang the hymn, *'Pour out Thy Spirit from on high, Lord, Thine anointed servants bless.'* He knew that was happening to him, that God was visiting him with His Spirit.

When he was in New Zealand he spoke at two young people's camps attended by well over a hundred people and on each occasion forty or fifty people were converted or brought to assurance. This affected him deeply and reaffirmed to him the power of the gospel. He remembers speaking on the *'I am'* passages in John's Gospel and the Lord dealt with these young people. It was a wonderful testimony to His grace and power.

As he looks back on those special times when he really experienced the presence of God, he said:

You knew it was God. It wasn't manufactured. It was a movement of divine grace, a downward movement from heaven to earth. God was just glorious in our eyes and Christ was supreme over all. I mean we just knew it was God speaking to us, and when you know that, there is only one explanation for it. In the 1950s and 60s there was a movement of God. Many of the men in the ministry at that time would testify to that. It wasn't revival but it was a reviving, it was a special touch of God's presence and power that animated, thrilled, stirred and moved us. He gave us an evangelistic zeal. We wanted everybody to be converted.

Andrew believes we should seek such visitations today and is concerned that there is not the same urgency for the work of the Spirit in the way that there used to be. It may be partly explained by the fact that people have never known, or have very little knowledge, of these things.

Can these things happen again?

Hence the reason for the interviews with these men who have known these things, *'before they leave the stage'*. So as Andrew warmed to his theme I interjected and said that I remember being quite young listening to him preach at the Aberystwyth Conference in Siloh Chapel, and his saying on one particular night that he felt the pulpit was on fire. On another occasion I remember him challenging the young men on how they looked at the girls and challenged the girls on how they dressed. He had authority and power. I also remember when he came as chaplain to our camps with the Heath Church and how the young people just gravitated towards him and wanted to be with him and his wife, Pam, to talk to them and ask them questions. With those memories, along with what Mr Davies said about his dad's preaching, I asked him in the interview, 'How can we get that back? How can we get our pulpits on fire again? How can we get that authority and directness in preaching? Lots of people can explain the text but not many preachers seem today to be able to "land the punch"'. To which he replied:

We have to go to God for that. You can't work it up. Revival can neither be worked up nor prayed down. God is more willing to revive His people than His people are to be revived. We need to believe that God can do this. Society has degenerated since our youth in a quite dramatic way, but we seem somehow or another not to believe that God can do this any more.

He went on to say that we've got ten times more commentaries than our forefathers had, we've got our Bible expositions, we've got our Bible readings and so on. We open up the Word, which is all very good, but at the same time there is this great need for the Holy Spirit to come down. Peter in his second letter says, *'I stir you up by putting you in remembrance.'* His aim was not to instruct them only, but also to inspire them. As far as Andrew is concerned, preaching is inspiration through instruction. You can have instruction without the inspiration, and by the same token you can have a kind of inspiration without instruction; but we need both together. We need to pray for this, and he remembers

Dr Lloyd-Jones saying that the reason we don't is because we are not desperate enough.

He believes if we were really concerned about the way in which society is moving and the plight of people, their need and their hopelessness, there would be a greater urgency. When they were young people, they were doing door-to-door work, holding regular open air meetings. They had this tremendous concern to see people converted because God wasn't being glorified and Christ wasn't being honoured. Andrew believes it all flowed from the spirit of prayer that the Lord gave them.

At this point, we were at the heart of why we were doing this series of interviews with these men, and so I pushed him further and, being totally honest with him, expressed my concern, maybe lack of faith, that these things seem impossible today, and wondered if we were living in the last days. To which he replied by saying that I was raising a controversial question about eschatology. Personally, he believes that Romans 9 to 11 is yet to be fulfilled, that there is to be a glorious gathering in of the Jewish people into the kingdom and a glorious revival among Gentile people. He thinks that is what Paul is talking about in Romans 9 to 11. Jonathan Edwards believed the same, and in his 'Concert for Prayer' spoke of the promises contained in Zechariah 8 and Romans 9 to 11, promises that are yet to be fulfilled.

Although we may well be approaching the end time, he believes, and is optimistic, that there may be a glorious gathering before the Lord returns.

Keith Batstone interjected at this point and remembered Morwen Higham in the prayer meeting at Heath praying fervently and using that biblical phrase from Jacob, *'I will not let you go until you bless me,'* to which Andrew responded:

You need to call on the name of the Lord, you need to plead with Him, argue with Him like the Psalmist does. You ask Him to arise again and to scatter his enemies and to draw people to the kingdom. He has given a people to our Lord Jesus, hasn't He? Those people are to be saved. So we need to plead with Him that He will do that in our day and do it for multitudes of people.

Chapter 11

Difficulties

As well as times of blessing, he had a really difficult time in New Zealand. The congregation were lovely folk: hospitable, warm-hearted, and he got to love them. But there was a real crisis in the denomination when the principal of the Theological College, a man by the name of Lloyd Geering, denied the existence and the immortality of the human soul. He also denied the bodily resurrection of our Lord Jesus Christ. He was tried for doctrinal error at the General Assembly in 1967 at which Andrew was present. The denomination dismissed the charges, declared his point of view to be valid, and closed the case. Now that posed a real problem for Andrew. Here were people whom he loved and didn't want to leave, but his conscience would not allow him to accept the decision of the Assembly. It was as if they had said 'No' to the Westminster Confession of Faith and 'No' to the gospel. So he and Pam agonised for months about what to do, whether they should stay or whether they should retire and withdraw from the denomination. In the end he decided to resign from the Denomination. He remembers the elders coming around to see them and pleading with them to stay. It was one of the most upsetting decisions he has ever had to make and yet he felt it was right to do so. That was a very real issue and in the end they came back to the United Kingdom.

Books

The books that have helped Andrew the most have been the sermons of Dr Lloyd-Jones, particularly on Romans 6. They completely changed his view of sanctification. Before that he had thought of himself as an old man, spiritually speaking, with a tiny little new nature so to speak. Then he realised that he was united to Christ, he had died with Him, been buried with Him, raised with Him to newness of life. He was a new man with an old nature and his trouble was with the old nature. But he was a new man. Reading Lloyd-Jones completely transformed his view and gave him great joy.

He has found J.I. Packer's *Shorter Collected Writings* immensely helpful, as are all of Packer's books. He also loves Sinclair Ferguson's writings. They're so rich, theological and Christ-centred. There are a lot of books that have really helped him, but those stand out.

Advice and the Need of the Hour

Andrew thinks that friendships are extremely important. Neville and Beryl Rees (see Chapter 2), for example, have been very close friends over the years. So have Jeff and Hannah Steadman, Hywel and Nansi Jones, Graham and Eluned Harrison, Philip and Kathleen Williams, whose daughter Debra married their son Stephen, and many more. These friendships have been tremendously helpful. They have been natural, normal friendships, but also with a deep spiritual dimension that Andrew thinks is very important and worth cultivating.

One thing he wishes he had known when he was younger is how to handle criticism. A minister is a public figure and so he is bound to be criticised in one way or another. Looking back, he doesn't think he always handled it very well. At times it was personally hurtful and sometimes he reacted in the wrong way. Now he realises the importance of facing criticisms honestly, and if there is substance to them to respond to those criticisms by improving, by doing better. If there is no substance to them, then leave the matter with the Lord. His brother Wynford said something to him once which helped him a great deal: 'Remember that the Davieses are not indispensable!' God does not depend on us. We are little and fallible. The work is God's and if He should choose to use people like us that is humbling and amazing. Pam was also affected by these criticisms, but the Lord gave them grace and they came through them.

He also thinks we need to pray more. In Acts 6 the apostles gave themselves to prayer and the ministry of the Word. The order is obviously very significant. We are to pray for God to work in a new way, beseeching Him and imploring Him. That element is largely absent today. He can remember prayer meetings where the whole meeting was taken up with a longing for God to visit us. He asked when was the last time we were at a prayer meeting, similar to the one in Acts 4, where everybody is coming to God with the same urgent request? Do we pray that God would work and visit us and pour out His Spirit upon us? Some of the people in Malpas

Road Evangelical Church have told Andrew of meetings when Hugh Morgan was the pastor when that happened and there was tremendous blessing. We need to call on the name of the Lord, believing that He is able to do what He has promised to do, and pray these promises back to him.

Aristotle used to say that in order to communicate effectively three things are needed. The first is logos, the word. The second is pathos, feeling or emotion. The third is ethos, the atmosphere in which you are speaking. Andrew believes we have the Word. We have a degree of pathos and feeling. But the ethos in which we are now operating is against us. It is against God. It is not so much individual people who are voicing their atheistic materialistic thinking, it is the mood, the ethos in which people are operating. Therefore, Andrew says:

Nothing is going to change that except the Holy Spirit. Nothing is going to blow away these spiritual and moral pollutants except the pure breezes from Calvary. So we need these breezes to blow again from Calvary, from that blessed place where heaven's love and heaven's justice have met. We need to put the cross at the centre of our living and preaching and Christ Himself to be central to everything we do.

He is passionate that we need a revival of spiritual life and godliness—authentic godliness, not just going through the motions. He believes we need to think about eternity far more than we do. This is not just an older man speaking. He thinks it is something very important to us all because our time on this planet is very limited and very short. We need to remind people of eternity and of the fact that they are going out to meet God; that there is a hell and a heaven; that there is a Saviour who can save them from the wrath to come. He loves Baxter's hymn about heaven and eternity:

My knowledge of that life is small,
The eye of faith is dim:
But 'tis enough that Christ knows all,
And I shall be with Him.

Andrew also believes that the one thing that is lacking today in our modern world is hope. People do not have any hope, but in the gospel there is glorious hope. We must get hold of that and plead with God that He will make it real to people; that He will give us the power to communicate with urgency, love and humble dependence on Him. This does not mean bombarding people, but gently and powerfully persuading them. The apostle Paul spent his time at the end of his life in Rome persuading people. Prior to the interview he had read an obituary in *The Times* newspaper of one of our most celebrated and greatest physicists. He was a Canon in the Church of England and when he was asked about his views concerning heaven he said, 'I cannot wait to begin to explore more fully and more deeply the wonder and the glory of the being of God, and of all that He has done and does. We have eternity to do that.'

As far as Andrew is concerned, this hope and sense of eternity is the urgent need today. He reminded us of the alcoholic man in Sydney who was converted and then went around Sydney writing *'eternity'* on the pavements. In the year 2000 they put *'eternity'* over Sydney harbour bridge to bring in the new millennium. According to Andrew, this sense of eternity not only fires our faith and love but also gives us a motive for praying and for desiring the salvation of our loved ones and our friends and our neighbours, the Lord being glorified in it all.

Chapter 12

Peter Milsom

Introduction

Peter Milsom is one of the three men we interviewed who were under 75. He is a real gentleman and I have fond memories, growing up, of him in Aberystwyth when he was the chairman of the Evangelical Movement of Wales (EMW). I also remember him preaching a sermon when I was a member at the Heath Evangelical Church many years ago. It was on the woman caught in adultery in John 8:1–11. One thing he said has always stuck with me. On that day, after the great festival in Jerusalem, it was actually two people that were committing adultery. The man must have thought he had got off scot free as he slipped away into the shadows whilst the scribes and the Pharisees frog-marched the woman to Christ. But wouldn't we all rather be the one who ended up at the feet of the Lord Jesus and hear those great words, *'Neither do I condemn you, go and sin no more'?*

Background and Conversion

Peter grew up in Cardiff and went to the same school as Keith Batstone, Cardiff High. He attended Park End Church, a Presbyterian Church in Cardiff. At the time it was a large church with five hundred members. As was the custom, he went through the senior Sunday school class and then became a member when he was about 14 years old. He was serious about Christianity and would have described himself as a committed Christian, but, looking back, he didn't understand the gospel. The minister for most of the time he was there was the Reverend Geraint Nantlais Williams, son of the great Nantlais. He was orthodox in his ministry and it was a very generous church. Mr Williams and his wife were very kind to Peter and his wife Margaret. When Peter and Margaret got married, Mr and Mrs Williams drove them to Pembrokeshire for their honeymoon.

But it was later, and in other places, that he began hearing the gospel. He remembers listening to Billy Graham in 1966 and being challenged whether he knew Jesus Christ as his personal Saviour. He never went forward at any meeting but would go home and pray. He never had assurance he was a Christian. He thought that if his prayer had been answered then surely his life would have changed more. It was through reading the parable of the prodigal son that he came to assurance. It was the picture of the father running to the son that really helped him. His image until then had been only of him coming to God and wondering if he ever actually got there. Then he saw this wonderful picture of the heavenly Father running to his prodigal son and having compassion on him, embracing him, and kissing him, and that brought him an assurance that God had heard his prayer. From that time on he knew that Jesus Christ was his Saviour.

It was in Park End that he met and married his wife, Margaret. They married early and have had quite a large family. They have six children, two of whom are long-term foster children, and have thirteen grandchildren and four great-grandchildren. Throughout his ministry Margaret has been a loving and wholehearted partner in everything he has done.

He left school after O Levels and for a time trained as a quantity surveyor in the City Architect's department in Cardiff. Then he decided that wasn't for him and joined an insurance company, the Guardian Group, where he worked for a few years, and eventually worked in Newport as an agency inspector with them.

The Call and Training

It was while he was in Newport that Peter sensed a call to ministry. At that time companies were wanting more and more commitment from their employees. They wanted them to really live for the company. Peter enjoyed his work but felt that if he was going to commit his life to something, he didn't want it to be an insurance company. He would rather live for the gospel and the kingdom of God. He discovered it was possible for him to have a grant to study and to go to college to prepare. So, he made it known to the church in Park End, went through the Presbyterian Church of Wales process, and was accepted as a candidate for the ministry. In September 1969 he went to the United Theological College in Aberystwyth and spent four years there doing his degree and also pastoral training. It was not an evangelical college but there were lots of evangelical students there at that time. One of the lecturers, Rheinallt Nantlais Williams, was an evangelical and a great encouragement to the evangelical students. Peter's fellow students included people like David Norman Jones, Gwynn Williams and Richard Davies, and so there was great fellowship. While he was at Aberystwyth Peter's own understanding of the faith definitely deepened, not so much from the lectures but through fellowship with other students.

Ministry

Mancot

When he completed his course in 1973, he accepted a call to the pastorate at a place called Mancot on Deeside. It was not an area that he knew, and it was a four-church pastorate. Mancot was the main church with one hundred and fifty members and there were three smaller churches with thirty or forty members each; so about two hundred and fifty people in the pastorate. He was ordained in September 1973.

He did not know if many of the people in the churches were Christians, but the Lord really encouraged him in the ministry there. There was a great openness to the gospel and during his very short time in the church he saw a good number of people coming to faith in Jesus Christ. They began having a prayer meeting for the first time and people started reading their Bibles.

At the same time Peter was getting to know the denomination better through attending Presbytery and Association meetings. At that time the Covenanting for Union scheme was being discussed and many evangelical Presbyterian churches had already seceded from the denomination. Those evangelicals who remained were, by and large, not that active at either Presbytery or Association level. There was a particular Association in April 1974 which distressed Peter in many ways. It became obvious that there was a certain amount of antagonism against evangelicals on the part of some, probably the result of secession by evangelical churches.

Then in the summer of 1974 Peter went to Lausanne to the first Congress on World Evangelisation. He found it a great privilege to meet with two thousand Christians from all over the world. It gave him a glimpse of the great task of taking the gospel to the whole world. There was a clock in the entrance to the conference which was counting the number of people born into the world during the time the congress was meeting. It was there he realised even more the urgency of reaching the lost with the gospel. Should he spend his life seeking to reform a liberal denomination or in taking the gospel to those who didn't know the Saviour?

That same summer he also took part in a Youth Holiday Fellowship in Aberystwyth and a teenage girl was converted. He was thrilled, but none of the other staff on that week seemed to think it was at all important. Sadly, he realised the things that thrilled him didn't really thrill other people in the denomination. So, many things were going through his mind that summer: his disillusionment with the denomination, the task of evangelism, the thrill of seeing people converted and also seeing God blessing the work in Mancot.

After the summer Peter did something he had never really done before and prayed that God would guide him. He opened the Bible, where he had been reading systematically through the book of the prophet Jeremiah, and read chapter 15. The first words he read were, *'Then the LORD said to me, "Though Moses and Samuel stood before me, yet my heart would not turn toward this people. Send them out of my sight, and let them go!'* Whilst Peter recognised this wasn't a prophecy given to him and that Jeremiah was in a particular historical situation, there were similarities with his situation which the whole chapter made clear.

In the light of this and all that had happened over the summer, Peter decided that he should step down as a Presbyterian minister. He would have happily stayed in the chapel at Mancot, but that obviously wasn't possible and he didn't want a secession to take place in a small community. The village was not a big one, and if there was a controversy in the chapel it would have taken a long time to recover from. He decided just to step down from the Presbyterian ministry and to seek to establish a new work in the wider area of Deeside. He completed his ministry at Mancot at the end of 1974 and the family were able to buy a house in the village and stayed there for another eighteen years.

While Peter felt it was right for him to leave the denomination, he has never thought that everyone else should do the same. Many of his good friends have stayed in denominations and have served the Lord faithfully there. Looking back upon his time in the Presbyterian church, Peter is delighted that Jonathan Hodgins, the son of Iain Hodgins, who was a student at Aberystwyth at the same time as Peter, is now the minister at Mancot. So another evangelical minister is serving in the chapel which traces its origins to the early days of the Calvinistic Methodist Church of Wales in the early nineteenth century. Peter did not preach in Park End for forty-two years, from 1974 until 2016. The congregation may have felt that Peter would not want to preach there, but that was not the case. When their minister retired, Peter was asked to help out by preaching one Sunday a month, which he was happy to do. He is delighted now to see Owen Batstone as the minister there; as far as Peter knows, Owen is the first evangelical minister at Park End.

Deeside

There was little animosity or bad feeling after Peter left the church in Mancot. He did not tell them he was going to set up a new church, because he didn't want people to feel that he was asking them to join him. Some Christians from Mancot chapel attended the early services of the new church and the midweek meeting was held in the home of a couple who were members at Mancot. At the beginning of March the first Mancot church member committed to the new work.

The first services of the Deeside Evangelical Christian Church were held on 5th January 1975. The first congregation was Margaret, Peter and their three children, Mark, Jon and Rebecca. They put an advert in the local paper and hired a very small local room. On a Saturday night Peter would go down, put some curtains and some posters up, put the chairs out and get everything ready. Then on the Sunday he would welcome people, give out the hymn books, lead the service, including playing the organ, and preach. He couldn't bring himself to take an offering!

Some friends came and probably wondered what Peter was doing, leaving a well-appointed building and a congregation of one hundred and fifty members and starting from scratch in a little place like this. The words of Hebrews 11 were very real to him at that time: *'Now faith is the substance of things hoped for, the evidence of things not seen.'* When he resigned as a minister of the Presbyterian Church of Wales, he didn't have a job and he and the family were living in a manse. At the beginning of November 1974, he applied for the post of Head of Religious Education in a senior boys' comprehensive school in Wallasey, the Henry Meoles School, and started teaching on 6th January 1975. Some of the boys Peter taught came to faith and later formed a small fellowship in Wallasey, which is still meeting.

The church at Deeside gradually grew. After six months the first sixteen members covenanted together. In 1977 they purchased a building in Shotton. Deeside is an area made up of a lot of little communities and at the time it was a difficult period for Deeside. Shotton steel works was one of the main employers and it closed in 1977–78, making thousands of people redundant. Nobody moved into the area for years because of the high unemployment. Other major companies in the area were also closing down.

Peter went to a deacons' meeting with his two deacons on 30th May 1977 without any idea what they were going to discuss, but as they talked they all felt it would be good for Peter to be free to give more time to the ministry. He resigned his teaching post the following day, and from September 1977 he became the part-time pastor at Deeside. The school kindly gave him a two-day part-time job.

They were there for twenty years altogether and quite a lot happened during that time. One big emphasis in his ministry was pastoral care. The ministers' fellowship Peter attended was studying *The Reformed Pastor* by Richard Baxter and Peter was struck by the importance of personal dealing with people. In the early years of the church Peter visited all members three times a year, just to spend time with them, get to know them and talk about their spiritual life. Being a new church, it didn't have any traditions. It was also an outward-looking church, and still is.

Bala

In 1981 Peter had contact with a few ladies in Bala who were wanting encouragement in their witness. Peter agreed to take a monthly service for the three ladies from September 1981 until May 1982. Amazingly, during that nine-month period, in a town of 1,400 people, two hundred different people attended at least one of those meetings. On the basis of that, they started Sunday services in September 1982 when numbers reduced to just a handful of people again. Peter travelled there every midweek and twice a month on a Sunday evening to take services for them. The church gradually grew and was formed officially in 1984 with eight members. In the past it had been difficult to establish a church in Bala but now, forty years later, there is a small but very active church in the town. Peter stepped down in 1989 so that the church could call a full-time pastor. Ioan Davies and Gareth Williams have served as full-time pastors at Bala. During the summer the church gets lots of visitors.

AECW, ETCW and EMW

In the early 1980s a number of ministers in the north-east of Wales, who had left the Presbyterian Church of Wales, felt there was a need to try to bring evangelical churches in Wales together. The group included men like Gwilym Roberts, Gilbert Evans, Peter Clement, Glyndwr Jenkins and Peter. Bob Horn, the editor of *Evangelical Times*, wrote an article about them and called them 'The Clwyd Five'. The group also approached Hugh Morgan in Malpas Road and Colin Davis in Cardiff to join them. Together they approached like-minded churches, encouraging them to come together to form a fellowship of evangelical churches. The new fellowship would be independent of the Evangelical Movement of Wales but in full fellowship with it.

The Association of Evangelical Churches in Wales (AECW) was established in 1988 with twenty-six member churches. One of Peter's burdens throughout his ministry has not only been the local church but also evangelical unity. AECW now has sixty churches. There are regional clusters where churches meet together to pray. Some clusters work together more effectively than others but there is a real sense of caring for one another. In 2018 Paul Daniel began a new ministry with AECW, visiting the different churches and pastors and helping them with evangelism. Today there are many challenges facing Christians and churches. Peter feels it is more important than ever to stand together, as churches are vulnerable, particularly the smaller ones, as we come out of the COVID-19 pandemic.

Peter also had the privilege of teaching at the Evangelical Theological College of Wales from 1992 to 2010 where Eryl Davies (see Chapter 9) was the principal. He coordinated pastoral studies and taught pastoral theology and evangelism and church planting. He was a Council member from 1985 to 2012 and was the Council Chairman when the Sarang partnership formed.

Peter was a member of the General Committee of EMW from 1978 to 1994. In 1991, following the retirement of Elwyn Davies, Peter became the Executive Chairman of EMW.

Malpas Road

It was encouraging to see the work in Deeside developing in an area where there had not previously been an evangelical church, but after twenty years in ministry Peter began thinking about whether he should remain there for the rest of his ministry or whether he should move on. He felt it would not be a good thing to stay there until he retired, a period of forty years, especially as he was the founding pastor. Then in early 1993 he received an invitation to go to Malpas Road following the sudden death of Hugh Morgan. He felt this was the right time to move and the right place to go. He was very open with the church in Deeside, and while there was great sadness he felt it was time to hand over the baton. In a relay race it is important to hand over the baton in full flight, not when you are slowing down. Peter feels the same about ministry, including retirement, so that those who follow enjoy the same freedom and opportunities as he did when he began his ministry.

Chapter 12

So Peter and the family moved to Malpas Road in June 1993. It was a larger church with lots of opportunities for ministry, but the time he was there was also a sad time for the church. In the just over four years he was at the church he took fifty funerals, many of them church members. Malpas Road Church was at a very different stage from Deeside which was a younger congregation. In the twenty years he was in Deeside, he took only twenty funerals.

UFM

Then in 1997 an approach came from UFM Worldwide (the Unevangelised Fields Mission) to ask if he would be interested in becoming the first director of the Mission. It was something that linked in to the previous convictions he had about reaching the whole world with the gospel.

Peter began his new ministry in November 1997 and it was a totally different experience. Up until then he had not been a great traveller. He had had two ten-year passports and used each of them once. He had been to Lausanne in 1974 and to the Reformed Conference in Zambia in 1992. But all that was to change during the fifteen years he was at UFM. He had the privilege of visiting about thirty-five countries and saw all kinds of really encouraging ministries. It was particularly encouraging to see the Lord calling a new generation of excellent people to serve in world mission.

When he joined UFM in 1997 there were sixty-eight missionaries in eight countries, half of them being in Brazil. By the time he retired only twelve of those were still serving. Some had died and some had returned to the UK because of children's education or care of parents. But the Lord was raising up new missionaries, and in 2012 there were one hundred and twenty missionaries in more than twenty-five countries. The UFM Council are excellent and were ready to take up new challenges and to adapt their approach to mission. They are committed to working in close partnership with sending churches to identify the people they recognise as being called to world mission. They then work with those churches to enable them to send their missionaries out.

When Peter started at UFM they had no one serving among Muslims, but over the fifteen years he was there, it came to the point where one in six of UFM's missionaries worked amongst Muslims. Moreover, in 1997 there were only two missionaries in Europe, which is one of the big missionary challenges of the world, but by 2012 there were more than seventy. This new pattern revealed God's actions in calling his people to strategic cross-cultural mission. UFM also partners with IFES in sending workers to Eurasia to reach students with the gospel.

Since 1997, Peter's ministry has really been to stand alongside others in the ministry. He has spent his time caring for missionaries, sitting and talking with them and praying with them. Often they have had very painful experiences in a struggling ministry and Peter has tried to encourage them and help them work through the crises that might have brought an end to their ministry.

Blessings

Peter has found it a great privilege to spend his time meeting people who were stepping out in faith, leaving their jobs, undertaking training for ministry, learning new languages and cultures, in order to take the gospel to the world. It has been a great blessing to see just a small part of what God is doing in His world. He has been encouraged by what he has seen in all the countries he has visited, but two stand out.

He travelled to Mongolia where a UFM couple were working in a place called Arhangai, about 300 kilometres from Ulaanbaatar. In 1990 there were about four known Christians in Mongolia, but then the church started to grow and now it is estimated at forty thousand. When Peter was flying, via Moscow, to Ulaanbaatar, he sat next to a Mongolian girl on the plane. They started chatting. She had been visiting her father who was in some kind of embassy in London. Peter asked her if she was Buddhist. She said that her grandparents were but neither she nor her parents were. They didn't follow any religion. Peter then asked her what most young people in Mongolia believe today. She said, 'They are believing in Jesus Christ.' The church in Mongolia is a very young church, which is a big challenge for the new leaders, who are also young.

It was great for Peter to see this missionary couple working in Mongolia. The temperature is −40°C in winter and +40°C in the summer. Their facilities were pretty basic with only an outside toilet. But they love the Mongolian people and want to serve them, whatever the cost. The couple are now involved in encouraging missionaries who are being sent from Mongolia into China and have a real passion to take the gospel to the Mongolian diaspora. It has been wonderful to see this church taking shape without the involvement of many outsiders as missionaries. It is a work of God bringing into being indigenous churches. They would not call it a revival, but many people are being converted.

The other place is Papua, which is the western part of the island on which Papua New Guinea is the eastern part. Some people may know it as Irian Jaya. It is part of Indonesia which has the biggest population of Muslims in the world. Papua has a population roughly similar to Wales but with a massive diversity of people living in remote communities. Two hundred and seventy two languages are spoken amongst the population of about two-and-three-quarter million people. The people live in remote valleys and mountains which are very inaccessible. The gospel first came to Papua around 1960 and, in an amazing way, out of two-and-a-half million people in Papua, a million and a half now profess to be Christian. It is hard to know if they are all genuine, but the pattern was that when one tribe was evangelised and came to believe, they would go to their neighbouring tribes. It is a difficult and dangerous situation. In 1968 two missionaries were killed by Yali warriors and were partly cannibalised. But God has done, and is doing, a wonderful work there.

Peter visited Papua in 2014, after he had retired, for the dedication of the Hupla Bible. There are about 15,000 people in that tribe and a UFM missionary had been involved, with a small team of local believers, in translating the whole Bible—a really massive task but a thrilling one. It is the fourth complete Bible in a Papuan tribal language. It is the only time Peter has seen people coming to church with spears and axes, but they don't use them to fight anymore! The people were in colourful tribal dress and looked amazing.

Peter also had the privilege of taking a brother called Otto Kobak to meet the leaders of the Evangelical Church of Papua New Guinea (ECPNG). Otto has since died, at the age of 50, and is now with the

Lord. Otto was a leader in the Evangelical Church of Indonesia (GIGI). Otto was from the Yalu tribe and had been one of the main translators of the whole Bible into the Yali language. Peter took Otto and one of the UFM missionaries in Papua to Port Moresby to meet the leaders of the ECPNG. The churches in Papua and PNG have much in common. There are over eight hundred languages spoken in PNG which has a population of five-and-a-half million people, so together, the two countries on the one island, have a total population of eight-and-a-half million and more than a thousand languages. Peter simply introduced the leaders. He didn't want UFM to get in the way, rather for church leaders to meet together and decide how to cooperate together. One of the things they decided was to undertake joint outreach to other parts of Indonesia. Their cooperation still continues. Otto told Peter it was like meeting the brother you had never known you had, because their backgrounds and history were so similar.

Books

The first book that Peter mentioned was a book that had been recommended to him by Pastor Vernon Higham called *More Than Notion*. It is about a work in the small hamlet of Pulverbatch, near Shrewsbury in the first part of the nineteenth century. One of the things that struck Peter from that book, which had an influence on his ministry, particularly early on when he was in Mancot, was a statement that the newly-converted rector of Pulverbatch made. He said that he wanted to try to be sure that the converts under his ministry were God's converts, not his converts. He didn't want people just to be influenced by him as a person but to know a real work of God in their lives.

The second book Peter mentioned was by Francis Schaeffer, entitled *The Church at the End of the 20th Century*. Schaeffer identified two things that he felt needed to characterise the church at the end of the twentieth century. Writing in 1970, Schaeffer anticipated Western society moving either to the extreme right or to the extreme left. In the light of this he said it was vitally important that the church held firmly to propositional revelation, 'true truth', and did not compromise this at all. The second thing Schaeffer identified was what he called a 'beauty of community', in other words, the truth being lived out by 'God's new humanity'. Peter tried to work these things out in the church at Deeside. He wanted the church not only to be strong in the truth, but also to be warm and relational, caring for one another and looking out to needy people around them. He and the church members had a lot of involvement in the community with people with problems of depression, debt, marriage breakdown, unemployment, learning disability and terminal illness. In 1979 the church set aside two ladies to the Bethany ministry reaching out to people with learning disabilities and their families and people suffering from terminal illness. The ministry to those with learning disabilities still continues and each week they get together for fellowship, Bible teaching and prayer.

The third book was Iain Murray's *The Puritan Hope*. Peter found great encouragement in post-millennial optimism. He read it before he was involved in UFM and what struck him was 'the conviction that led many people into the modern missionary movement, that the gospel would not only triumph but would be seen to triumph'. Peter said, 'I'm an amillennialist with a strong pinch of post-millennial optimism.'

Encouragements and Hopes

One of Peter's great encouragements is seeing God calling younger men to take up the baton in churches and missions. He remembers people asking some years ago, 'Where is the next generation of preachers?' Now Peter sees them emerging both in churches and in missionary work, committed to the task of taking the gospel to the lost. In 2004 it was encouraging for Peter to be alongside Ian Parry when the Bay Church in Cardiff was being established. Ian is a younger man with a strong sense of call and an ability to communicate clearly with his generation. He sacrificially committed himself, together with his wife and family, to planting a gospel church in the strongly cross-cultural community in Cardiff Bay.

Peter prays that the older generation of pastors and church leaders will be encouragers to the younger generations. For the work to move forward, the older generation, as well as remembering what God has done in their time, must get behind the men who are facing huge challenges today. Secession is not the issue today, but rather it is how to reach our post-Christian society with the gospel.

Linked to that is praying for a deeper unity. In John 17 the Lord Jesus prayed that we might be one as He and the Father are one so that the world may believe. On a visit to Bulgaria Peter took part in a Bible study for professional ladies who came from the Orthodox Church. They were seriously thinking about the gospel and had gathered in a missionary's flat to discuss these things. They asked all sorts of questions and turned to lots of scriptures. It was a lovely evening. Then towards the end one of the ladies said, 'I realise I need to know Jesus as my Saviour and, if I do, that I will have to leave the Orthodox Church. So which church should I join?' She went on to ask Peter the difference between all the denominations. As Peter explained it to her, it struck him that the differences between evangelical Christians are just a small part of the things we believe. The things which unite us are eternal and are the things that really matter. So, Peter told the lady that if she found a church where Jesus is loved and the Bible is preached, to go there and not be too concerned about the denomination. Our divisions, and our separateness, confuse the people around us. We need to stand together and warmly endorse one another.

Peter is encouraged by God's promise to be with us. The promise God gave to Joshua when he succeeded Moses, that giant of the faith, was, *'As I was with Moses, so shall I be with you.'* Sometimes we look back to previous generations and think that they must have been giants and that we are pygmies. We thank God for all that previous generations have done, but at the same time we must hold on to God's promise that as He was with them, so He will be with us. He will never leave us nor forsake us. 'Jesus Christ is the same yesterday and today and forever.'

It is quite clear to Peter that we need to know more of God and His blessing upon us and that we must pray that He would raise up powerful preachers. But he also believes that God accomplishes more through His people than He does through great preachers. The task of pastor-teachers is to equip God's people for works of ministry, and we need to keep this always in mind.

Chapter 12

René Padilla, who was a missiologist in South America, was asked why the Pentecostal churches in Brazil have grown so rapidly. He said that one of the reasons was because they believed in, and practised, the priesthood of all believers, whereas the historic denominations put more emphasis upon leaders. Whilst there is a lot of confusion amongst the Pentecostal churches in Brazil, and they are not an exclusively good paradigm, Peter thinks that it is important to learn from their emphasis on equipping the saints for the work. We can be too passive in our Christianity and need to get out into the world and amongst people to tell them the gospel. Aceh, in Indonesia, experienced great devastation in the 2004 tsunami in the Indian Ocean. It is a Muslim closed nation, but the tribal people in Papua said, 'We've got to go to them and show them the love of Jesus.' They were living in remote villages in the hills but had a passion for the gospel and a sensitivity to God's leading. So they sent gifts to Aceh in the name of Jesus. We need that same vision, that same heart, for the nations in our troubled world.

Chapter 13

Stuart Olyott

Introduction

There are two main reasons why I am so thankful to Mr Olyott. Firstly, when I was in Cardiff I led some of the Heath Evangelical Camps. One year we didn't have a chaplain and a lady called Jean Hate told me that Stuart Olyott had said one of the best preachers in the British Isles is Gerard Hemmings. I spoke to the elders and then phoned Gerard Hemmings to ask him to be our chaplain. He initially said he couldn't do it but then he phoned me back a quarter of an hour later and said, 'Actually, Alun I feel I should.' Gerard Hemmings was our chaplain on camps for many years and is now my pastor in London, and I agree, he is one of the best preachers in the country.

The second reason that I'm indebted to Mr Olyott is because, a year or so ago, my wife and I were listening to a series on knowyourbible.org called 'Aspects of Spirituality' by Mr Olyott, where he talked about meditation, solitude, prayer and fasting. They were so helpful and I highly recommend listening to them. Around the same time Mr Olyott preached three sermons consecutively via Zoom for Amyand Park Chapel, on Titus. He also wrote an article in the *Evangelical Times* on revival and, because of these three things, I felt compelled to email him. In the email I received back, I cannot recall exactly what he said, but it put the idea in my head that we should really interview men like Mr Olyott because we may not have much longer with them, and that is how *Before They Leave the Stage* came about.

Background

His father was an Englishman and was brought up in a little railway terrace house behind the station in Colchester, Essex. He was converted as a young man in the Railway Mission and when he found out he wasn't growing very much in the faith, he walked up the hill to the Baptist Church. He left school at 14 and worked as an engineer.

On the other side of Colchester was a Welsh family and Eileen, one of the daughters, went to the Baptist Church. Her father had served in the Welsh Highland Artillery and on leaving the army, became a SASRA Scripture Reader for the Colchester garrison.

In the Baptist church these two young people met, they fell in love and they married. Stuart's father joined the Royal Engineers and went straight from sapper to staff sergeant, and straight from staff sergeant to captain; and at the time he was captain, Stuart was born.

He was born in Lahore, which is now in Pakistan. It was then in India and he spent his early years on the North-West Frontier. They went back to Colchester for a little while and then he spent the remainder of his childhood, up to the age of 10, in Malaysia. When he was 10 the family moved to Chester. Stuart went to his ninth primary school in Chester and then, by the grace of God, he amazingly got a free place in a local public school and, even though he was from a military family, had all of his secondary education at that school without interruption.

Conversion

In his teens he came under tremendous conviction of sin. He knew he needed to be saved but he didn't want to be because he knew he would probably lose all his friends. He was very, very torn. He knew his parents were right and respected them enormously, but he didn't want to go their way; and yet he was very burdened by his sin.

In the summer of 1957 he went to stay with his grandmother in Colchester in the little house behind the station. Sunday came and she didn't make him go to church, which Stuart was very pleased about. He thought that this was the moment he would make the break. But, in Stuart's own words:

In the afternoon of that Sunday I felt strangely hungry. I just felt I needed to be in the presence of the Bible. I needed to be where the Bible was opened and explained. The last thing I expected to feel was that. That's what I felt. I have felt it most days since.

At the time it was a new experience for him, so he went to the Baptist church up on top of the hill and he didn't think anything would happen there because, although the church had an evangelical history, there was very little gospel preaching there at that time. The pastor led the service. It was completely unmoving, and as he came to preach he told the congregation that he wasn't going to preach that evening but that he had asked somebody else to tell them his life story. As this man told his life story, Stuart had an enormous sense of God. He recalls:

I had a sense of judgment and bewilderment and lostness and sadness and fear, but overwhelmingly I had a sense of God and it overcame me, it invaded me, it conquered me. I knew I needed to be saved. I knew Jesus had done something on the cross. I could never have explained to you at that moment, or for several months after probably, what Jesus had done on the cross, but I knew that what Jesus did on the cross saved sinners. Before the service was over there I was, a Christian young man, just short of 15 years old.

He went back to school; it was the beginning of the new school year, and something must have happened because a new teacher saw him and said to him, 'Olyott, you and I are going to start a Christian Union,' which they did.

The Call and Training

He left the church he was currently attending and went to a church which was filled with young people who loved the Lord, loved His day, loved each other, loved the work of the gospel and loved to pray. There he made his first steps in the Christian life and before long, very soon in fact, he had an extraordinary desire to preach. He went to the deacons and said, 'I must preach.' But they insisted he was too young. So he went to the Methodist minister down the road and said, 'I must preach,' and he replied, 'Great, we can't get preachers on the circuit these days.'

Stuart began to preach with the Methodists, and also in some of the Presbyterian churches of North Wales. After a year his deacons came back to him and said, 'You're preaching for the Methodists! Well, you had better preach for us too, then.' So he then began to preach in his home church. They had no pastor, which meant that he had quite a lot of opportunity to preach. The desire to preach got stronger and stronger and he knew in his soul that this was God's call on his life. He came to believe that the reason he had been put on the planet was to preach the gospel.

He went off to the London Bible College and met people there who greatly helped him in his faith. Brian Edwards was one of them, Paul Bassett another and Bruce Powell (see Chapter 10) followed on, along with others. The principal at the College, Dr Ernest Kevan, was wonderful. He built college life on spiritual-mindedness and hard work. Stuart was sure he was going to the mission field because he knew a lot of missionaries. But he didn't know any ministers who were really keen.

However, he started worshipping at the East London Tabernacle, where he sat under the ministry of Paul Tucker. As time went by he became increasingly convinced that maybe he should be in the pastoral ministry and not in Brazil. He made a covenant with God that if he had a unanimous call from a church he would accept it. In the seventh term, the first term of the final year, he had a unanimous call from Poplar Baptist Church. So his future was settled. In 1964 he went straight from college into the pastorate at Poplar Baptist Church. He was 21.

Ministry

Poplar

It was a difficult church. It was a small church. It was a worldly church. There were also some lovely Christians in it, and best of all, there were three district nurses who worshipped there. One of these was the greatest Christian Stuart has ever met, Doll. But he had also made a covenant with God that he would never go out with a girl from a church where he was the pastor because, if it went wrong, it would spoil everything. After three years there, for reasons which will become plain later, and nothing actually to do with Doll, he left the church and accepted a call to an independent Baptist Church in Liverpool, called Belvidere Road Church.

Belvidere Road

He had been teaching two days a week in London, and once he got to Liverpool and settled in Belvidere Road he also began to teach a few hours, or a day a week, in the local secondary modern school.

After a year he moved out of the suburban manse into a little terraced house in Toxteth, just a few hundred yards from the church. It was then that he opened negotiations with Doll. They got married in 1970 and the busiest part of his life then started. They were married on 3rd January 1970 and twenty days later the first boy arrived at their home. Over the next ten to twelve years they adopted eight boys and had eight other children live in their home for significant periods of their childhood.

As well as the home and family, the church was also very busy and God's blessing was on it. He began preaching abroad from 1973, began writing, began reading books with potential leaders, as well as knocking his French into shape, because he had this burden that he really needed to learn it. It was a very significant pastorate of 15 years.

Switzerland

He was called to the French-speaking Baptist Church in Lausanne, in Switzerland. In 1982 he and Doll moved there and the two youngest boys moved with them. It was a little church, made up of twelve elderly people who had been gathering together for twelve years, but the Lord was pleased to bless it. For three of those years he also pastored the little English church in the city. He was able to leave the English work after three years because a man they had trained up was able to take over the pastorate.

They started satellites, as well as a pastors' conference in France, and Stuart continued writing, as well as reading books with potential leaders. He was able to leave the church in 1991 and to return to Belvidere Road, because it now had a Swiss pastor of its own and was able to support him.

Back to Belvidere

Back to Belvidere Road they went, which was less frantic than the previous time, and Stuart's mother went to live with them. He did some school teaching again, began to teach part-time at the Evangelical Theological College of Wales and was going abroad quite regularly to preach, mostly at pastors' conferences.

ETCW and EMW

The Evangelical Theological College of Wales (ETCW) eventually asked him to go full time, which he did from 1999, for four years. Then he was approached by the ETCW to help churches in Wales with problems, especially church leaders and pastors, and so he moved sideways. He still had an office in Bryntirion but was actually working for the Evangelical Movement of Wales (EMW) until he officially retired in 2008.

Retirement

Stuart and Doll retired to Connah's Quay, in North Wales, to be near Liverpool, but also to remain in Wales, as he was still doing a lot of pastoral work among church leaders and churches in Wales. Doll's problems at that point were beginning to become visible and it became clear that something wasn't quite right. It was the beginning of her dementia which was to become more and more obvious as the years went by.

For two of those years, however, he did pastor Christ Church Deeside which had had to remove its pastor for a moral reason. He was able to lead it through the process of calling Matthew Francis who is there today and very happily settled as a respected gospel preacher in North Wales.

Doll's dementia was now extremely serious and Stuart had to devote all his time to look after her. The Lord took her in 2017, and after some months Stuart moved back to Liverpool to be near the boys so that they could look after him should he become unwell.

He is very happy to be back in Belvidere Road Church as a member. He spends most of his time giving advice to people. He still preaches at home and abroad, and especially in Caergwrle, where he pastored the Evangelical Church during 2018 and 2019. He also still writes articles, and tries to shepherd his large family in a way which is meaningful at this stage of their lives.

Times of Blessing

As he looks back, Stuart can testify to the Lord's kindness and grace. Throughout his life he has seen people come to Christ through personal conversations, but what thrilled him the most, in Poplar Baptist Church, was the first time that somebody came to Christ through his preaching. According to Stuart, 'I cannot imagine any joy or any thrill on earth which is greater than that.' There were a number of conversions during his brief time there. The youngest was 13, the oldest was 88, and they came from a wide variety of backgrounds.

But the time of greatest blessing was undoubtedly Belvidere Road Church in the middle of the 1970s. The prayer meetings they had in the church were unforgettable, characterised by what Stuart calls 'serious joy'. The Lord seemed to be at work in everything. There were children converted in the children's meetings, children converted in the Holiday Bible Club, children converted at the annual camps, young people converted in young people's meetings, and students converted in the church and in the Christian Union. He remembers baptising nineteen people one Sunday and then a fortnight later baptising fourteen more. It was an exceptional time. He thanks God for the privilege of going through a time like that.

Then he went to Lausanne. When he got there it was twelve discouraged people. But when they left, there were a hundred encouraged people, because the Lord had been pleased to bless the work. They had also started some satellites, some of which have become churches since.

When he returned to Belvidere, the church had been discouraged because it had been through some troubles, but God blessed it at last by encouraging it again.

There were blessings in the College. The spiritual tone of the Evangelical Theological College of Wales was very good. There were some fine young men, and it was thrilling to see that God was raising up another generation.

When he worked for the EMW, he felt the Lord's blessing was on the work. There were men kept in the ministry who otherwise would have left it. There were churches kept united which otherwise would have divided; and there were office-bearers ready to hand in their badge who didn't.

As he looks back over his ministry, all Stuart can testify is that, *'Goodness and mercy have followed me all the days of my life.'*

Hard Work and Difficulties

In saying that, it has been hard work. A typical Sunday in the summer at Belvidere would be: The Lord's Supper at ten o'clock on two Sundays of the month, followed by the morning service (and there were a lot of people at that), very often followed by about an hour's talking afterwards. They would have people for lunch, after which Stuart always went to the Sunday School or the Bible class. They had a different set of people for tea, before going to the open-air meeting and on to the evening service. Sometimes there was a young people's group at home afterwards, and if there wasn't, there were people who came to the house for counselling. It was a very busy time, but the Lord sustained them.

Lausanne was also busy. For a period in Lausanne, Stuart was pastoring two churches at once, as well as several satellites, meaning that there was a period of three years during which he took nine meetings a week. It was very hard work, and there's no way of explaining it except that God was in it. The Lord was doing something special in Stuart's own physical stamina, because he does not know how otherwise it could have happened.

Moreover, another thing that was difficult in the Liverpool days was that they were poor. When Stuart got married he had no money and Doll had very little. They lived in a tiny house. There were fifty-four houses in their street and fifty-two of them had no bathroom, and theirs was one of those fifty-two. They had no running hot water. It was tough. They started saving up to build a bathroom, but the Lord kept sending people to live with them and to become members of their family. They bought their house for £1000 and Stuart's mortgage was £9 a month. Then they bought the house next door for £1,050 and joined the two houses together. But they still had no bathroom. They just had all these little rooms with people in and were really poor because each of their boys came to them in unusual ways. Four of them were self-invited; they just turned up. One was given to them. Only three of the boys they adopted came through any normal means, and for nearly all their boys they received no financial help at all. In addition they had all their part-time children. They had three girls who came for part of the week, and often for the weekend and long periods in their school holidays. They had other children who lived with them for long periods. Two boys lived with them for a year each. Stuart recalls:

It was a very tough time financially, but we can say that we never ever went into the red. We had a plaque on the bedroom wall which read, 'My God shall supply all your need,' and it is still up there. We once got down to 51 pence, but we never ever went into the red.

Doll's dementia was a tough time because looking after someone with dementia is physically exacting and emotionally exhausting. As Doll did less and less, Stuart had to do more and more, until he did everything. However, there were no spiritual problems during Doll's dementia. She remained the praying, loving person that she had always been. Even five days before she died, when he was reading with her about the need for us to love God, she just stopped him and said, 'Well, I love him, I really love Him.' She had a model death and Stuart thanks God for the privilege of witnessing it.

Preparing messages and seeking the Lord during his ministry was hard, but Stuart believes you have to make time. He reminisced with a pastor not long before we interviewed him, about the years during which they never went to bed on the same day as they got up. He has always found great help in getting outside walking and does most of his praying while walking.

As a Baptist, Stuart has never believed that there is any form of ministerial accreditation except the call of the local church, but the church in Poplar was in the Baptist Union and there was no chance of it leaving. He found in Galatians 1 that if someone preaches another gospel we must not even accept them as a fellow Christian, but found in the Baptist Union that he was expected not only to accept them as a fellow Christian, but as a fellow minister. In all good conscience, that was something he could not do. He was already on his way out of the BU, but that famous day in 1966 when Dr Lloyd-Jones gave his appeal in the Methodist Central Hall put the cap on everything. Leaving Poplar Baptist Church was hard, but he knew that, although he loved these people to bits, he had to leave because he could not in good conscience remain in a church which was joined to an association of churches to which he could not be committed.

Belvidere was tough to begin with. The office-bearers were wonderful and were already reading good books before Stuart arrived. But many of the members had no understanding of, or desire for, the doctrines of grace, and some of them were dyed-in-the-wool dispensationalists. He would come home from church on a Sunday morning and the telephone would be ringing with people objecting to something that they had heard in the morning service. This did not last long, but there were two or three years where that was very difficult.

Most difficult of all in Belvidere Road was the church discipline. There were occasions when the church had to discipline people and it was unbearably trying. One man was so offended by the discipline that for several years he followed Stuart around in his car, hoping to find him guilty of some traffic offence. He interrupted meetings when Stuart was preaching away from home and sometimes he interrupted meetings at Belvidere Road too. Those things are hard and quite disturbing, particularly when you are a young man.

Lausanne was tough because he arrived in a church that was non-charismatic, which was virtually unknown amongst the evangelicals of the city. He was a five-point Calvinist and they had never heard of such a thing—and this was Lausanne where Pierre Viret, the successor to Calvin, had ministered! Moreover, because Stuart was amillennial, the local evangelicals all assumed that he was a liberal. He had no trouble with his church members, but it was a very difficult time with the other pastors in the area. However, as he puts it, 'If you have got convictions, you have got convictions; and you have to be prepared to carry them, come what may.'

Advice

When asked what advice he would give to a young Stuart Olyott now, and subsequently to all young men in the ministry, Stuart said, 'As a young man you have temptations to dishonesty and to pride and to immorality and to unbelief. With the years those temptations get greater, not less. Therefore, you have got to guard your own soul.' Even now in his late 70s, the temptations to dishonesty, pride, immorality and unbelief are significant.

Another thing he believes is that to say Christ is the centre of the Bible is not enough; rather it is that the centre of the Bible is Christ crucified. That is what must be preached. He used to think as a young minister if he was preaching about Christ as prophet, or priest or king, or about his exaltation or his humiliation, then he was preaching Christ. But, as he has gone through the years and looked at the Bible more closely, he has concluded that one is not preaching Christ unless he is preaching Christ crucified. The great theme of heaven is the Lamb who was slain.

Another thing he would say is that he had no idea that the ministry would be so lonely. As an older man looking back he realises that he has literally a couple of thousand good friends, which is a great privilege. Many of them he made at the Banner of Truth ministers' conferences and in local fraternals. He reckons he has dozens of close friends, but he does not have many soul mates. If he had not had Achille Blaize as a soul mate in the first ten years of his ministry, he does not know where he would be. According to Stuart:

When you've got yearnings for God which you can't express, but you want to talk about, you need a soul mate who can understand where you're coming from. When you have agonies of soul which affects you at every level because of the spiritual conflict that you're going through, you need some form of soul mate with whom you can talk. And there aren't many of them. When you're overcome with such a sense of the holiness of God that you're stunned into silence, you need some form of fellow spirit with whom you can share this.

As well as Achille Blaize, if it hadn't been for Bill Hughes, Bernard Lewis, Paul Wells and Gerard Hemmings through the years, and Matthew Brennan more recently, he does not know whether he would have survived in the ministry. At certain times he would go to these men and open his heart and have fellowship together; it could be on the phone or face to face, but there are times when you just need someone who understands. Deep calls to deep. Of course he had the advantage of having Doll, with whom he could talk about anything at any time, but sometimes he needed to talk to a fellow minister.

Books

Stuart is a man of three books. The first one is *Power through Prayer* by E. M. Bounds. It is not a perfect book, it doesn't have enough about Christ in it, but it is a book which he has read most years since 1961. He reads it sentence by sentence, and every sentence prompts him to pray. But the book he loves above all other books, and of which he recites one-sixth every weekday, is *The Shorter Catechism.* If it was not for the answer to the 95th question, he would actually think *The Shorter Catechism* was divinely inspired. It gives you all the basic gospel beliefs; then it gives you all that you need to know about the Christian life and its ethics (how to behave); and finally it gives you a pattern of godliness by its teaching on the Word, sacraments and prayer. Stuart has built his Christian life on *Power Through Prayer*, *The Shorter Catechism* and, thirdly, *Matthew Henry's Commentary*, because that commentary teaches you to state the truth, to illustrate the truth and to apply the truth. Other books he has loved include *Search the Scriptures*, because again and again, when he has been unable to break down a scripture passage, he has gone to *Search the Scriptures* and suddenly found that it is obvious. But next to *The Shorter Catechism*, the book which he loves above every book is *The Incomparable Christ* by J. Oswald Sanders. Other books which have helped him enormously are *The Forgotten Spurgeon*, which clarified all sorts of things for him, and in more recent years, the biography of Daniel Rowland by Eifion Evans. There are also three secular books that he has found helpful. The first one is, *Getting Through: how to make words work* for you by Godfrey Howard, which is a simple book on communication. The next one is called *Total Fitness in 30 minutes a Week*, so for the last forty-five years he has done exercises in his bedroom every day except the Lord's day, resulting in being reasonably fit and not having too many health issues. And the book we may laugh at is, *How to Win Friends and Influence People*. Stuart maintains that the people who laugh about it have never read it!

People

The people who have influenced him are first of all his parents. Before he was in his mid teens he knew two things and he knew them right deep in his soul: he knew that spiritual things are more important than anything else on the planet, and he knew that the personal quality which you must always have, and which you never need to give up on, is integrity. You can lose your reputation, you can lose your health, you can lose your life, but you never need to lose your integrity. He got that from his parents.

Then there was Doll, the greatest Christian he has ever met, because she understood that everything the Son of God did, and everything the Son of God does, was and is for others. According to Stuart:

In forty-seven years of married life I cannot think of a single occasion where she put herself first. I cannot think of one. She was the most welcoming, loving, outgoing, inclusive person imaginable. Now just think of the effect of that on your life for forty-seven years.

Then there were the boys. They have taught Stuart that there is no such thing as an ordinary person; they are bursting with flair and intelligence and talent and creativity—and, given the right opportunities, that is true of everyone.

But amongst preachers, supremely the preacher who has had the most influence on him was Hywel Griffiths. Again and again, after hearing him preach, Stuart has seen the congregation just sit there in stunned silence, sometimes for ten minutes, sometimes for quarter of an hour, and then often they would burst into spontaneous prayer. Stuart tried to analyse his preaching and then realised that the same thing was in Paul Tucker, his pastor when he was a student, and the same thing was in Harry Matthews, the third minister who took Stuart under his wing. First of all, Hywel Griffiths loved everybody to bits and you could see that by the way he preached; he just wanted to do you good. The second thing was that he informed the mind, he informed you about Christ crucified, and he did it by story. The third thing was that he spoke to the conscience. He insisted that the truth he was preaching must change you. The fourth thing was that he prayed for the Spirit; something must happen during preaching; those who hear preaching must engage with God, they must have dealings with God or, to use an expression that he and others use, 'they must do business with God'.

In June 1964 Stuart was leaving college and he knew he was going to be the pastor of Poplar Baptist Church, but he had a moment of enormous doubt: can the prayerful preaching of the Word actually do the job? For several days he was in total disarray because of this doubt. Can the prayerful preaching of the Word actually do the job? He went to Westminster Chapel to the Campbell Morgan Memorial Lecture given by Dr Martyn Lloyd-Jones in June 1964. There the Doctor spoke on 'The Weapons of our Warfare' (you can still find it in print in the book published by the Banner of Truth called *Knowing the Times*) and Stuart's life was transformed. He was rescued from his doubt by that one address.

Legacy

Stuart decided, for what he believes are Biblical reasons, not to build his ministry on what he would call the *'literacy model'*, where a man preaches in detail through parts of Scripture and leaves his congregation to read up the rest for themselves. It is a model which assumes the literacy of the church members and congregation. He believes it is important for a Christian to know that the whole of Scripture is given by inspiration from God and is profitable, so that the man of God may be complete. So it seems to him that the literacy model is not the Biblical one. Personal Bible reading was unknown in the early church. Obviously there was no printing and, even after the invention of printing in Europe in the fourteenth century, personal Bible reading wasn't known really until a couple of hundred years ago. It was in the *church* where people discovered the whole counsel of God. So he felt in his preaching he must sacrifice some depth and go for breadth, in order preach the whole Bible. He has therefore adopted a model of preaching which is simple, serious and vivid, but does not assume literacy. And also, because most people are unaware that they don't have any powers of synthesis, he believed that it was important not only just to preach Bible books, but to preach themes and topics. Otherwise people can read the whole Bible and then, when asked what the Bible teaches about leisure or race or some other topic, they can't give an answer. So Stuart felt all this had to be tackled from the pulpit and built his ministry on paragraph preaching and on topical preaching, not assuming literacy in anyone.

The State of the Church Today and The Need of the Hour

One of the good things is that there are now Reformed churches everywhere. When he went to Liverpool in 1967, apart from one little tiny independent Baptist Church on a housing estate, there wasn't a single Reformed church in the city. Nowadays, Stuart could recommend twelve Reformed churches in Liverpool.

Another is all the resources which are available. The books which have been published by the Banner of Truth, Evangelical Press and Bryntirion Press, and a number of other publishers, Stuart thinks are extraordinary. Then there's YouTube. While there is a lot of nonsense on YouTube, if a young Christian says today, 'Who is Hudson Taylor?, he can go to YouTube and find a film on him. All sorts of information and resources are available there.

Then there are some extraordinary young people. Stuart loves going to the Aberystwyth Conference. There are hundreds of young people present and Stuart often asks them why they are there. They reply by saying they are there for the preaching. As he talks to them he finds that they are serious about their Christian life and that they are brave in their comprehensive schools and universities. Many of them are standing up for

Christ and are being despised and abused on a daily basis. But they are not flinching. Stuart thanks God for them.

As for bad things in the church, Stuart thinks the Americanisation of the church is not healthy. The culture and mind-set of North America is so different from ours and does not translate well into our British context. He is distressed that so many of our young ministers are completely infatuated by what is going on in North America and, as a result, neglect reading the likes of Luther and the Puritans and Spurgeon.

But what troubles him most is, that while there is an interest in doctrine, which is great, and there is an interest in ethics, which is also great, in Scripture there is an emphasis on experience—that is, we know God and we deal with God. He is concerned that this emphasis is largely missing today. Sermons are not to be prepared in the study but, to use a Puritan expression, 'sermons are prepared in the closet'. The 'closet' is the place where you engage with God. Open before you is the text of scripture which you're studying, but you're having dealings with God as to how He would have this particular passage of scripture preached to this particular people on this particular occasion. This involves a lot of labour and agony of spirit. Then, when it is all prepared, preachers have got to pray for the blessing of God upon it, because such blessing does not come automatically. Stuart feels that the church today is far too Lutheran. In Lutheranism there is the belief that the Word and the Spirit are so tied up together that when you faithfully expound the Word, the Spirit is automatically let loose. Stuart believes that the Bible is the Word of God. Every time the Bible is read, and every time the Bible is preached, God is shouting and trumpeting, as well as speaking gently. But the problem is the human heart. People are not hearing the voice of God in Scripture. So something has got to happen in their heart. The Spirit must so work in them that the whole direction of their soul is changed. They have got to have a direct miracle wrought on their soul by God Himself and Stuart does not think that this is recognised in modern evangelicalism. Therefore, he does not think that people today understand what our forefathers used to call 'praying through'. In Stuart's own words:

I believe that part of my ministerial duty is to pray for every single person individually, as far as that is possible, before I preach. I must deal with God and talk to Him about my people. I do not believe that when preaching is powerful it is just that the Word has been supercharged. I don't believe that's what happens at all. The Word is always supercharged. I believe that when preaching is powerful it is because God is doing a direct work upon the human soul. That's the work of God. We can't do it. But He can. Therefore we should pray to Him about it.

When Paul talked to Lydia and opened the Word, it does not say that the Word opened her heart, neither does it say that Paul opened her heart. It says that the Lord opened her heart. Stuart believes that that is the great need of the hour.

Final Exhortations

At the end of the interview, Stuart asked if he could make some final exhortations.

His first was that we should not take literacy for granted. He thinks that PowerPoint is a step in the wrong direction, partly because most preachers who use PowerPoint make their structures too complicated and therefore not memorable, and partly because by using it you're actually discriminating against the folk who have reading difficulties. If a minister responds by saying, 'Well, we've got no people with reading difficulties in our church,' then, that speaks for itself.

Secondly, almost two-thirds of the Bible is story and almost two-thirds of our Lord's recorded ministry is story, so why isn't two-thirds of our preaching story? The purpose of every sermon ever preached is that men and women and boys and girls should *pray*. If all a sermon does is inform the mind, it isn't a sermon, it's a lecture. The purpose of every sermon is that every person listening, whether they are a Christian or non-Christian, is that they will engage with God and that they will pray. Stuart recounted the story of when a theological student came to see the great Welsh preacher, Henry Rees, in Liverpool, and said, 'Please give me some advice.' He simply said, 'Read those books which will stir up in you a spirit of prayer.' Stuart thinks there are too many ministers who are studying the great commentaries that are available, but they are not reading devotionally and not stirring up their own spirit to pray. In Stuart's own words:

Ultimately preaching is the action of the preacher's soul upon the hearer's soul, under the blessing of God, and revival, for which we long and pray, is essentially a personal experience. In widespread revival there may be thousands of people having that personal experience, but essentially revival is a personal experience and the only thing in the universe that can stop me having a personal experience of God is my sin. So I need to get alone with God and ask Him to search my heart, so that I can confess my sin to Him. And, instead of praying for power, maybe I should first of all tell the Lord that I haven't got it.

But Stuart ended by exhorting us all to ultimately live in the light of the second coming of our Lord. He had recently told two friends that they might have wasted their money during lockdown, because they had bought two graves. According to Stuart:

The sky, not the grave, is our goal. We don't live on earth just waiting around to die. We live on earth constantly remembering that the great Christ who died for us and rose again from the dead, who is seated at the right hand of the majesty on high, is coming for us:

> Coming suddenly! Coming soon!
> Coming certainly!—night or noon.
> Jesus, I humbly pray,
> Wash all my sins away,
> And keep me to that day
> When Thou shalt come.
> (C. H. M. Foster; CSSM Chorus 249).

Chapter 14

Maurice Roberts

Introduction

In March 1994, when I was in my first year
at university, I remember reading an article
that Mr Roberts wrote in the Banner of Truth magazine. Nearly thirty
years on, it is still the best article I think I have ever read and seems more
relevant today than it was back then. It is called *More than a Dream* and
is also a chapter in Mr Roberts's book, *The Christian's High Calling*, also
published by the Banner. I cannot recommend it highly enough and would
urge you to get either a back copy of the magazine or buy the book.

Background and Conversion

Maurice Roberts was brought up in Sale, Cheshire, a few miles south of
Manchester. He lived there with his mother, father, and his sister, Ann.
None of them was very religious at the time but by the grace of God they
all became Christians. The Lord has been very good to them as a family.
His sister married an excellent minister from Manchester called David
Winch, and they became missionaries for many years. David passed away
a few months before we interviewed Maurice.

Maurice's own conversion occurred when he went to university at the
age of 18. He went to Kings College in Durham University to study classics:
Latin, Greek and Ancient History. He was there with a view to becoming a
secondary school teacher. While he was there, he met a student from Wales
who was a Christian. He was the son of a minister and began to gently,
kindly and affectionately talk to Maurice about the gospel. Maurice had
never heard it before; never knew about his need to repent and believe on
the Lord Jesus Christ. He came under conviction of sin but really did not
want to be a Christian and wanted to enjoy the world. But through the

Holy Spirit, God graciously continued to convict Maurice, and day after day, in spite of his trying to get rid of this fear that came upon him, God was prodding his conscience that he needed to be converted. The day came when he could not put up with this conflict any more and he remembers sitting on a chair in the university library and praying, 'Oh Lord, I will do anything to get peace.' By the grace of God he got peace there and then. He knew that his sins were forgiven and that he was a Christian.

He went back home and told his father, mother and sister. As time went on, they all became believers: first his mother, then his sister Ann.

His father came to Christ late in life. He was in Manchester Royal Hospital and Maurice went to visit him when he was on his deathbed. Maurice by now was married. His wife, Sandra (née Macleod), came from Stornoway, Isle of Lewis. They had a little daughter. The three of them stood by the bed and he said to his father, 'Father, as you leave this world, are you trusting in Jesus?' He could not speak but nodded. Maurice asked him a second time, 'Are you sure you are trusting in Jesus only?' Again he nodded. 'Well,' said Maurice, 'it won't be long, father, before you and I are together up there in glory.' Tears came into their eyes.

Teaching

Maurice did not go immediately into the work of the ministry. For fourteen years he was a schoolteacher in several different schools. He first of all taught in a grammar school in County Durham and had the opportunity there to teach the Bible in the Religious Education classes. After school hours he invited children to a meeting in a hall and there taught them the Bible and explained to them what it is to come to Christ and be converted. He would have maybe twenty, or twenty-five, young people and a number of these were truly blessed and genuinely converted. One or two who came to saving knowledge of Christ became missionaries abroad. Maurice is still in touch with one of them who is living in Mexico City.

He not only taught these boys and girls the Bible outside of school hours but also during their Religious Education lessons. He taught them to treat the Bible as a divinely inspired book. The head of his department was a liberal Christian and did not accept the Bible to be divinely inspired. When he discovered what Maurice was doing he was furious. He took him to the headmaster and sat him down in a chair. He said to the headmaster, 'This man ought not to be teaching anyone anything. He's not fit to be teaching anybody, he should be out there on the road sweeping the streets!' He did all he could to get Maurice thrown out. But the headmaster was more sympathetic to Maurice than he was to his accuser and it was his accuser who ended up leaving the school. Another Religious Education teacher tried to do something similar, but again was unsuccessful.

Maurice believes that the Bible must be handled as a divinely inspired book. We must not add to it or take away anything from it, and this is where our nation is going wrong today. He is also sad that children are taught that the world came about millions of years ago with a big bang. They should know that, *'In the beginning God created the heaven and the earth'* (Genesis 1:1).

The Call

In 1964 he met a lovely lady named Sandra Macleod from Stornoway, a town in the Western Isles of Scotland. They married in 1965 and they have lived in Scotland all their married lives.

Following their marriage they attended a congregation of the Free Church of Scotland in Edinburgh, and he loved it in every way. There was sound theological teaching, respect for the Word of God, biblical worship, and there were godly men and women in the congregation. Some of them were exceedingly fine examples of godliness and spirituality. The effect of meeting these people was that, more and more, Maurice felt drawn to the importance of preaching the gospel to save souls. This impulse got stronger and stronger, and so he sought the advice of a friend who was a minister, who urged him to go ahead. Maurice began to prepare for the ministry. He trained in the Free Church College in Edinburgh and externally did a BD with London University.

Ayr

Maurice Roberts ministered in two congregations. The first was in Ayr in south-west Scotland. He was inducted in 1974 and was there for twenty years, until 1994. It was a time of real blessing and delightful increase in numbers. When he went to the congregation in 1974, forty or so people were in the morning service and about thirty in the evening. By the time he left it there were about a hundred. The prayer meeting midweek had about six people in it when he first began and had about sixty-five people when he left.

In addition to systematic preaching they had lots of fellowships, following the example of what they did in the Island of Lewis. When he first met his wife and went to the Island of Lewis in 1964, he thought he had stepped into heaven. It was a wonderful place. It is not quite as good now as it was then, but it is still better than anywhere else he knows in the UK. In Lewis, people very often after a service would go to one another's homes, maybe five or ten of them. They would sit around together and talk about a text of scripture or some spiritual experience that they are aware of, or some problem that has arisen in their lives. Maurice tried to cultivate a similar approach in Ayr. They had lovely times together, people gathering, talking about the holy Scriptures, giving their testimonies one to another. It really was a delightful experience and they had many examples of God working.

In the first year or two in Ayr there was no growth and no development, and so Maurice started to pray earnestly, 'Oh Lord, let there be a blessing.' There was one lady who was a businesswoman, and somehow she came along to talk to Maurice about a problem that she had. He talked to her about it, but then said that her real problem was that she needed to be 'born again'. She smiled and said she had never heard of that. However, she started to come to church with her children and after a whole year she came to the wonderful experience of being born again, and what a change came into her life. She was on the telephone night and day telling all her friends and family and connections what had happened to her. At least thirty people came to church in the next few years through her influence. She witnessed to people diligently and the congregation grew rapidly. It was the beginning of a time of blessing. A number of other people came and similar things happened.

There was also a lovely case of a young girl of eight or nine. She went back home one evening and said to her parents, 'I was converted tonight.

Can I become a church member?' The parents said they were delighted to hear that she had been converted but told her she could not become a member until she was at least 14. Another young girl was at a wedding and as she listened to the minister preach, she was converted—again at about the age of eight. In both girls you could see the change in their lives.

Maurice's pattern was to preach primarily to the Lord's people in the morning to build them up in the faith and in the evening he emphasised the need to repent and believe on the Lord Jesus Christ. In his own words:

Oh, what matters most is to preach Christ and to show people how they must repent of their sins and flee to Him. A tremendous emphasis surely in preaching ought to be upon the need to get right with God, and that was the emphasis I tried to make.

He did some writing for the Banner of Truth in those years, editing the Banner Magazine, and in total wrote ten small books, some published in the UK and some in America. Maurice counts it a great honour and privilege to have done this work for the Lord Jesus Christ.

In communion seasons in the Free Church of Scotland and at their annual Bible Conference, he had excellent times. The visiting preachers would come along and had a slightly different emphasis from Maurice which he welcomed. Bill Hughes (see Chapter 8) was one of the men who came to preach and they got to know him well and loved him very much. They had conferences where Iain Murray (see Chapter 16) and others would come along and preach the Word of God.

Inverness

After twenty really happy years in Ayr, there was a congregation in Inverness that needed a new minister and they called him to be their minister in 1994. Inverness is in the north-east of Scotland, so they moved quite a distance, all the way from the south-west to the north-east.

He cannot say why, but he didn't get on with the people quite so well, and says that it was probably his fault rather than theirs. The culture was different. The big problem, however, was that the whole denomination was divided at this time. There were allegations of immorality against a prominent minister. Some felt that the matter should be ignored, but others like Maurice felt it should be dealt with in the church courts. For protesting, he and around thirty other ministers were suspended. The suspended ministers there formed the Free Church of Scotland (Continuing) with about thirty congregations and 1,500 members and adherents.

Maurice was very, very sorry that this happened, but felt it was his duty to stand by his conscience.

Maurice lost a lot of friends, which was heartbreaking, but there were also practical problems. They had to buy manses for the ministers to live in and buy buildings for public worship. That took some time, and in the wonderful kindness of God He provided an excellent building in Inverness which they were able to buy. It was not only big enough to be a place for worship, but big enough so that part of it was a house for the minister, and there were rooms for other uses. Eventually they were able to form a seminary for training young men for the ministry in the Free Church Continuing, and there was sufficient room in the building for this.

In the Inverness Free Church Continuing there was a very good spirit among the people. They were happy and united. Maurice was the minister of that congregation until 2010, for sixteen years. Maurice hopes he never has to go through anything like the Free Church division again. In his own words:

It's terribly painful when you love a congregation and love a denomination when a division like that comes. It's very, very painful.

Throughout those difficult times, though, God drew near to him and he had precious promises from the Word. For example, *'All things work together for good to them that love God'* (Romans 8:28). Another verse he often liked to quote was from 2 Chronicles, *'If my people, which are called by my name, shall humble themselves, and pray, and seek my face, and turn from their wicked ways; then will I hear from heaven, and will forgive their sin, and will heal their land'* (2 Chronicles 7:14).

His comfort is that if we do the right thing, no matter how much we suffer, it will enjoy God's blessing in the end. In the Old Testament many times the Lord's people just had to humble themselves in dark days. His hope is that the Lord will yet bless us even more in a time to come.

Advice

When asked what advice he would give young ministers, he said, firstly they must adhere to their ordination vow under all circumstances. Everything that is done in public and private worship must be thoroughly biblical. They must adhere to the principles of the Bible in everything they do in the worship of God.

Secondly, they must not make their own feelings the rule of life. We must go by the teachings in the Word of God. The Lord Jesus suffered to redeem us and shed his precious blood. The apostles also suffered, and we must be willing to suffer for the cause of Christ as well. It is always better to suffer doing the right thing than to turn a blind eye to it and neglect our duty. God sees it all. The text that often influences Maurice is, *'Be sure your sin will find you out.'*

The Banner of Truth

Maurice Roberts' editorials for the Banner of Truth magazines were outstanding, including, *More than a Dream*. He did them for a long time and we asked him how he went about preparing them and managed to be so consistent.

His method was to be in prayer often, that the Lord would give him suitable subjects to write about. He always bore in mind that he must speak to people's hearts as well as their heads. True religion is not simply an intellectual thing—although, of course, it is intellectual. As far as Maurice is concerned, we have to believe the right doctrine, but alongside that we need to be stirred up and our emotions touched. This was very much what the Puritans did. The Puritans touched the head and the heart; they stirred the conscience and they aroused the emotions too. Maurice tried to write in a similar way. He remembers lying in bed one morning and the idea came to him for the *More than a Dream* article. He jumped out of bed and started writing at once. He felt the article was given to him by God. He felt the thoughts were being put into his mind, which he was able to put down on paper.

He is deeply interested in the subject of revival, has a burden for it, and has written much about it. On a Monday night he and dozens of people would meet to pray for revival. It seems to him that this is what we desperately need today. He longs to see the Spirit of God coming down again. When revivals occurred in the past, suddenly the whole world changed. Mr Roberts gave a good example from China.

There was a wonderful man raised up in China in the 1920s. He died in 1944. His name was John Sung.

His father was a Methodist minister in China—preaching, of course, in Chinese. He was academically brilliant and went to America to study. Very soon he got his PhD and other degrees. The downside was that in America he saw that Higher Criticism was being taught and the Bible was said not to be divinely inspired. He was so upset by what he discovered from these teachers in America that he nearly went out of his mind. He had to be given medical help for a month or two, but, eventually, God gave him an assurance that the Bible is the Word of God. So he came back to China from being in America. All the prizes and medals which he had been given whilst he was there, he threw into the sea. And, as soon as he got back to China, he started to preach in the open air like Wesley and Whitefield. Literally thousands and thousands went to hear him, and thousands and thousands were converted. In China and Singapore today there are very many Christians, and it is very much down to the influence of this dearly beloved man. He saw revival and he died in 1944. Maurice said, 'Oh, wouldn't it be good to see somebody like that being raised up again.'

Books and Preachers

The writings of Dr Martyn Lloyd-Jones have profoundly influenced him. He had the greatest respect for him and thinks he was nothing less than a genius. He loves the books the Banner of Truth have produced, both Puritan and Reformed, and the excellent sermons of Whitefield and Spurgeon. He has read these books over the years. At a slightly different and more technical level he has studied the Westminster Shorter Catechism, the Larger Catechism, and the Confession of Faith. In his circles they often read these books again and again because they give wonderful, well-defined doctrine, which is good for the mind, good for the soul and good for life. One thing he gets out of these books is the importance of the Ten Commandments, and is afraid that a lot of evangelical churches have lost the sense of the importance of the Ten Commandments. While we are saved by faith alone in Christ alone, we honour God by keeping the commandments as carefully as we can.

This is what Christ teaches in the Sermon on the Mount: *'Think not that I am come to destroy the law'* (Matthew 5:17). We are not saved by our good works. But when we are saved our duty as believers is to keep God's Moral Law. Not all professing Christians believe this. But our peace in heaven will be related to our obedience to God's Moral Law (Matthew 5:19).

The State of the Church and the Need of the Hour

He does not know the state of the church in England as well as he does the state of the church in Scotland. He believes the Scottish churches have, sadly, undergone a terrible decline. There are very many female ministers in the Church of Scotland today. He is, however, delighted to know that the Presbyterian Church of England and Wales is now growing and that they have a seminary in Newcastle where they are teaching the Westminster Confession doctrine, and there are many young men training for the ministry. This is very encouraging. He longs for God's Holy Spirit to be poured out upon us. That is what he prays for every day.

He is of the conviction from Romans 11, similar to Andrew Davies' (see Chapter 11), that the day will come when the Jewish nation, as a nation, will be brought back again to the Christian faith and grafted back into the church. He believes that when that happens it will result in revival to the whole world. He is encouraged because there are more and more Jews being converted in the world at this time. Mr Roberts hopes and prays that the darkness that we see in the country today is the darkness before the dawn.

Mr Roberts' high view of God and His Word came through strongly throughout the interview, as well as his longing for revival. He believes that as Christians and ministers we must do all we can to promote the Word of God. We should put the Bible back into schools, back into homes, and back into pulpits. It grieves him that in Religious Education today, children learn about different religions which are all given equal status. The Bible must be treated as the inspired, holy Word of God.

As he ended the interview, he said:

We must add nothing to the Bible, we must take nothing from it. Liberalism has been the curse of this country. We need revival and I long therefore that God will pour out His Spirit and do a great work and raise up eminent preachers like Whitefield, Wesley, Spurgeon and Lloyd-Jones. Let us all pray for this.

Chapter 15

Mike Mellor

Introduction

Nearly all of the men we interviewed for this series were over 75. Mike Mellor is one of the three who were not. But when we had the idea for this series, my son said to me, 'Dad, you've got to get Mike Mellor.' Jack is one of his biggest fans, and so am I. He was my chaplain when I went on EMW camps thirty-five years ago and it is now my privilege to serve alongside him on Heath Church camps. He is so winsome and the way he lives out his faith is so attractive. He has written several excellent books. One in particular worth mentioning is *Preaching the Heart of God*, published by Day One. It is a book about the importance of pathos in preaching, a theme that has come up time and again throughout these interviews.

Background

Mike was not from a Christian home. His mother came from Liverpool but originally the family were from southern Ireland. His grandfather was from County Cork. He was an Orange man but Mike doesn't know if he really knew what it meant. Like many families, they made the trip from Ireland to Liverpool, and they lived in Anfield. Even though his parents were not Christians, they were good parents; very caring and loving. Mike's father was a professional musician, as his father was, and his father before him; they were all string players, generations and generations of string players. His dad played the violin and double bass and played in various orchestras, including the prestigious orchestra on the Queen Mary which took the rich and famous backwards and forwards from New York to Southampton.

Chapter 15

Mike was born in Liverpool in 1948, in Mill Road Hospital. During the war, Hitler really gave a peppering to Liverpool and the Mill Road Hospital was bombed, including the maternity ward, and mothers and their babies were killed. Mike does not remember much about Liverpool because his father got a job as a musician in Bournemouth when Mike was very young, and so the whole family moved down to Bournemouth. He has a sister who was born in Warrington.

Mike had a happy childhood and would never have imagined that by his mid-twenties he would have become an alcoholic. There was no indication of that. He was a happy child, loved playing football and loved music. He learned to play the trombone at school and played in the band and the orchestra. He was not too motivated academically and loved school for all the wrong reasons.

When it was time to leave, he didn't know what he was going to do. He had no qualifications but a friend of his got a job on the *Bournemouth Echo* and asked Mike if he fancied a job there as an office boy. So that is what Mike did. He started at the very bottom, making the tea and posting letters, but he did it well and was promoted. As time went by he got a very good job at the paper with excellent pay and a car thrown in as well. He had freedom to do what he liked, but looking back that was where the trouble really started.

Addiction

His boss was a heavy drinker and there were a lot of other heavy drinkers on the newspaper. Mike was invited to join them. There were no signs of trouble in the early days, but he started drinking more frequently, then going every day to the pub, but again all seemingly under control; you do not become an alcoholic overnight and Mike did not think it was a problem.

Then musically, Mike was offered a job as a trombone player in a big band in the area. He thought it was great as he got paid even more money and there were bars and there were breaks, and so he started to drink there. It was at this point he met a very attractive girl vocalist called Gwen. Things took their course and they ended up getting married, settling down and having a family.

The problem was, he didn't settle down. He just began to get more and more into drinking and gravitating to the company of heavy drinkers, both on the newspaper and in the music business. He was now in his mid-twenties and knew that he had a problem. He just wanted to be in that state all the time. Things were getting tense at home. He was becoming an irresponsible husband and father.

As he looks back over his life he can see turning points, and one was when musically he and Gwen went their separate ways, she went to sing in the pavilion ballroom in Bournemouth and he started doing freelance trombone playing in theatres and on the *QE2*, and drinking more and more heavily.

Everyone could see that it was getting worse. He was falling into the car paralytic almost every day and just letting people down all the time. By his late twenties things went from bad to worse. Alcohol had taken a hold of him. Every day was a drunken spree and he lost his licence for drunk driving. The police took his licence from him, and even his own newspaper printed the headlines, 'Newspaper man three-and-a-half times over the limit'. He remembers when he got his licence back telling himself he must be good now, he must not start drinking and driving again, but he couldn't help himself and within months he was back falling into the car day and night, and it was chaos at home. It wasn't that he didn't love his wife and children, it was just that he was in the grip of an addiction, being controlled and taken over. People would say, 'Well, why doesn't he change? What's wrong with him?' But there was this threefold grip: he loved the flavour of drink, he loved being drunk and he loved being with hooligan drunkards. As Mike looks back, he thinks, 'Poor Gwen'. She would tell him to go to Alcoholics Anonymous but he would say back to her, 'They'll tell me to stop drinking, won't they? Well, I can't and don't want to.'

By the time he was thirty years old, things were getting really bad. He went on a three-day drinking spree and on the third day he did the usual thing of falling into the car and started weaving his way home. He hit a parked car and thought he dare not stop as the police would get him again, and then he hit another car. When he got home, he knew that was it. He can still remember the look on Gwen's face when the phone call came through that the police were on their way around.

He remembers that in those days he would wake up every morning with this tremendous ton of weight on his chest, of hopelessness, despair, feeling he was trapped, not able to see a way out, knowing he was going to die, either suddenly in a car crash or just become a hopeless wreck. His marriage was hanging by a thread and Gwen could not take any more. Mike recalls, 'The whole of today was taken up by trying to piece yesterday together and apologising to the people I had let down. Meanwhile God was at work and I didn't know it.'

Conversion

A young man came to work at the newspaper and his desk was slotted right into the side of Mike's. He was a joyful, happy chap, and there could not have been a greater contrast between this young man and Mike. He was a Christian and had a Bible on his desk. He was a nice guy and he liked football. Mike thought, if he likes football he can't be that bad. Bit by bit Mike heard him speak about Jesus, and he would roll his eyes and think, 'Here he goes again', without really thinking that it was going in subconsciously. One of the things that went in, he realised afterwards, was that this man used to go to a Baptist Church and he was the editor of their youth magazine. He would come in every month and say, 'Mike could you just check this magazine through for spelling mistakes for me?' Mike would read it through for him, and what stuck out was a one-frame cartoon about the second coming of the Lord Jesus Christ, and that if you were not ready you would be in trouble and it would be too late. Mike remembers thinking, if this stuff is true, that was him.

On 8th September 1979, with another court case looming, it was just Mike and this young man in the office. Mike found himself unusually sober. He hadn't been drinking and found himself asking questions about this young man's faith, not expecting an answer, and not really sure why he was asking him. The man turned to Mike and asked him if he believed in God. Mike answered, 'Possibly, who knows?' He then asked Mike if he believed in Jesus Christ. Mike again said, 'Possibly'. But could not see the relevance of Him, having lived two thousand years ago and two thousand miles away. The man then said to Mike, 'Why don't you ask God to forgive your sin and come into your life and take it over?' Mike had never heard that before, but something started to stir inside him. He went out of the room to this toilet, a little cubicle, got down on his knees and prayed, 'God if you are there, please help me.' He went back to his desk and didn't tell the man that he had prayed, he was too proud and it was also time to go home. He went to his car and as he drove home he just broke down in tears of joy. He knew it was all true. He knew that God loved him. He knew that Jesus died for him and that if he crashed the car and died now, he was not going to hell but was going to heaven. He drove the car rejoicing.

When he got home, he tried to tell Gwen what had happened and that he had become a Christian. She thought, 'Oh no, what's he up to now?' She was absolutely mystified and a bit afraid. He tried for days to explain what had happened, but she couldn't understand. It was on a Saturday that he had prayed, and on the Monday the man gave him a Bible and Mike could not put it down. It explained everything that happened to him, that *'If anyone is in Christ they are a new creation, the old is gone the new has come.'* He thought, that is me! He read that Jesus said, *'You must be born again'*, and Mike thought, 'I've been born again.' But as he tried to explain it to Gwen, she got more and more annoyed, especially when he told her that she needed to be a Christian or she would go to hell. She had been holding the family together all this time, but it goes to show how amazing grace is, she's now the sinner and Mike is the saint.

Mike started to go to church, to Moordown Baptist Church. Peter Williams was the minister. He was a Congregational minister but Dr Martyn Lloyd-Jones advised him to leave the Richmond Hill Congregational Church which was liberal and go to Moordown. The first service Mike went to was a baptismal service which he thought was a bit strange, but felt he belonged there.

Gwen was getting more and more agitated because he was still leaving her out. He left her out before as a drunkard. Now he had this Christian faith and it felt like he was leaving her out again. She said, 'Mike, what are you doing? You went to church last week.' To which he replied, 'Well, Christians do that, they go every week and go to prayer meetings.' She could see something supernatural had happened to Mike, but it worried her. Is it voodoo? Is it black magic? There were arguments all the time and tension was building.

Gwen was still singing in the pavilion ballroom and one night when she was in the bar with the rest of the band the topic of conversation was Mike. He had been infamous for his lifestyle and so they started asking her what had happened to him—had he become one of those religious nutters? Even though Gwen would argue with Mike about it all, she said, 'I don't know what's happened, but it's great. He's become the husband I always wanted. He is coming home for his meals and he is kind to the children.' One of the men in the bar said, 'If you ask me, Gwen, you'll become one of those Christians and he'll become a minister,' at which point they all roared with laughter.

Like Mike, Gwen had no upbringing at all in the church apart from when as a girl she went for six weeks to a Sunday School where they taught the life of the apostle Peter and gave an exam at the end of it. But as she was driving home late that night, it was as though the Lord said to her, 'Gwen, why are you denying me?' and she thought to herself, 'Why am I fighting this?' It was now three months after Mike's conversion and she got on her knees and asked the Lord to save her. She knew the same joy and peace that Mike knew, and from that moment on Mike could do nothing apart from talk about the Lord Jesus.

The Call

Nine months later, Mike still really could not get enough of the Bible. He was reading it from cover to cover. He got to the Psalms and Psalm 61, but instead of turning to Psalm 61 he turned to Isaiah 61 by mistake. *'The Spirit of the Lord is upon me because he has anointed me to preach good news to the poor.'* It just struck him. He thought, 'Is God calling me to preach?' He pushed it aside and tried to forget all about it, but it began to grow and to grow and to grow.

It was 1980 and he was doing summer season at the Winter Gardens, a large theatre in Bournemouth. The band was on stage and Mike could see these thousands of people coming in night after night, and he looked at them all, wondering who was going to tell them about Jesus. Between shows, instead of going to the bar, he went, with his dinner jacket and bow tie on, up on the West Cliff in Bournemouth to give out tracks before getting back for the second show.

He was reading a book at the time and the writer asked, 'Who will be willing to obey the Holy Spirit and do whatever God wants him to do?' It hit Mike like a rock and he could hardly play the second show or even hold his trombone. It was as though God was saying to him to leave everything and go.

When he got home at about 11 pm, he phoned his pastor, Peter Williams, and asked him could he go and see him and talk to him about the fact he felt God was calling him. He tried to put Mike off at first, but he could see that this was of God. Mike could not stop speaking about the Lord Jesus and the burden continued to grow. He came home from a show one night and said to Gwen, who was just beginning to think things were settling down, that they had to be ready to go wherever God took them.

Training

Although he had been accepted to go to a local Bible College, he felt more and more uneasy about it. Reading *Evangelical Times* one day he saw an advert and it said South Wales Bible College. What really caught his eye was that it said, 'Abundant preaching opportunities'. Even though he didn't know where it was or what it was about, he thought, 'That's the place for me!'

When we interviewed Mike on 6th June 2021, it was forty years ago that week that he set off to South Wales with Gwen and, at the time, three girls (they had another daughter later). They did not know what lay ahead, only that God had called them on this tremendous adventure.

Mike loved his time at the South Wales Bible College. John Waite was the principal and John Cook and Noel Gibbard made up the faculty there. He thinks that if he had been a more mature Christian he would have benefited a lot more, but is so grateful for that time and says, 'Over the three years they did their best with me.'

Ministry

Over the last forty years Mike has had a varied ministry. It was in the final months at Barry that he got a call to a Baptist church in the South Wales valleys, Glandwr Baptist Church, in Aberbeeg. He was there for five years from 1984 to 1989.

After that, he became the pastor of Litchard Mission in Bridgend, from 1989 to 1993. They had five happy years there, but God began to stir him to do something different.

The man who had witnessed to Mike in the office was Paul Pease, who was also called to the ministry and ordained at the same time as Mike. He is the pastor at Hook Evangelical Church and they have kept in touch. Paul was on the committee of the London In-reach Project who were church planting in the West End of London. Michael Toogood was in Soho, but they had now set their sights on Covent Garden. Mike felt God was moving him on from Bridgend, and on the very day that he was going to have a word with the elders, a phone call came from London. It was Paul who said, 'Mike, you're not thinking of moving on anytime are you?'

Mike knew that Gwen was terrified of London and it was the last place she wanted to live, but God was calling them to go there and they ended up in Covent Garden, spending eight years, from 1993 to 2002, church planting. It was a tremendous opportunity. Mike loved the west end of London, the buzz of it, the cut and thrust; but after eight years they thought their work was done there and Mike felt he should give himself fully to evangelism.

He got in touch with the Open-Air Mission who said they had a vacancy for an evangelist. From 2001 to 2008 he spent seven tremendous years just being able to focus on evangelism.

In 2008 he felt God was calling him back into more church-based ministry and he received a call to Moordown Baptist Church. They were about to do a church plant in a place called Ferndown and Mike became the pastor there from 2008 until 2015. Mike retired in 2015 but is still an elder at the church and engaged in itinerant preaching and evangelism.

God's Providence and God's Provision

Mike said that he has never known a particular season of blessing but has known really obvious interventions of God, peppered throughout the years. He can break it down into two 'Ps': God's providence and God's provision.

The greatest thrill for him over the years has been to see God at work in someone's life, to see evidence of the Holy Spirit at work. One of the books he has written is called *The Pursuit: the Work of the Holy Spirit in Evangelism*. It is about how the Holy Spirit works in people's lives, which has thrilled Mike over the years. Sometime Mike has seen this in people coming to faith; other times he has felt like a link in the chain. It is all God's work, the sovereign work of the Spirit, who lovingly pursues people through men and women, not just through preachers. Jesus, the good shepherd, seeking the wanderers.

He remembers the first time that he was conscious of this real leading of God to talk to people about the gospel. When he was in Bible College, the students would be sent out to preach each Sunday. On one particular Sunday he was in the Rhondda and it was awful. He preached in a dying chapel. As he got there one of the deacons was putting out his cigarette and then rushed to switch on the lights and then the chapel goers turned up for their Sunday night out. It did not matter if the preacher preached on the glories of heaven or the terrors of hell. They would just say at the door, 'Nice service'. Mike got out of there feeling quite depressed having preached to people who did not want to know. But as he was driving home in his little car through Porth, he looked up at the side and on the hillside he thought it was a mirage. He saw this long line of young people, about fifty metres long, all queuing up to go to a nightclub. He felt God prompting him to go back and preach to them. Mike says he is a born coward, so he thought, 'Oh no, I can't do that,' and carried on down the road. But the Holy Spirit wouldn't let him. He got two miles down the road, stopped the car, turned it around, drove back and parked the car. He could see the crowd in the distance and he could feel his mouth drying and his heart beating. He got out of his car, wearing his reformed outfit: black suit, white shirt, black tie and Bible in his hand. He got near the crowd and could hear their sarcastic comments, but once he started to speak he had liberty and there was a good response. He had a pocket full of tracts which he gave out. He has no idea what the result was but sensed that God was at work and maybe one day in heaven he will meet some people who were in the queue that night in Porth.

At his first church in Aberbeeg he had the greatest battles but also the greatest blessing. He recalls once taking a funeral on a particularly dark, stormy day on the Welsh hillside. He didn't know the person who died, but attending the funeral was a couple who were in the cabaret business. From then on they started to come to church and God saved them and called them into the ministry. There were many things like that, but the blessings were always side by side with the discouragements.

When Mike was church planting in Covent Garden, before they had their nice new building, they were in an old smelly London City Mission hall which been a base for homeless people. It stank badly and was dark and dingy. They started with a small number of people and a man started coming to all the meetings. His face was badly scarred and he had a black patch over his eye. Mike spoke to him and said it was nice to see him. His name was James and Mike asked how he knew that they met there. He had received a leaflet about their Christmas service, but now it was Easter, so it had taken him quite a while to actually come. It turned out he was a playwright, his wife had left because of his addictions and he had tried to kill himself. He had put his head in the gas oven but it had gone terribly wrong and was so depressed that he couldn't even kill himself! Mike gave him a Bible and he devoured it. He kept coming back for more, and some weeks later Mike asked him how he was getting on reading the Bible—was he understanding the message of it, that he needed to come to Jesus Christ, to repent and be saved? He said, 'I do, I do.' They both got down on their knees in this smelly place and, according to Mike, 'Something of glory came down.' He prayed this lovely broken prayer of repentance. Mike opened his eyes and there was a tear trickling down his patch and he thought, 'Well, this is what it's about.' Mike could give many similar examples and also had several opportunities to speak to Peter Stringfellow, the playboy nightclub owner.

As well as God's providence, he has known God's provision throughout the years. When they set out for South Wales in their car, God gave him as a verse, Psalm 37:25, *'Commit thy way unto the LORD; trust also in Him; And He shall bring it to pass.'* As an old man looking back over his life, Mike has never seen the righteous forsaken or their children begging for bread. God has provided for them right the way through the years, just when they needed it. It has been a struggle, still is, but always God has provided for them—sometimes in amazing ways.

They could not get a house in Covent Garden when they first went to London and they had to live out in Finchley. He had to get the tube in every day and it was hard work church planting at a distance, one man and his bag full of tracts and booklets. They prayed about it as a committee that God would provide. They organised a day of prayer. As they started to pray, Peter Jermyn, who was the treasurer, interrupted and said, 'Brothers, can I just share something with you? We've come here to pray, but God has already answered our prayers and I've had this cheque.' Someone had sent in a cheque which meant that the committee could buy a house in Covent Garden. It is still there today, a three-bedroom cottage right in the heart of Covent Garden, off Drury Lane.

Advice

When we asked Mike what advice he would give to the young Mike Mellor, he said, 'Oh boy, wouldn't I say a few things to him!' To a young Mike Mellor and all young ministers he would say to be yourself. As a young preacher you obviously have role models and people you seek to emulate, but you are still you. Mike thinks it takes a while to find out who you are and have the courage to be who you are without looking over your shoulder. Even being part of this series with these other men, there was a temptation to be someone that you are not. Mike believes you have to develop your own preaching style and your own way of relating to people. He says, 'You must be spiritual in your natural life and natural in your spiritual life.'

He also thinks it is important to be patient. He can be very impatient and impulsive, but people need time to change. You cannot just preach one sermon and think, 'They've got it now.' We must be prepared for disappointments. The Christian life is a battle, and being a minister certainly is. You have to be called, otherwise you will not stick at it, and you must be convinced that God has put you in the ministry. Then it does not matter if men and devils are against you—and they will be.

He has known times of oppression, especially when he was in the Welsh valleys. It was a very dark place and probably still is. It is why he wrote another of his books, *Ice and Fire*. It is a book about the battle of the Christian life. We must be aware of the warfare we are involved in. The Christian life is not a game, there is cosmic warfare going on, and so we have to be prepared for disappointments. It was Adoniram Judson who spoke about how suffering and success are bound up together. He said that if you are succeeding without suffering it is because others before you have suffered. If you are suffering it is because others after you will succeed. Young ministers must brace themselves that it is going to be tough, and to be ready to fight their battles, but to be patient, loving, kind, always remembering it is God's work and that He will fight their battles. We do not need to defend ourselves or be defensive.

As he looks back, he has noticed that if God gives him an encouragement, he graciously will send a discouragement. He has had enough encouragement to keep him going and enough discouragements to keep him humble. The blessings are in the battle.

Books and People

Paul Pease is one person who has obviously had a huge impact on Mike's life. He first shared the gospel with him and was like a little pastor at his side when they were at *The Echo* together for all those months before God called them both into the ministry.

The ministry of Peter Williams, who was his pastor when he first went to his church, had a big influence on him. By listening to him week in, week out, he knew what preaching was from the word go. It was consistent, passionate preaching, and he was also a great pastor, especially when Mike was being called to the ministry. He got him to read *A Body of Divinity* by Thomas Watson, which is based on the Shorter Westminster Catechism, and he got Mike to write out the answers to it in his own words, which he did—but doesn't think Thomas Watson would have felt threatened in any way! It was not only Peter Williams, but also his wife, Brenda: they were such a godly couple and a great support. He can see, time and again, God's hand providentially upon his life.

Mike did not read much before he was converted, so when he became a Christian, all of a sudden a whole new world opened up to him with the Bible as well as a raft of Christian literature. He couldn't get enough of books and there have been so many that have helped him. *The Attributes of God* by A.W. Pink, *A Body of Divinity*, that he has already mentioned, *Passion for Souls* by Oswald J. Smith, *With Christ in the School of Prayer* by Andrew Murray, *Power through Prayer* by E.M. Bounds, *Knowing God* by J.I. Packer, *Preaching and Preachers* by Martyn Lloyd-Jones. Then a whole raft of biographies: Wesley, Whitefield, Jim Elliot, C.T. Studd, George Müller, Hudson Taylor … the list of goes on and on.

The early years of being a Christian are so foundational, and in God's providence these men and books came into his life. He was thankful for the start he had in the Christian life and how, providentially, he did not have to battle with liberalism like so many men had to.

The State of the Church Today and the Need of the Hour

Mike doesn't think that any of us fully knows the state of the church and believes our view of the church is too small. He thinks there are things to be encouraged about it, and what personally encourages him is the number of church plants and revitalisations that are going on. At the time of interview he was praying for two church plants, one in Brighton and another in Morecambe.

He is always encouraged that God can bless people we would not want to bless, and thinks we need to be more large-hearted and rejoice wherever we see God at work. We can get overwhelmed by the state of our nation today and almost think, 'Poor God, what is he going to do?' But according to Mike:

Our greatest danger as a church is not the power of the LGBT movement or transgenderism or the battle for freedom of speech: the greatest problem is we are losing sight of the greatness of God and His power to break in at any time. It is important to read church history, to read about the revivals of the past, not for nostalgia's sake, but to realise, this is our God. I mean, God could break into individual lives like mine and yours, and He can break into this nation again; so keep going, wherever you are serving God, as a Christian, as a preacher; just keep going and expect God to break in.

Chapter 16

Iain H. Murray

Introduction

Mr Murray was the oldest of all the ministers we interviewed and celebrated his 90th birthday just before we spoke to him. It was commemorated in the May 2021 edition of The Banner of Truth magazine. He founded the Banner of Truth from which many thousands of Christians have benefited enormously. When I was in university, one of my favourite times of the year was the Banner of Truth student sale, and we had a saying, '*The Truth, the Whole Truth and nothing but the Banner of Truth*'. Before interviewing Mr Murray I had just read his two biographies on Dr Martyn Lloyd-Jones. The first one is called *The First Forty Years* and the second one *The Fight of Faith*. I can honestly say I have never read two better biographical or historical books than those two. Being Welsh, growing up, all I heard about was Dr Martyn Lloyd-Jones, and there were times when I thought, 'Oh no, not more Dr Martyn Lloyd-Jones!' But after reading these books I can see why people talk about him so much. He was an absolute giant of the faith and I found both books, particularly the first one, so stirring. They are must-reads, as are his sermons on Romans and Ephesians, *Studies in the Sermon of the Mount* and *Spiritual Depression*.

Overview

Iain Murray was born in Liverpool in 1931 and since then has lived in five different countries. For the first forty years of his life, with some interruptions, he lived in England. One of those interruptions came when he and his sister were evacuated to Caernarfon during the time of the heavy bombing of Liverpool in the Second World War. The school he attended in Caernarfon went by the very distinguished name of 'Miss

Tompkins Private Academy'. He doesn't think he was a great credit to Miss Tompkins, but he remembers those days in Caernarfon with pleasure, and after that he did somewhat better at school.

Another interruption to living in England came when he went to the Isle of Man from 1945 to 1949 for school. In the school holidays he would return home to the Wirral. After finishing school, like all young people at the time, he was enlisted for National Service. It was a wonderful experience that took him to the jungle of Malaysia with the Cameronians from 1950 to 1951. He then returned home to England to university. He remained in England until 1972, at which point he went to Edinburgh in Scotland for ten years. In 1981 he went to Australia for approximately ten years before returning to Edinburgh in 1991 where he has lived ever since, combined with a number of overseas experiences.

Calling

He believes his calling had a twofold part to it. The first part, and the most important part in many ways, was the work of the pastorate. He began as an assistant in Oxford and then in London at Westminster Chapel. He then served a church in South London, Grove Chapel, Camberwell, and finally in South Sydney, in Australia.

The other part of his calling has been connected with teaching by means of publishing and writing. He did not find it easy to combine these two roles. If anyone asks him the part he enjoyed the most, it is the first part, but he is convinced that books have a large part to play in the growth of the kingdom of God and so it has been his privilege to have a share in that.

Conversion

Mr Murray was clear that nothing good he has done, and that is lasting, originated with himself. It is a wonderful truth that it is God that *'worketh in us both to will and to do of His good pleasure'*. All good things are from His hand and, the truth is, we cannot draw a line between actions that spring from ourselves and those which come from God's guidance in us, and that is what makes it serious when we talk about our lives. The apostle says, *'Judge nothing before the time, until the Lord comes'*, because on the Day of Judgement there will be those who engaged in Christian work, and perhaps what we thought were precious stones, will be wood hay and stubble, and that is a very sobering thought.

For seventeen years he did not know that he was not a Christian. He was born in what is known as a Christian home, and in a sense it was. His father was a godly, praying man and an elder in the Presbyterian church. They had Christian books in the home and they were at church twice every Sunday. But as he grew up his religion was all external and the internal part was not a pretty sight. It was self-serving, self-pleasing, self-satisfied and wanting people to think well of him. He set out to be proud of himself, but in God's mercy the opposite happened. He got a sense of real despair. Slowly he came to see that it wasn't simply actions that are wrong and sinful, it is much worse than that: we have a fallen nature and we need saving from ourselves. We all must be saved because we have an evil heart and a bad nature.

When he was 17 years old, his sister, who is two years older than him, had some friends who told her about Hildenborough Hall in Kent, which was a centre started by Tom and Jean Rees after the Second World War, with the objective of reaching young people. In 1948, Iain found himself there and at the end of the week he was like the man in John 9:

I could begin to say, *'One thing I know, whereas I was blind, now I can see,'* and the thing that amazed me was that the truth I had heard and I suppose read, suddenly came to life with meaning. I had heard about the death of Christ, but I had no idea that meant that He died in the place of sinners, that He died as a substitute. He died, *'the just for the unjust, that He might bring us to God'*. I remember saying to the first Christian who pointed it out to me, 'Is that really in the New Testament?' 'Oh yes,' he said, 'it is!' What a wonderful thing it is. We can sing hymns such as *'There is a green hill far away'*, and we can still be blind to the fact that everything in salvation depends on Christ acting for us.

The New Birth

In our interview, Mr Murray stressed the importance of the new birth and regeneration. While some people can remember the particular date of their conversion, although the date of conversion may be helpful, it is not the most important thing to be known. The most important thing is the new birth by the Holy Spirit. The new birth is the beginning, there's no question about that. The Bible says, *'the natural man receiveth not the things of the Spirit of God, neither indeed can he'*. So how do people receive the Spirit of God? The apostle John says, *'not by blood, not by the will of the flesh, not by the will of man, but born of God'*, which means that something marvellous and hidden happens to us before we are actually aware of what is happening; something happens that makes a natural man desire spiritual things. The Lord Jesus describes it in John 3 through the ignorance of Nicodemus. This teacher in Israel did not know that that which is born of the flesh, that of the unregenerate man, is flesh, but that which is born of the Spirit, is Spirit. A decision for Christ is not enough to make a Christian, and Iain stressed the importance of this truth. The Lord tells us plainly that when the sower goes to throw out seed to sow (maybe a good orthodox preacher), the seed is sown, and when they have heard, the Lord says immediately there are some who receive it with gladness but it does not last because the heart has not been changed. The ground is stony and the roots of the seed do not get into the soil. This is where regeneration comes in. We read of Lydia, *'whose heart the Lord opened'*. Our stony heart is taken away and a heart of flesh is given. It is a great mystery; *'the wind blows where it listeth'*. We very often cannot put a date on that. It may be almost simultaneous with our conscious conversion, but it may not. We do not know. But we do know that at a real saving conversion there is not only a decision for Christ, there are a new nature, new ambitions, new desires, a new life: *'old things have passed away, behold all things become new'*. Before we are converted we have to be born again, and God has to do something to turn us and to humble us and to prepare us for that.

Meeting Jean Walters

Iain went back to Hildenborough Hall the following year, in August 1949, for a week. At the end of the week, Friday 27th August, he was due to go home the next day, but Jean Rees heard that he had no commitments in the following weeks and suggested to him that he might like to stay on for a month. He later discovered she did that with a number of young men, and the purpose was of course to get some help with hosting, but more importantly she had her eye on helping young men who might be of help to others in years to come. The first year that Iain went to Hildenborough Hall, Eric Alexander was there the same week, and he was another that Jean Rees had her eye on helping.

Iain agreed to stay for a month and the next day was 28th August. It is an important date in his life because one of his first duties was to welcome newcomers at the door. Hildenborough Hall was a beautiful mansion country house in the countryside of Kent. Iain was there to welcome the young people as they were dropped off by the coaches. He opened the door of a coach and helped a young lady down and offered to take her case. She gave it to him and he took her up and showed her to her room. He was thinking he had done quite well. When he came back down to the front door to continue, Jean Rees quietly got hold of him and said, 'Iain, you look after the boys, please, and we'll welcome the girls.' But, as Iain remembers it now:

If I was briefly out of order, it was worthwhile because it was an example of how marriages are made in heaven. A lifetime of happiness followed carrying that one case. Six children were born from it. We've been happily, wonderfully married for 66 years [she was only a few feet away from him during our interview]. Next to our conversion, if God calls us to be married, then to whom we are married is the most important thing in our lives.

The Banner of Truth

Sydney Norton

1955 was a real turning point in Iain's life. His experience of guidance is that sometimes when we are proceeding and thinking of going ahead, God shuts doors. Other times we are left, as it seems, to our own decisions and we have to make a choice between alternatives, and that is what happened to him in 1955. He had been accepted for the ministry as a candidate for the English Presbyterian Church a few years earlier on the understanding that after he had finished at Durham University he was to go to their College in Cambridge. By the time 1955 came, he was convinced that this denomination was not where he was meant to serve, but he didn't know where he should go. For some months he and his fiancée at the time were exercised about it, particularly because for a few years they had been looking forward to getting married and had decided they were not going to wait any longer.

In the mercy of God a door opened in a small church in Oxford. The minister was a man called Sydney Norton. He had been a bandsman in the Royal Marines and was converted in the South China Sea in the 1930s and called into the ministry. He had three great characteristics. Firstly, he was a man of real prayer; secondly, he had a strong attachment to the doctrines of grace and he saw quite clearly that his own life had been intervened by God Himself; thirdly, he was a great lover of books: he enlarged Iain's knowledge of books and helped him.

In their first months they often prayed together and talked together. They shared a conviction that there were great books that needed to be reprinted. Out of that came their expedition up to London with the purpose of finding out what it would cost to buy a printing press and to start some publishing work. They discovered very quickly how little they knew about printing or publishing and had no idea of the costs involved. They went back to Oxford rather subdued, but God continued to give them faith that something could, and should, be done.

They started a little magazine in September of 1955 and Mr Norton gave the name to the magazine, *The Banner of Truth*. He got the name from Psalm 60: '*Thou hast given a banner to them that fear thee, that it may be displayed because of the truth.*' Mr Murray did most of putting together the twenty pages, but their friendship was all of God in enabling the beginning of *The Banner of Truth*.

They did not ask people to subscribe to it because, the simple truth was, they did not have the money to print a second issue. The first issue was the result of £40 that Mr Norton was given. A second edition would come a few months later, thanks to £20 from Westminster Chapel and £20 from dear friends in Swansea. £40 was enough to produce a magazine in those days!

Jack Cullum

Two years before, in 1953, a middle-aged businessman called Jack Cullum was crossing the Atlantic on the *Queen Elizabeth*. In God's providence, in the restaurant he sat next to Stanley Clark and his wife, who were Christians. They sensed that they had been led to a needy soul and gave Jack Cullum a New Testament and they spoke to him of our Lord, and the Lord used it to begin an opening in his heart.

Jack Cullum had some Methodist and some Congregational roots and had gone to the Congregational school, Mill Hill, many years before. So when he got back to his home in Highgate, he took himself to Highgate Central Hall Methodist Church where the minister was the Reverend Joe Blinco. He was an affectionate, warm-hearted Christian, and as an illustration of what a humble man he was, when he talked with Jack Cullum, God seemed to give him a sense that Jack's conversion could lead to repercussions perhaps far and wide. So he told the visitor, instead of retaining him as he would love to do, that he should go to Westminster Chapel.

When Jack Callum got to Westminster Chapel he soaked up the preaching and everything else that was available at Westminster Chapel.

All the while, back in Oxford, Iain and Sydney Norton still had no money for publishing, neither did the Murrays really have any money to live on because the church in Oxford was so small and just couldn't provide a salary, only a very suitable accommodation for Iain and his wife. They had a wonderful time there until after a year, their savings almost exhausted, they were getting near the penniless condition.

At which point, Dr Lloyd-Jones invited Iain to go to Westminster Chapel to assist him. Iain thinks it really meant Lloyd-Jones assisting *him*, but the Doctor put it the other way around. When Iain asked him what help he could give, he was pointed to the need for addresses on church history. Iain scarcely knew Dr Lloyd-Jones before he went to Oxford. It was when the latter heard that Iain was going there, that he urged him to study the English Reformers and encouraged him to find out how the reformation happened and particularly, he told him, to write something about the Calvinism of the English Reformers.

So Iain arrived at Westminster Chapel and gave some addresses on church history. Sat there, listening to Iain, and all ears, was Jack Cullum. After a few weeks he came to Iain and said, 'Why is it that not everyone knows these wonderful things?' He was thinking of men like Hugh Latimer and William Tyndale giving their lives for the gospel; Hugh Latimer at the stake saying to his companion, 'Play the man, play the man, Master Ridley, be of good comfort, we shall by God's grace this day light such a candle as I trust will never be put out.' Jack was thrilled with these truths and asked why people were not reading about these things in books. Iain told him it was because many of the best books were not available.

Jack Cullum thought he had wasted his life thus far and had prayed, 'What am I to do, Lord?' Various people had suggested ways he could use his wealth, but God put it in his heart to make the republishing of Christian books his primary concern.

So that is how the Banner of Truth started at Westminster Chapel, London, in 1957 with Jack Cullum and Iain Murray as the founding trustees. Primarily, fundamentally and ultimately, it was the providence and sovereignty of God.

Advice

Iain Murray is sure that the most important thing for young pastors to learn is that the risen Lord Jesus Christ is the one on whom the work of the church depends. It is His work. He has His servants here for a little while, they come on the stage and have their entrance and their exit. But it is all under the Lord. This is a great liberating thought for men who are concerned that the work is too hard. It is too hard for everyone. It was too hard for the apostle Paul. He says, *'Who is sufficient for these things?'* But faith in the risen Christ is the transforming difference. There are degrees of faith and it is by the Spirit of God that faith is strengthened in answer to prayer. In revival, man is filled with faith and the Holy Spirit transforms preaching. That is how Latimer and Tyndale did the work they did, along with those in the 'hall of faith' in Hebrews 11: *'Through faith, they subdued kingdoms, wrought righteousness and obtained promises.'*

Iain believes that God encourages us by giving us special help from time to time. This has been his experience on several occasions.

In Malaya in Singapore a missionary helped him enormously by giving him a book. It was the life of Robert Murray M'Cheyne and that led him to seek more such works. When he went to university in Durham in 1951, after being there a few months he met a lady in the town who was the daughter of James Shiphardson, a Methodist minister who had died in 1927. In her home was a fine library which had been shut since that date as she did not know what to do with it. Her father was a faithful preacher with a very good library, and his old study was now opened for students who would value the works of Jonathan Edwards, George Whitefield and the best evangelicals. It was a wonderful providence of God. There have been other situations that Iain has found himself in where there has been a rich heritage of books. Grove Chapel had the best library that he had ever seen in any church in England and which had been safely preserved down through the years.

But what Iain would put at the top of his list of advice for younger men is to believe that present usefulness is not the great and ultimate thing that God is working for. Present usefulness in the ministry is much to be desired, but we go wrong if we think that the immediate is the main thing. *God is preparing a people for glory. To that end, all things, including trials, disappointments and hard days are working for closer resemblance to Christ.* That is the prospect with which pastors are to live. It is not the present moment that is all-important. God has a long-term purpose.

Books

The first book that Iain recommended was the *Westminster Shorter Catechism*, which he thinks is wonderful. One hundred and seven questions like, *'What is prayer?'* and the answer it gives: *'Prayer is the offering up of our desires to God for things agreeable to His will through Jesus Christ'.*

The second book was Andrew Bonar's, *The Life of Robert Murray M'Cheyne*. After that, there were so many books that he loves, that he found it too difficult to narrow it down to give a third.

However, when asked what his favourite book that he has written was, he said it has often been the last book he wrote because, in his own words:

In order to write a book you have to live it and get into it and live with the author, and doing that is a happy experience. This experience will remain uppermost for a time after. Books that will change the lives of others have to help our own first.

The Need of the Hour

On the state of the church today, the great thing to know and to believe is that God is doing exactly what he purposes to do.

We are not in a situation of defeat, God is not puzzled about what to do with Britain or any other country. Christ is building His church. The purpose of God is certain. Now sometimes that has a solemn side, as presently what is happening in Britain. We are being brought low, we need to believe we have sinned with a high hand. But the church is not Britain. The church is something different, and when we talk about the different churches there is a vast variation. Some churches have shut, and sometimes that is well. Other churches are being helped, and so it is a very diverse picture, and it is the same across the world. But in every part of the world God is doing what He means to do and we can be thankful.

To know God better will make us more humble. '*The more thy glories strike my eyes, the humbler I shall lie*' (Isaac Watts). Knowing God brings truer knowledge of ourselves. When someone asked Lloyd-Jones if revival is near, he thought not, 'because we are too healthy'; we are coping, very busy in all our activities, imagining all is in our hands. We need more of Scripture and more of God's presence to learn we are poor and needy sinners. That is the path to true riches.

Chapter 17

Philip Eveson

Introduction

Philip Eveson has written many books, including commentaries on Genesis, Leviticus, Chronicles and the Psalms, all of which have received excellent reviews. He has also written books on Matthew Henry and Dr Martyn Lloyd-Jones, and a great book about *When God came to North Wales.* He was the principal of the London Theological Seminary (LTS) and also the minister of Kensit Evangelical Church in Finchley. He lectured my brother-in-law and my nephew, both of whom said he was one of their favourite lecturers.

Background

He was born in a little village called Caego, near Wrexham on the Brymbo Road. His wife, Jenny, also comes from North Wales, from Connah's Quay, but they met at university in Bangor. Since retiring, they have moved from north London back to Wrexham. They live within walking distance of their church, Borras Park Evangelical Church, where Mark Thomas and Sam Oldridge faithfully minister the Word and are caring pastors. They have a loving church and their only child, Ruth, together with her husband Andrew and Philip's four grandchildren, live close by and attend the same church. He feels wonderfully blessed and can say with the Psalmist, '*The lines have fallen to us in pleasant places.*' Throughout his entire life, he has been very aware of the unseen Sovereign Protector who has graciously led him and kept him all down through the years.

He was born into a Christian home and was an only child. His father was a blacksmith with the county council roads and bridges department in Wrexham, and latterly, before he retired, was Transport and General Workers Union shop steward. He had been a local parish councillor and a school manager and was also a keen violinist. He tried to teach Philip the violin but not very successfully! His mother had been in domestic service and was from a very Welsh-speaking home.

His parents were members of Trinity Presbyterian Church of Wales, Wrexham where in those days, D. O. Calvin Thomas exercised an influential ministry in the town. Philip was baptised by him and the church became his second home: from a young boy it was three times on a Sunday as well as midweek meetings. His mother prayed with him each night at his bedside, while his dad got him to learn verses from the Bible each Sunday. It started with the ones that he was teaching his Sunday School class, like John 3:16, Romans 1:16 and Romans 3:22–23, and so on. Although Philip sometimes objected, he is very grateful to him for making him learn the key gospel verses and chapters of the Bible. By the time he was thirteen years old he could recite Isaiah 53 and so many of the great passages of the New Testament like Romans 5, 8 and 12.

There was never a time he did not believe the gospel truths or objected to going to church, but he certainly lacked the assurance that he was the Lord's. He rested at first in belonging to his parents in their faith, but by the time he was ten he began to feel the implications of Jesus' words about *'one being taken and the other left'*. He began to wonder what it would mean if his parents were taken, 'raptured', and he was left. It also concerned him when the age of accountability and responsibility would apply to him. This really troubled him: was it 10 or was it 12 or 13 as it is in Judaism? He cannot actually remember what made him think like that. Around the same time his Sunday School teacher asked each boy in turn in his class one Sunday afternoon whether he was a Christian. They were all saying they were. When the question came to Philip, everyone thought for sure that he would say that he was a Christian because he attended all the church services, but his reply was, 'Not yet'. He lacked assurance and it worried him.

Conversion

At the age of 12 he was prompted through a special Scripture Union meeting in their church to ask the Lord to save him, which he did one night at his bedside. According to Philip, 'It was nothing dramatic, but it was a great relief. Now I knew Christ for myself and was not relying any more on my parents. I've never lacked assurance since.'

After that he began praying and reading the Bible each day, at first with Scripture Union notes. He used to wear his Scripture Union badge to school and as a result one or two lads came up to him to say that they also belonged to the Scripture Union and were Christians.

A year after he was converted, when he was 13, his mother died of cancer. He was at her bedside when she was dying and it was remarkable to see her pray in her final moments expressing her trust in the Saviour. She asked the Lord Jesus to receive her and told Philip's father to take care of him. It left an indelible impression on him. In the light of his mother's death and the struggles of life without her, he experienced and benefited from the caring love and kindness of the people in the church at Trinity, which he has never forgotten. Glyn Owen was the minister at the time, who prior to coming to Wrexham had been the minister at the Heath Evangelical Church in Cardiff. He and the previous minister, Calvin Thomas, were both influential in Philip's early life. During Glyn Owen's time Philip became a member of the church. It was Easter Sunday and about twenty of them came into membership that Sunday, all of them young people, including Philip Davies who later became an elder at the Heath but on retirement returned to Wrexham.

Education and Training

Philip was unsure about what he wanted to do in life but had ideas even as a young boy of preaching and lecturing. He even used to compose lectures in psychology with the help of an encyclopaedia that he had been given, and would deliver these lectures to make-believe students when no one else was around.

In God's wise providence he found himself in a class at grammar school that studied classical Greek to 'O' level. When the Greek master knew that Philip was a Christian and interested in the Bible, he gave him his old Greek New Testament. He also remembers from his school days how the Scripture master was livid with him because he was insisting that the death of Christ was a substitutionary propitiatory sacrifice. Philip recalls, 'Oh, he was so mad at me for saying it!'

He then went up to Bangor University for an interview but did not really know what he was going to study there. The professor of Hebrew took him aside to his study room and encouraged him to read classical Greek and Hebrew and Biblical Studies. So that is what he did. He learned a lot of liberal teaching, but the Lord kept him. He was so grateful for the Christian Union where he matured spiritually. The first term the students read together *Holiness* by J. C. Ryle, a book that had not long come out. They used to read it on a Sunday night after church in one of the student rooms. He has happy memories of his time in Bangor and, much to his surprise, they made him the President of the Christian Union. At the same time the Hebrew and Biblical Studies students in his year elected him Chairman of the Departmental Society, which meant working alongside the most liberal of his lecturers. He did, however, manage to arrange for Dr Guthrie, the New Testament lecturer at the London Bible College, to come and speak to the department.

During those years he went on a couple of Christian Union missions. The first time, he went to South Wales (he didn't know there was a South Wales much before that!), to Gorseinon, and then the following year to the Forward Movement Church on the Gabalfa estate in Cardiff where he met Richard and Joyce Akrill.

His time in Bangor came to an end and he was awarded a scholarship that gave him the option of furthering his studies at either Oxford or Cambridge. He chose Cambridge and his intention at the time was to end up teaching or lecturing in an Old Testament department, or something similar.

The Call

But during his second year in Cambridge, God had different plans. Philip saw the attraction of academic life at its best. He was surrounded by all the books that he needed and actually had a table at Tyndale House where the warden was Derek Kidner. But he felt also an increasingly nagging desire to be a preacher of the gospel.

He had taken services when he was in Bangor, and even prior to university he had been involved in a lot of the evangelistic outreach that was going on in Wrexham. Open-air meetings were held by the bus station just outside Trinity Church and sometimes Philip was asked to speak. The leader of this outreach was Mr Mawdsley, whose son, Keith, later became a minister. The place was bustling in those days as people had nothing else to do on a Sunday night since at that time in Wales all the pubs and cinemas were closed. Philip remembers the Teddy Boys standing in front of them, just propping up the wall, and so they had this wonderful captive audience and some would even go back to the church with them for a cup of tea and a talk. Philip can see that the Lord was preparing him in these ways for his future ministry.

He had to go and tell the minister of his church that he felt the Lord was calling him to be a preacher. His dad tried to put him off, not because he didn't really want him to be a preacher, but because he knew the difficulties and the problems that ministers experienced.

However, Philip went through the various channels to become a ministerial candidate of the Presbyterian Church of Wales. This included being examined about his calling before all the members of his church in Wrexham by the Reverend Gwilym Roberts.

Because of his previous biblical and theological degrees from Bangor and Cambridge, he was only required by the denomination to take the Pastoralia year at their Theological College in Aberystwyth. Like Andrew Davies (see Chapter 11), Philip did not find this very profitable, but the college library was wonderful. He found all the works of Gresham Machen and devoured them. He only wishes he had read them earlier so that he could have replied to liberal scholarship in a better way.

Ministry

He had a summer pastorate in a Forward Movement work on the Ringland housing estate on the edge of Newport. They had had a sister of the people there who had done a good work: sister Joan was her name, but she had left to get married to John Davies, the brother of Eryl Davies (see Chapter 9) four years before Philip arrived. Since that time, they had been starved of biblical truth. Philip felt really drawn to this place and the people themselves wanted him to be their pastor. So he wrote to Rev. Ieuan Phillips, Dr Lloyd-Jones' brother-in-law, who was the Forward Movement superintendent, but he wrote back a sympathetic letter stating, in effect, that his hands were tied. Philip was very disappointed that he could not go there, but at the same time his name had been put forward to two other churches in Monmouthshire who were interested in him. One was Park Place in Tredegar where John Pugh the Welsh Forward Movement leader had ministered in the early days, and the other was Havelock Street in Newport.

He thought it was only right to make clear to them his position on baptism, as well as on jumble sales! Jumble sales were how many of the churches in South Wales at the time raised money. Park Place in Tredegar could not accept this, but the church in Newport did not object at the time.

While these possibilities were in their earlier stages, Dr Oliver Barclay, the General Secretary of the IVF (UCCF as it is now called), wrote to Philip asking whether he would consider being the next IVF travelling secretary for Wales, in place of Geraint Fielder. Philip went to see him in Highgate and also had to go to Ashford in Middlesex to be interviewed by Derek Swann. He was really torn between entering immediately into a pastorate or encouraging student work in Wales for two or three years beforehand. In the end he did not feel at all at ease about taking on the student work, and when the invitation came from Newport he felt strongly he should accept this call.

The Newport pastorate also included the little Bethania church in St Mellons, so it was a joint pastorate between Bethania and the larger church, Havelock Street in the centre of Newport.

He was ordained at a special association meeting in his home church, Trinity Presbyterian Church, in 1968. The moderator was Geraint Nantlais Williams, one of the sons of Rev. Nantlais Williams, the Welsh poet whose life was spiritually transformed by the 1904–5 Welsh revival, and uncle of Dr Stephen Williams of Union Theological College, Belfast. Philip was the only one being ordained and the father of Mostyn Roberts (currently pastor at Welwyn Evangelical Church) was given the responsibility of questioning him very closely on his theological position, giving him an especially hard time with regard to the Bible.

The following year Philip married Jennifer who was converted in Bangor under the ministry of Vernon Higham. Mr Higham also preached at his induction service in Havelock Street in 1968.

After three years in this pastorate, he resigned over the World Council of Churches issue in the denomination, and so he was out of the ministry for two years working in an insurance office in Cardiff. His wife was a teacher and taught modern languages in a secondary school in Newport. They had to leave the manse, of course, but they moved into a little terraced house and attended Malpas Road Presbyterian Church, where Hugh Morgan was the minister. They loved being there and benefited greatly from Hugh's and Mari's wise counsel and friendship, and so in God's providence it was important that he had those two years with them in the church. Hugh Morgan allowed him to attend all the elders' meetings. It was a real privilege for Philip and it was at a time when God was clearly at work there. The early Saturday morning elders' prayer meetings were particularly special. Nevertheless, it was also a difficult time of feeling in the wilderness and wondering what God had in store.

Interestingly, during this period Philip was invited to do some lecturing at Heath Church in conjunction with the Evangelical Movement of Wales on Saturday mornings, which he thoroughly enjoyed. And then, one day his wife was handed an advert by Rev. Graham Harrison when she had been speaking at the Ladies fellowship in his church. Mr Harrison indicated it might interest Philip. It was advertising a post for vice-principal of a Bible college in London, plus to share in the preaching at the attached college chapel. As soon as Philip read it he was convinced that this was where he was to go, even before he knew anything further about it or had an interview. That was the one and only time Philip received such an immediate and overwhelming sense that this was the Lord's will for him. Letters of recommendation were sent by Graham Harrison and Glyn Owen, who was then at Westminster Chapel, and after various interviews he was duly appointed to the position.

Chapter 17

They moved to London in 1973 where he became vice-principal of the Kensit Memorial College, Finchley, later becoming its principal in 1975. Again, in the amazing providence of God, he was privileged to be involved with Dr Lloyd-Jones in encouraging the Kensit College Trustees to allow London Theological Seminary to meet on the premises beginning in October 1977. As well as being the head of the Kensit College, he became the resident tutor of the new seminary. For twenty-five years he was also the minister of the Kensit Evangelical Church. He was appointed the seminary principal in 1997, where he continued until his retirement in 2009.

Times of Blessing

When Philip first went to Kensit, you couldn't really call it a church. It was more like a college chapel. It took some time to persuade the Kensit trustees to allow them to become an independent church, but they managed it eventually in January 1982. They had about ten members, but in the goodness of God, by the time Philp became the principal of LTS, there were about sixty members, with many more attending morning and evening Sunday services. In London there are lots of comings and goings, with people settling for a time from all parts of the world. Philip loved this about London and had wonderful fellowship with people from many different countries and cultures.

At the 1983 Bala Ministers' Conference many of the ministers covenanted to pray each Saturday evening from nine o'clock to ten o'clock for God's Spirit to move among them. Philip found this a great blessing. Some of his church members found out that he was doing this and wanted to meet with him, and so eventually they started an early Saturday morning prayer meeting, which continued until he left London. As a result, gradually they began to see things happening in the church. More and more people started to come in. Some were saved and a number of younger people were baptised on confession of their faith. One young man was converted and later took the seminary course in preparation for preaching back home in his country of Ghana. Philip, along with his wife and daughter, went out to Ghana with him in 1988. Philip had never been to Africa in his life, he had actually never been on a plane before, and yet here he was in Ghana. It came about because a doctor in London, Dr Felix Konotey-Ahulu, gave him contacts with people in Ghana who had started an outreach mission. The family had an amazing time there and the pioneering work undertaken by the young student has prospered and continues to this day.

Difficulties

When he was at Havelock Street, he realises with hindsight his time there could have been managed better. The church was not run by elders, but by a committee. They did have elders but they did not work as elders. Philip tried to change this, but without any success. The committee people were opposed to his evangelistic preaching and were pro-ecumenical. He remembers one of them saying to him one day, 'Why are you always on about sin?' Matters deteriorated further when he put his name to a letter to the *South Wales Argos*, along with other evangelical ministers in Newport, against the local ecumenical activities that were taking place in the town. The church arranged a special committee meeting without his knowledge, with the aim of censuring him. He only learned about this proposed plan because the appointed chairman, a former minister who was himself a member, informed him in advance and asked whether Philip would like to intervene and chair the meeting. Philip declined but attended and sat in the middle of them. They discussed the issue and decided to write a letter to the secretary of the Newport Evangelical Ministers objecting that Havelock Street's name had been associated with the letter. They clearly didn't realise who the secretary was, a Rev. Graham Harrison, who knew how to respond to letters of this kind. In his reply Mr Harrison stated that, whether they liked it or not, Philip was in fact the Minister of Havelock Street Church.

There were some who supported Philip which he only learned after he had resigned. He kept in touch with a few of the members until they recently passed away. There was a large family in the church who were the main ones giving him a hard time, especially after he read out his letter of resignation. Some were particularly nasty to his wife as well. Ministers' wives have to put up with a lot behind the scenes. One of the members of the difficult family came to take the manse keys from Philip but could not bear to talk with him or be in the house, simply demanding the keys and leaving. It was a sad end to ministry in Havelock Street, and even sadder in view of the plight of those who rejected the gospel.

The church in St Mellons was so different: though smaller in number and hard work, there was a happy relationship in the fellowship. They were very kind to him, and when he resigned he encouraged the faithful in the church to go across the road to the local Baptist church where Russell Williams was ministering at the time, which some of them did.

Books

He remembers having to give a talk in the sixth form to the school Christian Union. It wasn't run by evangelicals and they knew his position. So he gave them a talk on his beliefs. His dad had recently bought *Fundamentalism and the Word of God* by J.I. Packer and Philip more or less cribbed everything from that to give them. He has also found Packer's book *Evangelism and the Sovereignty of God* very useful in understanding the importance of the sovereignty of God but also the responsibility of human beings.

When Iron Gates Yield by Geoffrey Bull also affected him a lot when he first read it, where he talks about his ministry in China and how they brainwashed him. From his early teens he had a particular concern for the people of the Far East, especially after seeing a Christian film on the Korean War (1950–1953). Little did he think that he would have the privilege of teaching men from South Korea and visiting their country. He also thinks Dallimore's *Life of George Whitefield* is a great book. He would also encourage young ministers to read Dr Lloyd-Jones's biography and to note particularly how he dealt with people in Sandfields who were not believers. Many books, too numerous to name, have impacted him over the years.

The State of the Church Today and the Need of the Hour

The first thing Philip wanted to stress was that the church belongs to the Lord Jesus Christ and it is important that we keep in mind the worldwide work. He has had some connections with this from the days of going to Ghana, but also through being involved with LTS and students attending from many nations. As a consequence, he has been invited by former students to lecture and preach in numerous countries across the world. He has preached for former students in Indonesia, Malaysia, Madagascar, Japan, Hong Kong, Taiwan, Australia, Romania, and so on. We have to keep in mind the big picture and that it is a global work. There is a lot going on and we must give thanks to God for it. As Philip puts it, 'We belong to something huge and it puts the likes of Richard Branson and Bill Gates and their enterprises into perspective.'

Concerning our own land, he thinks things are pretty desperate. There are some encouraging signs in places, but generally speaking it is hard going and the fruit is small. Most churches are just about holding their own and some are going down. As a result of the pandemic many have seen losses and there are lots of unresolved problems in many churches that need sorting out. There are many tensions and numerous pastors are under a great deal of pressure. We need to pray for them. What saddens him most of all is to find reformed churches, evangelical churches, so judgmental towards other Christians and churches who don't exactly cross their t's or dot their i's. He believes we need to pray for more humility and understanding and to encourage one another more. The days are evil and it is vitally important to be slow to criticise and judge and quick to encourage and support, and to go the extra mile.

He went on to say that preachers should pray for their people daily and preach evangelistically and not be afraid of preaching the great key gospel verses. As he puts it:

When was the last time you heard somebody preach John 3:16? Come on, preachers, preach these great verses! They will inspire believers and they will convict unbelievers. Always have a message. Don't do a running commentary.

He urged pastors not to be too despondent when members move on. We are links in a chain and sometimes God uses us to help people for a time and then they move elsewhere. We are part of something big and something glorious. We must keep in mind that we are working for eternity, we are not just working for time.

He would encourage pastors not to be loners. Ministers, pastors, preachers need each other for support and encouragement and challenge. They should join local ministers' fraternals.

Never take your wives for granted, either. Make time for them, listen to their concerns and do all in your power to love them and to treat them with respect. Also, do not ignore or resent advice and constructive criticism from others, especially from your wife if you have one. He remembers an old lady telling him that his main prayer in the church service was too long. He was praying like Lloyd-Jones used to pray, who in the main prayer would pray for twenty to twenty-five minutes and it was only as if he prayed for five minutes. Philip realised he was not Lloyd-Jones and this lady was good to tell him that, even though he didn't like it at first. He thanks God for old ladies, and remembers another old lady who, as she was leaving the service when he was at the door one morning, said, 'I pray for you every day.' What an encouragement!

Finally, Philip believes today there is little in the way of repentance and despairing of self. There is too much self-sufficiency and empire building. In his own words:

How we need to have that persistent, persevering cry that Jesus calls for. The days are evil and we all need to give ourselves to praying that God in his mercy for Jesus' sake would rend the heavens and come down and make a thousand hearts his own. Pray that the Lord would raise a new generation of preachers. All the Bible colleges and theological colleges should be full; they're not. Very few are coming forward and we need preachers who will catch the ear of the ordinary people as well as those in high places. This is an important part of praying for revival. Pray the Lord of the harvest, that he will thrust out labourers into his harvest field.

Chapter 18

Austin Walker

Introduction

Even though I have never met Mr Walker, I feel I know him. Over the years, Geoff Thomas has often talked to me about him. He was in Alfred Place pre-Geoff Thomas, which is quite something! Almost fifty men who are now in the ministry have sat under Mr Thomas at Alfred Place, but Austin Walker was the first.

Moreover, when I was Headmaster at The Fulham Boys School (FBS), it was a privilege to have two of Mr Walker's grandsons as pupils at the school. They were two fine boys and one became an internet sensation clocking up over 80 millions views—almost as popular as *Before They Leave the Stage*! It was great having Jeremy Walker as a parent at the school and we have become close friends. Dan Walker is also a good friend and has done video messages and spoken at FBS over the years.

Background and Conversion

Austin was born immediately after the Second World War and therefore was raised in what is known as the austerity years. For the first eighteen years of his life he lived in north London where he was born. His parents were Christians but not well taught, and in the early days of his life they did not often go to church. The war ruined the pattern of their lives quite dramatically.

Austin was converted at the age of fifteen. He knew he was a sinner and knew that Jesus Christ died for sinners, but aside from that, he knew very little of the gospel. He was brought up in a Baptist Union church that was evangelical at the time. Their practice was to call people to the front to make their decision for Christ. Austin went forward in one meeting but doesn't believe he was converted at that point. He thinks he was converted between that time and the time when he was baptised. He noticed three things in his life during that period which were not there before, and believes God must have done something in his heart and life. For the first time in his life he wanted to read the Bible, he wanted to pray and he wanted to worship with God's people.

However, he was also very keen on sport which dominated his life. He played football, cricket, basketball and table tennis. It meant that on Sunday mornings he would not be in church because he was doing his school work that he didn't have time to do on Saturday when he was either playing or watching football.

But changes were taking place in his life and other interests began to develop. He was on the fringes of Operation Mobilisation (OM) through two brothers who attended the same church as him and worked for OM full time. But his main involvement was with the National Young Life Campaign. They did coffee bar evangelism and sometimes a group of them were asked to go and take services elsewhere. The first sermon that he ever preached was in a London City Mission Hall, behind King's Cross Station. In those days it was a pretty bad area. It was a red light district and had a lot of problems with alcohol abuse. He did not know what to expect, but when he got there, in front of him were a group of men and women who were hardened drinkers. Most of them could not sit up straight and were horizontal lying on their chairs. He had taken as his text, John 5:8, *'Rise, take up your bed and walk'*.

Education and Training

When he was eighteen years of age he went to Aberystwyth University to study Geography and History. It was, for several reasons according to Austin, *'a master stroke of divine providence'*. He began to sit under the ministry of Geoff Thomas (see Chapter 7) who began his systematic preaching through the Bible. He preached through Genesis and through Matthew's Gospel and Austin had never heard anything like it. As Geoff Thomas worked his way through the first chapters of Genesis dealing with creation, the fall and the beginnings of redemption, it transformed Austin's whole understanding and outlook.

Austin also began to exercise leadership skills as he took on responsibilities in the Christian Union and he began to preach regularly. The Christian Union in Aberystwyth had a number of services during the weekdays in some of the old people's homes. He was preaching regularly in these homes and that proved to be quite a formative influence upon him.

But the last, and most important thing, was that he met the lady who was to become his best friend, his lifelong companion and a helper in his ministry; his wife, Mai. She is Welsh and a Welsh speaker and was brought up on a farm on the hills that surround the Brecon Beacons where her family raised sheep and some cattle.

He stayed in Aberystwyth for four years, from 1964 to 1968, and then in 1968, he sailed to New York. He was under the conviction that God was calling him to minister the word of God, to be a preacher. He wanted to be exposed to the best, the most biblical theology that he knew of. Geoff Thomas obviously had a big influence on him, and as he had been at Westminster Seminary Austin also went to study there for three years. He sat under men like Cornelius Van Til, Ed Clowney, Palmer Robertson and Jay Adams. From 1968 until 1971 he was consistently exposed to reformed theology.

He and his wife married in 1970. He wanted her to have an experience of America, so they spent one year together in America. They settled in Philadelphia, but within a few months he had to undergo life-saving surgery. That was a very testing time, but God preserved his life and, at the time of interview, he was seventy-five and still able to preach and teach God's Word.

Ministry

They left America in 1971 and returned to Sussex, to Cuckfield Baptist Church, where Erroll Hulse was the pastor. It was a Reformed Baptist church and Austin, along with two other men, was sent from there to plant a church in Crawley, 23 miles south of London.

So in 1972 he moved to Crawley and secured a post in a local comprehensive school. At that time Crawley had a population of about 56,000 and they took over an old Particular Baptist chapel that had recently closed. There were about fifteen or sixteen of them in those days. The church was constituted in 1975 and Austin was recognised formally as an elder, although he had been doing much of the work since 1972.

In 1979 he gave up teaching in a local comprehensive school and became the full-time pastor of what was then Crawley Reformed Baptist Church. He remained there for over forty years. Their two sons and two daughters were raised in Crawley, and in those forty years the church went through all sorts of ups and downs.

In the 1990s, Crawley Reformed Baptist Church moved to Maidenbower, a new neighbourhood in Crawley. They renamed themselves Maidenbower Baptist Church. In March 2018, on the anniversary of the founding of the church, he stepped down from pastoral responsibilities and his son Jeremy became the sole elder.

Since retiring, he has fought two rounds with cancer, and at the time of interview he could thank God that he was cancer free and enjoying good health. He is a member of Castlefields church in Derby, where Dave Fielding is the pastor, and he still preaches occasionally.

Blessings and Difficulties

There are many examples of times of blessings and difficulties that Austin could mention, but one in particular stands out, a time when he certainly knew God's blessing and when he was put to the test and had to really prove him.

They had been in Crawley about ten years and one Sunday a lady came up to him and said, 'No one will ever be converted through your ministry.' She was quite angry, upset and distressed. He cannot remember what he said to her, only that he didn't say very much because he didn't really know what to say. What he did do, though, was spend many hours over the next few months and years in prayer. The lady's comment drove him to his knees to cry out to God to, first of all, vindicate the appointed means of preaching, to vindicate the name of Jesus Christ and bring glory to Him, and in the process, if God was pleased, to vindicate Austin as a preacher of the gospel.

Within a couple of years the church had doubled in size. There were a growing number of younger people in their 20s and 30s, some married, others single, but all of them in their testimonies mentioned how the preaching of the gospel had changed their lives. It was a time of great blessing, and for a short period people were being converted every single week. The strange thing was, the lady never came back to him to withdraw what she had said. Perhaps she had even forgotten she had said it, but through that comment and that time of testing God proved that he would honour the preaching of the gospel, and honoured his servant.

As he looks back, Austin is able to say, it was good to be afflicted. While he cannot remember the details of his prayers, all he knows is that he took some of the promises that God had given in the Scriptures, that preaching the gospel was the means that God had ordained for the spread of the gospel, and turned them into petitions. He did not change the style or content of his preaching, but he was more prayerful and more expectant. It was an exciting time and a very busy time. With new converts every week, he had to spend a lot of time talking with them, listening to them and then preparing them for baptism and church membership. In Austin's own words:

It was a time when I was cast upon God. Our problems and our difficulties are meant to drive us into the arms of God, and he doesn't fail us. He came alongside me and he strengthened me and encouraged me and enabled me to preach faithfully his Word with fruitfulness that was everywhere evident in the life of the church.

Advice

There are things that he knows now as a retired man, that he wishes he had known as a young man entering the ministry. One of the things that he has learned, and no one ever really told him, is how difficult a Monday could be after preaching twice on a Sunday, and sometimes three times if he had to lead an adult's Bible class as well. He found it so difficult to pray and to read the Scriptures on a Monday morning. His friend Jack Seaton used to say, 'Never resign on a Monday', and with good reason, because on a Monday Austin often felt discouraged, weary and tired, and that is when Satan would attack and assault and falsely accuse him. He remembers times when he came out of the pulpit and wanted a six-foot hole to climb into and disappear because he felt he had been a total failure. He always took Mondays off, but it would take him most of the day to recover.

Another thing he wishes he had known was how demanding and how important public prayer and leading the people of God in the service is; not that a minister is in any way a mediator, but they are the mouthpiece of the people of God. When he looks back on those early days, he is not sure he wants to be reminded of some of those prayers again. But he learned over the years how important it is to prepare, to lead a congregation in worship, and to lead them to the throne of grace in prayer. In some senses he thinks it is more important than preaching because you are speaking as the mouthpiece of the congregation to God. When you preach, you are preaching in the presence of God but you are preaching to men and women and to boys and girls. In prayer you are addressing the throne of heaven and that is a huge responsibility. He was not ready for it forty or fifty years ago.

The other thing he has noticed is how easily Christians forget what they have been taught in the public ministry. He came to realise that he had to tell people again and again and again. He took heart from Peter's words in 2 Peter, when he was at the end of his life, and yet still has to put them in remembrance of the things he had taught them. But there were times when he did not understand people's forgetfulness or the fact that they might have missed the whole point that he was trying to make. He was at times too impatient and frustrated and got cross with them. He should have been more sympathetic. Sometimes people are suffering too much and are too weary and too sick to really receive what is being said. Exodus 6:9 talks about the time when Israel was in such anguish of spirit and under cruel labour and hardship in Egypt that they couldn't hear what Moses was saying to them and they could not take it in. It was just beyond their capacity because of their sufferings. He has learnt these things as he has gone through his ministry, especially being in the same place for over forty years. You get to know people and realise some of the trials and difficulties through which they are going. You learn to minister into that situation and weigh what you're saying to them publicly and privately. It is something that has taken him a lifetime to learn.

Burden

Austin's one great aim and determination throughout his ministry was to preach the whole counsel of God, and to preach it in such a way that young and old could understand it. Aberystwyth was a good training ground for that because when preaching to the older people in the homes you had to be fairly short, you had to be clear and plain and pointed. He believes that if a minister can learn to preach to young children and to old people then they will not have any problems communicating with anybody else. He would encourage young ministers to take Sunday School classes and learn to get into the hearts and consciences and minds of children. He thinks it would be of great benefit to them in their ministries.

He tried to preach as a watchman, like Ezekiel who was a watchman on the city walls. If he doesn't sound the alarm, then God will require the blood of the people on his head. Austin does not want God to call him to account in that way and so he has tried earnestly to preach as a faithful watchman; not to be a coward and simply tell people what they want to hear, but tell them what God says and what they need to hear. To that end, he made 1 Timothy 4:16 his motto from day one, '*Take heed to yourself and to the doctrine continue in them, for in doing this you will save both yourself and those who hear you.*'

That has been Austin's great concern because he must be a pattern and an example for other people to follow. Sadly, as he looks back, he knows a number of men who have made shipwreck of the faith and have ruined their ministry because they have not taken 1 Timothy 4:16 to heart. Austin has been determined to be a pattern to follow, to his children, his grandchildren and to the church where he was a pastor. He is a morning person and has always been an early riser and that is when he is at his best. He would be early every day in the study to read the Scriptures for himself and to pray to God. That would be his pattern even when he was under great pressure.

The legacy he hopes he will leave is that he has been a faithful servant of Christ and an example and a pattern to others, even though they may have forgotten about what he preached.

He also has a great concern that God's people know church history and would hope that through the many talks he has given on church history he has passed on something of the heritage of our forefathers.

Books and Preachers

Like so many others, in the early days he read A.W. Pink's *Sovereignty of God* and Packer's *Evangelism and the Sovereignty of God* and *Fundamentalism and the Word of God*. But the books that have really shaped him over the years are books like John Murray's *Redemption Accomplished and Applied*, Herman Bavinck's *Wonderful Works of God*, formerly known as *Our Reasonable Faith*, Geerhardus Vos's *Biblical Theology*, the works of Warfield, particularly his topical studies on various biblical themes; John Owen, *Communion with God*, transformed his prayer life; John Flavel *Keeping the Heart* and *The Mystery of Providence*, Thomas Brooks' *Precious Remedies Against Satan's Devices*, John Newton's Letters and Calvin's letters, tracts and treaties and his *Institutes*, particularly the chapter on prayer. Austin found that so helpful the first time he read it and has returned to it again and again.

As for preachers, Geoff Thomas has been a huge influence on Austin. He was, in effect, his mentor. He taught him and showed him what the reformed faith was all about, what it was to preach the Scriptures.

There were other sermons while he was at Aberystwyth that stood out. He remembers a sermon by Eric Gurr who at the time was the pastor at Melbourne Hall in Leicester. He came to Aberystwyth and preached on Isaiah 6 and the holiness of God. He was so struck by that sermon, focusing on the greatness and the glory and the holiness of God. He was also privileged to hear Professor Murray preach in Aberystwyth and remembers him preaching on the economy of God's salvation. Austin remembers him saying those words from Hebrews describing Christ as *'holy, harmless, undefiled, separate from sinners'*. He said it with such feeling, with such force that it is still stuck in his memory after fifty years or so. There was also a sermon by a friend of his, Richard Holst. It was at a Welsh IVF (as it was then, now UCCF), Leaders' Conference. Richard was preaching from Galatians 1 and there was one phrase that stuck in Austin's mind and struck him, namely that the gospel is God's gospel; whatever else we think or whatever else we are doing, it is God's gospel. He is the source, the origin and we are to faithfully declare it.

Then, when he went to the United States, for a while he sat under the ministry of Al Martin and later on he listened to a lot of his cassettes, as they were then, when he taught pastoral theology in the Trinity Ministerial Academy. Those have now become three volumes of pastoral theology.

He was privileged to be at Westminster Seminary when Dr Lloyd-Jones gave his lectures which became *Preaching and Preachers* and he learned a lot from just listening to him. He has read and re-read that book.

There are also a lot of men who have become lifelong friends and a great influence on him. One of his best friends is Achille Blaize who was a pastor in East London for many years. Others include Bill Hughes and Ted Donnelly, and men in America like Jim Sevastio in Kentucky and George McDearmon in up-state New York. He and Keith Underhill, who spent most of his life in Nairobi in Kenya, have been friends since university.

He highly values all these friendships along with many others. He still speaks to some of them regularly and seeks their counsel and advice.

The State of the Church and the Need of the Hour

Austin thinks it is important to say at the very outset, that Christ will build his church and the gates of hell will not prevail against her. We need a strong confidence and faith in Christ. He is sovereign and the head of the church. Austin is thankful that many churches hold fast to the faith and the gospel is being preached and it is being preached in places where there were no gospel churches forty years ago, particularly in the north of England.

But, having said that, we need to be realistic. The churches in the New Testament had all sorts of problems, and when Christ addressed the seven churches in the book of Revelation there were both good things and bad things. Likewise today, there are certain things that concern Austin.

He thinks this generation has lost something of the greatness, the glory and the holiness of God. There is a general lack of reverence. There is a complacency at times, and an over-confidence in man. Over the years he has seen initiatives come and initiatives go and we are no better off. These things peter out.

He thinks there is also a doctrinal ambivalence. We are too content with the minimal statements of faith of what we believe. Our forefathers were much stronger. From the very beginning, the church in Crawley was a confessional church. They adopted the 1689 second London Baptist Confession of Faith as a clear summary of what they believed. He is concerned that this generation confesses less truth than our forefathers did. It is common today to hear people talk about primary and secondary truth. Obviously there are things that are absolutely fundamental and primary, like the Trinity, the two natures of Christ and so on, but he thinks this division into primary and secondary truth is misleading. At its worst Austin thinks it is dangerous because it blurs the distinctions and it means that historic biblical Christianity is not being expressed by the churches. There is a great danger of compromising the truth and of losing certain things which are fundamental. To Austin, if it is in the Bible, it is primary. But he worries that there are Christians who do not always appreciate the sufficiency of Scripture or trust it sufficiently to put it into practice. It is seen in certain aspects of the church where there is ecclesiastical confusion and an absence of what he would call, 'biblical churchmanship', by which he means an appreciation of what it is to be a member of the church of Christ. Christ has not left us to organise ourselves as we see best. There is an order and a pattern to follow. A person said to Austin a long time ago, 'I can say whatever I like in a church meeting.' He pointed out to her that he was an overseer in the church and he could not just say what he liked. He had to weigh and measure the words that he spoke, and so does every member of the church. The Banner of Truth brought out a book, a modern version of John Owen's *The Duties of Christian Fellowship*, which deals with the rules for walking and fellowship with respect to pastors and elders, and rules for walking and fellowship with other believers. He believes that if people read those two sections it would radically alter the pattern and practice of church life.

But the primary need of the hour, Austin believes, is the standing need for every generation of Christians. In his own words:

We need to pray to God and heed his Word and pray that God will pour out His Spirit and raise up men who are full of the Spirit of God, full of the Scriptures, full of zeal and courage and conviction, willing to suffer for the sake of Christ, men who understand the times, men who understand and preach to the times, men who love Christ, men who love His church, men who are like Christ, men who preach judgement and sin and wrath and condemnation faithfully, yet at the same time proclaim the gospel and freely offer Jesus Christ as the all-sufficient Saviour. We need a full-blooded confidence in God.

Finale

This series of interviews had its birth in a burden that an older generation of preachers should have a voice today by telling their experiences of God and His word and so encourage today's and tomorrow's men. Have we, have they, brought godly desires to you as you have read their testimonies? Or if you have seen the original interviews, how would you summarise the lessons of their lives? I have been asked to write about the things that struck me as, week by week from February to June 2021, we listened to their responses to the questions sent to them beforehand, and to the issues which arose spontaneously from the live conversations. What spoke to me will probably not be what spoke to you, but let me challenge you to compile your own list. Here is mine.

1. For a brief while before and after each interview, Alun and I, along with the techies, would talk about what was to come, or what had been. Without exception these shepherds of God's flock displayed an un-self-conscious humility. Our interviewees are mostly well known in our circles, some as national figures, and some international, yet there were no airs and graces. Each was nervous beforehand, believing they had little to contribute, and anxious afterwards, that they had been helpful to the viewers. I remember my pastor at the time, Vernon Higham, recounting how at Bala Minsters' Conference of the Evangelical Movement of Wales, Dr Lloyd-Jones had stated that 'if we (ministers) lose our humility, we lose everything'.

So there is one lesson for all Christians in leadership, not just preachers, 'to walk humbly with your God', and 'to let this mind be in you which was in Christ Jesus'. I felt it a privilege to have met and interviewed them.

2. It is an evangelical cliché that we wish we prayed more or were more faithful to the church prayer meeting. Well, our interviewees said the same, but here's the thing: it wasn't a cliché with them, but a genuinely heartfelt sense that 'without Me you can do nothing'. We knew that we

were interviewing men who prayed, of course, but they expressed an awareness that for their own walk with God, and for the benefit of their people, hindrances to prayer must be overcome.

In his sermons 'The Christian Soldier', Dr Lloyd-Jones is quite forceful that the armour is rendered powerless if prayer is neglected. So let us encourage Christian leaders and churches to maintain a strong prayer life. Pastors, how can your churches do this? Leaders, how can we better encourage the church to pray? Christians, are you praying Ephesians 6:19 for your preachers?

3. Some believers are raised up and bring widespread blessing to Christ's church. If we try to raise ourselves up, however, or make self the important one, we will damage His flock. One who was raised up, and I have mentioned him twice already, was Dr Martyn Lloyd-Jones. Most if not all of the interviewees spoke of his help and encouragement. Having a person to whom one can look can be vital at times of trial in the ministry. It is wise to have such a friend and productive to seek their help.

4. We live in an age where we have sound, reformed seminaries, ministers, churches and books by the billion. For this we should be grateful. However, it is possible in life for our strength to become a weakness, and there were concerns expressed by a number which arose from this.

First there is the gospel. A number of them said that if they were back in harness they would preach the gospel more regularly, that is, probably every week, and even if the congregation are all believers: it is for believers as well as the unsaved, as it reminds us of our raison d'être, and the Cross is the basis of all we have in Christ. This does not mean, of course, a simple ABC message every Sunday; gospel principles can be drawn from throughout Scripture.

Second, there is the question of preaching. They discerned a tendency to lecture and impart knowledge to congregations, with a bit of application, and to leave matters there. The calling however, is to preach; to search for a message from God for His flock and to bring it, whether it is a gospel or teaching message, and to preach it with pathos.

Third, and linked, is the whole question of preaching 'with the Holy Ghost sent down from heaven'. The concern was the danger of dependence upon soundness and accuracy to achieve spiritual fruit through preaching, rather than dependence upon the life-giving Spirit. The word 'unction' was used by several to describe what had been their heart's desire for their own ministry and their prayer for today's ministers. I was surprised when I asked Iain Murray, prolific author as he is, about his books. He felt that his most significant book was *Revival and Revivalism*. In this he draws out the important difference in the two concepts but reminds us of the reality of the real thing. 'O that Thou wouldest rend the heavens and come down!'

5. A woman in my church once said to me, 'If we don't know what God is like, we won't feel the need of a Saviour.' This theme was also touched on by the men we interviewed. Another way of putting it would be 'preaching the God-ness of God'. This they felt was more important than ever in our godless, secularised nation. God and His attributes and eternal Being, so different from us and so pure, needs to be set against the sins of the day.

6. Two 'domestic issues' were regularly referred to and touched my heart. The first was the deep affection for and appreciation of their wives. In response to the question on the advice they would give to a young minister today, Ian Hamilton said very concisely, 'Marry well!' How true—and we must remember to pray for and encourage ministers' wives, and pray for our young men to find godly partners in life.

The second was the number of men who had faced real financial hardship and distress at some time in their ministries. My thought at the time was that as churches we can do better than this. Perhaps with some of the old-fashioned 'piety' fading away, this now is an area able to be more easily and robustly discussed, and so it should be. I do not believe in making millionaires of our ministers, but correctly caring for them should be an important duty for churches.

A summary of all the things said is possibly found in the words of one of them concerning the work of the ministry: 'Pray. Preach. Pastor. Plead—for an unction, and for the unity of the brethren.'

We hope you were blessed and moved by the interviews we did with these best of men, and that this book has blessed you also.

Keith Batstone